D1094372

TWAYNE'S WORLD AUTHORS SERIES

A Survey of the World's Literature

Sylvia E. Bowman, Indiana University

GENERAL EDITOR

SPAIN

Gerald Wade, Vanderbilt University

EDITOR

Leandro Fernández de Moratín

(TWAS 149)

TWAYNE'S WORLD AUTHORS SERIES (TWAS)

The purpose of TWAS is to survey the major writers —novelists, dramatists, historians, poets, philosophers, and critics—of the nations of the world. Among the national literatures covered are those of Australia, Canada, China, Eastern Europe, France, Germany, Greece, India, Italy, Japan, Latin America, New Zealand, Poland, Russia, Scandinavia, Spain, and the African nations, as well as Hebrew, Yiddish, and Latin Classical literatures. This survey is complemented by Twayne's United States Authors Series and English Authors Series.

The intent of each volume in these series is to present a critical-analytical study of the works of the writer; to include biographical and historical material that may be necessary for understanding, appreciation, and critical appraisal of the writer and to present all material in clear, concise English—but not to vitiate the scholarly content of the work by doing so.

Leandro Fernández de Moratín

By JOHN DOWLING
Indiana University

Twayne Publishers, Inc. :: New York

LIBRARY
COLLEGE OF SAN MATEO

Copyright © 1971 by Twayne Publishers, Inc.
All Rights Reserved

Library of Congress Catalog Card Number: 70-120486

TO ALBERT AND GEORGIA DOWLING

MANUFACTURED IN THE UNITED STATES OF AMERICA

89599

Preface

When the armies of Napoleon invaded Spain in 1808, those cosmopolitan Spaniards who admired France and who had absorbed European ideas found themselves in a dilemma. While they regarded the French as the bearers of the enlightenment against the forces of darkness, they could not help but see them also as armed invaders. The liberals of Spain divided on this issue. Some either tacitly accepted or actively supported the French who organized a constitutional monarchy with Joseph Bonaparte as king. These Spaniards have gone down in history as the *afrancesados*, French sympathizers, a word which carries the connotation that they were tainted with French ideas and disloyal to Spain. The liberal patriots, on the other hand, supported Fernando VII, whose father Carlos IV had abdicated the throne only weeks before the French invasion. They organized a peripatetic government that finally established itself in the south of Spain. They wrote the liberal Constitution of Cadiz, but they also found themselves allied with the traditionalists. When they succeeded, with the help of the British, in driving the French from Spain and restoring Fernando to the throne, they discovered that they had given the upper hand to the traditionalists. In the years that followed, Fernando clapped them into jail, or else they fled abroad to share exile with the *afrancesados*.

Thus, either side was the wrong one for the enlightened man, but his reputation suffered more if he chose the side of the *afrancesados*. The dramatist Leandro Fernández de Moratín elected to remain under the French in the government post that he had held in the reign of Carlos IV, he accepted the Cross of the Royal Order of Spain from Joseph Bonaparte, and he took the post of Royal Librarian. Later the government of Fernando VII, in the "purifications" that traditionally follow political upheaval in Spain, cleared him and restored his property to him. Even so, his personal reputation forever suffered, and he has been known as an *afrancesado* in literature, with little justification, as well as in politics, which did not much interest him.

Moratín's literary fame has been diminished by the fact that he wrote little and polished much. In literature Spain has been noted for outbursts of genius that manifests itself in a prodigious creative capacity. One thinks at once of the more than four hundred extant plays of Lope de Vega. Quantity has been one measure of an artist's worth. If his work has contained parts of undisputed beauty, it has not much mattered that it was marred by carelessness and flaws. Polish has not commanded much respect.

On one point concerning Moratín, however, everyone is in agreement: he is a master of the Spanish language. Federico Ruiz Morcuende, who compiled the two-volume vocabulary of his works, says: "It would be difficult indeed to find among our writers of the first rank anyone who surpasses Leandro Fernández de Moratín in his vocabulary, such is the eloquence, wealth, variety, quality, distinction, and elegance which characterize his control of the language."[1] Whatever the views of his critics, friendly or adverse, toward his literary works or his public conduct, they agree in according him the distinction of being an indisputable model for correct Castilian usage.

To his command of the language may be attributed in part the enduring quality of his literary works. He has also served many Spanish playwrights as an exemplar of dramatic form, and this study is devoted principally to showing him as a writer of comedies. Moratín was the first successful dramatist to write in a new vein after the decline of the Golden age *comedia*. He himself recognized that comedy necessarily belongs to a particular period and that it is not likely to last beyond the age for which it was written. His own comedies did survive the end of the *ancien régime* in Spain, and it is my purpose to illuminate the qualities in them which have given them enduring appeal.

Moratín was also a man of the theater, deeply concerned with the status of dramatic art in his day, and for this reason I devote much attention to the performance of his comedies. I have given the cast of characters and the actors who played the parts in the premières when I introduce each of the plays. Although I have been searching a long time, I have not found the complete cast of *El viejo y la niña* (*The Old Man and the Girl*), and strange as it may seem, I have not found nor have I seen anyone else publish the complete cast of the première of *El sí de las niñas*

(*When a Girl Says Yes*), the greatest of all his plays.[2] In these cases, I have had to be content with giving a partial cast.

I have also presented Moratín's translations from Shakespeare, Molière and Voltaire, and I have treated his notes to an account of an *auto de fe* which is related to his interest in Voltaire. I have omitted a discussion of his travel books and his correspondence, which were published posthumously, although I have used them incidentally to complete the portrait of a writer who was a cultivated man of his century. I have purposely neglected his poetry. Some of it is occasional verse that belongs more properly to biography. In general, it has passed out of fashion although it had admirers at one time.

This study is not a biography, but I have used the facts of Moratín's life when they throw light on his works and on the production of his plays. Also I have tried to clarify one story which has mistakenly made *El sí de las niñas* directly the result of an experience in his life. The chronology at the beginning of the book will serve those who wish to relate the main facts of his life to his literary production.

For the reader who has little Spanish, I have translated the title of a work the first time it appears in a chapter. For Moratín's works, the reader may also refer back quickly to the Chronology where he will find the title of each work translated. In the text I have used italics only for those Spanish words that do not appear in *Webster's Third New International Dictionary* (Unabridged). I have endeavored, however, to explain even these words in the text on the first occasion of their appearance.[3]

John Dowling

Acknowledgments

I began my studies of Moratín when I was a visiting professor at the University of Texas in the fall of 1957, and I have continued them since with the financial support of the Guggenheim Foundation, the Research Committee of the Texas Technological College, and the Office of Research and Advanced Studies of Indiana University.

I have worked in many archives and libraries, and I am grateful for the assistance that I have received from archivists, librarians and attendants, who often work under adverse conditions. As principal sources of original materials used in this study, I am indebted to the Biblioteca Nacional in Madrid, where the bulk of Moratín's private papers are kept; and also in Madrid to the Biblioteca Municipal, the Hemeroteca Municipal, the Archivo de la Villa, and the Archivo Histórico Nacional; in Paris, to the Bibliothèque Nationale and the Archives Nationales. There are numerous other collections which I have used for special purposes and which I recognize in the footnotes.

Many have been my professional friends to whom I owe debts of gratitude, more than I can mention by name. I am grateful to Professors Emeriti Eunice and Bryan Gates for their reading of the manuscript. I particularly express my thanks to Don José López de Toro and to Don Antonio Rodríguez-Moñino; they have often given me orientation which has enriched the depth and scope of my investigations.

Finally, I express my appreciation to my wife Constance, who unselfishly indulges me in my scholarly pursuits; and to my son Robert, who gallantly accommodates himself to my way of life.

Contents

Preface

Chronology

1. How to Write a Play   15

2. December Matched with May   26

3. A Play about Playwrights   38

4. An Impostor   60

5. A Pious Deceiver   76

6. School for Parents and Guardians   92

7. The Foothills of Parnassus   129

Notes and References   145

Selected Bibliography   157

Index   165

Castigat ridendo mores.

He corrects manners with laughter.

Chronology

1760   March 10: born in Madrid to Nicolás Fernández de Moratín and Isidora Cabo Conde.

1779   His narrative poem *La toma de Granada* (*The Conquest of Granada*) won honorable mention in the contest of the Royal Spanish Academy.

1780   May 11: father died in Madrid at the age of 42.

1780-   Employed in a silversmith's shop in Madrid.
1786

1782   His *Lección poética* (*A Literary Lesson*), a satire on the literary vices of the day, won honorable mention in the contest of the Royal Spanish Academy.

1785   Published his father's epic poem, *Las naves de Cortés destruidas* (*Cortés' Ships Destroyed*), with a commentary by himself.

1785   Death of his mother, Isidora Cabo Conde.

1786   Read his first play *El viejo y la niña* (*The Old Man and the Girl*) to the dramatic company of Manuel Martínez.

1787   January: appointed secretary to the Count of Cabarrús, director of the San Carlos Bank, whom he accompanied on an eleven-month trip to France. Composed the musical play, *El barón* (*The Baron*).

1789   Took minor orders becoming an abbé, a secular ecclesiastic, eligible for a church benefice, a sort of fellowship, which he held for many years.

1789   Published his prose satire *La derrota de los pedantes* (*The Defeat of the Pedants*).

1790   May 22: première of *El viejo y la niña* at the Príncipe Theater, Madrid.

1792   February 7: première of *La comedia nueva* (*The New Play*) at the Príncipe Theater, Madrid.

1792   May-August: in France with a fellowship from Manuel Godoy. He fled from Paris to England in the face of the mounting Terror.

1792-   In London, learning English, attending the theater, and ex-
1793   ploring British life and customs.

1793   August-September: traveled to Italy by way of Flanders, Germany, Switzerland.

1793-   In Italy with headquarters at Bologna.
1796

1796 Appointed Secretary of the Interpretation of Languages, he returned to Spain.
1798 Published his translation of Shakespeare's *Hamlet* with notes.
1803 January 28: première of the play *El barón* in the Cruz Theater, Madrid.
1804 May 19: première of *La mojigata* (*The Pious Deceiver*) in the Cruz Theater, Madrid.
1806 January 24: première of *El sí de las niñas* (*When a Girl Says Yes*) at the Cruz Theater, Madrid.
1808 Fled Madrid temporarily when the French invaded Spain, but returned to his post as Secretary of the Interpretation of Languages, and served under José Bonaparte.
1811 Accepted appointment from José Bonaparte to the post of librarian of the National Library.
1812 March 17: première at the Príncipe Theater, Madrid, of *La escuela de los maridos* (*The School for Husbands*), adapted from Molière's *L'Ecole des maris*.
1812 Republished, under the pseudonym of Ginés de Posadilla and with his own Voltairean notes, the seventeenth-century pamphlet *Auto de fe celebrado en la ciudad de Logroño en los días 7 y 8 de noviembre del año de 1610* (*Auto de Fe Held in the City of Logroño on November 7 and 8 of the Year 1610*).
1812 August 10: abandoned Madrid, never to return, with the French forces which retreated to Valencia.
1813 July: fled from Valencia with the French forces and took refuge in Peñíscola, which was later subjected to seige.
1814- Lived quietly in Barcelona.
1817
1814 December 5: première in Barcelona of *El médico a palos* (*The Doctor in Spite of Himself*), adapted from Molière's *Le Médecin malgré lui*.
1817- Fearful of the Inquisition, he went to France and later to
1820 Italy.
1820 Returned to Barcelona after the establishment of the new constitutional regime.
1821 Fleeing the pestilence in Barcelona, he went to France, establishing himself definitively in Bordeaux with the Manuel Silvela family.
1827 Moved to Paris with the Silvela family.
1828 June 21: died in Paris.
1830- The Academy of History published his collected works in-
1831 cluding the first edition of his *Orígenes del teatro español* (*Origins of the Spanish Theater*).

CHAPTER 1

How to Write a Play

I The Rise and Fall of the Comedia

IN the seventeenth century in Spain, it seemed that almost everybody knew how to write a play and that almost everybody wrote one—from a Madrid tailor to a court wit who was reputed to be King Philip IV.

The man who set both the example and the precept was Lope de Vega. Miguel de Cervantes, who would have liked to possess such facility, called him a monster of nature; and the appellation has stuck, for succeeding generations are astonished that a man should have written so prodigiously. Contemporaries and posterity have admired him, pillaged him, berated him, and have gone back to see his plays, read them, write about them, and simply enjoy them.

Writing two centuries after Lope's triumphs, Leandro Fernández de Moratín commended "his exquisite sensitiveness, his burning imagination, his natural eloquence, his harmonic ear, the naturalness of his language, his erudition, his wide reading of both modern and classical authors, and his practical acquaintance with the national character and customs."[1]

There was a time toward the end of the sixteenth century when the Spanish theater might have followed the dual road of tragedy and comedy which the French theater was later to take. But neither the study of the drama of antiquity in the Jesuit schools nor the work of contemporary imitators could withstand the powerful impact of Lope de Vega's genius. Lope created a structure into which he poured all the variegated products of his own imagination. The same structure served that whole school of dramatists which flourished in seventeenth-century Spain.

The *comedia*—the word should be taken to mean simply play—was a quick-moving, exciting, and romantic drama which Lope divided into three acts. In the first act he presented the situation;

15

in the second and most of the third he complicated the action; and as near the end as possible—for the audience would walk out as soon as they guessed the end—he presented the denouement. The tone of the play might vary from farce through witty comedy to passion and even tragedy, and a single play could move an audience to both laughter and tears.

While every sort of character from saint to emperor walked the boards of his theater, Lope made use of handy types—the graciosos or comic servants, the lovelorn gallants and amorous damsels, and the *barbas* or sage old men. The types of characters he used came to govern the composition of the theatrical companies. In turn, the companies required plays with parts for their actors, and self-interest demanded continued adherence to the structure that Lope created.

The characters spoke in a variety of verse which changed to reflect the situation or the emotion of the moment, and the author put into their mouths clever ambiguities which brought pleasure to audiences that were in love with wit.

In the hands of Lope, his contemporaries and his immediate followers—the great names are Tirso de Molina, Juan Ruiz de Alarcón, Pedro Calderón de la Barca, but there were dozens of others of genius—this structure, this method, produced the greatest theatrical flowering that the world had known. Lope himself wrote the precept when, in 1609, he addressed a poem to the Academy of Madrid entitled *Arte nuevo de hacer comedias en este tiempo* (*The New Art of Writing Plays in These Times*). A modern critic has said that the poem is "an ingenious academic game . . . which in practice would only have resulted in dramatic abortions."[2] This indeed happened as genius spent itself, as the Spanish dramatic tradition fell into the hands of men of little merit, as the Spanish theater fed on itself unnourished by freshets of new genius.

For a century after the death of Calderón de la Barca in 1681, the Spanish theater found no new directions. Dramatists pillaged their predecessors by doing *refundiciones*—revisions or adaptations of earlier plays. If they experimented at all, it was with the use of stage machinery. Hence, the heroic *comedia*—in the Golden Age it was known as the *comedia de teatro, de ruido*, or *de cuerpo*—enjoyed a vogue. In *La comedia nueva* (*The New Play*), Leandro Fernández de Moratín gives us an excellent idea of what such a drama was like without our being obliged to read one. His fictitious play *El gran cerco de Viena* (*The Grand Encirclement of Vienna*)—everything was on the grand scale in these comedias—masses an army on the stage in an effort to blast away the critical faculties of the audience.

One of the few developments of the eighteenth century was the *comedia de magia,* in which the dramatist put to use all the tricks of the stage machinist in order to beguile the audience with scenes of magic. Calderón had pointed the way in *El mágico prodigioso* (*The Marvelous Magician*). In the early eighteenth century a tailor, by name Juan Salvó y Vela, gave impetus to the *comedia de magia* with *El mágico de Salerno Pedro Vayalarde.* (*The Magician from Salerno Pedro Vayalarde*). So warmly did both actors and public receive it that Salvó spun out his theme into five parts, and Pedro Vayalarde was still mystifying Madrid audiences well into the nineteenth century.

The eighteenth-century theaters of Madrid had changed less than the plays. Until almost the middle of the century, they were the simple *corrales* or courtyards of the past. The public was accommodated in the patio either seated or standing, or in boxes, or in a special section for women alone. The patio was open to the sky, and an awning was drawn if it began to rain. Stage scenery was limited. Ordinary plays merited but a few hangings of calico prints or damask. When a *comedia de teatro* was performed, flats, flies, and backdrops painted especially for the particular play were used. For these delectable additions the public paid a higher admission price.

The first theater to take on a modern appearance was the Teatro de los Caños de Peral, which presented chiefly Italian opera. When it was refurbished around 1738, the authorities in charge of the two old *corrales* were stimulated to rebuild, on the same spots, the Teatro de la Cruz and the Teatro del Príncipe.

This commendable step [wrote Leandro Fernández de Moratín] gave the Spanish court suitable and comfortable theaters; but it had no effect at all on anything else connected with them. The prompter still hid in the curtains or wandered backstage from one side to the other, his cap on his head and a taper in his hand. A chief burgess presided over the spectacle seated on the proscenium with a scrivener and two bailiffs behind him. The orchestra, composed of five violins and a contrabass, was as wretched as ever. An old man playing a guitar still came on stage when an actor or actress was to sing comic verses between acts.

Costumes [Moratín commented] were as inappropriate as everything else. For example, Semiramis appeared before the audience with her hair in sausage curls, wearing earrings with pendants, a taffeta gown with a knotted collar and flowing cuffs, a dainty apron over a hoopskirt, and high-heeled shoes. Julius Caesar performed with a laurel crown adorning his curled wig, a plumed hat under his left arm, wearing a silk frockcoat under a velvet cassock, a lace necktie, stockings rolled at the knees, and a shell-handled rapier. Aristotle (as an ecclesiastic) wore the dress of an abbé: a round wig with a cap, a buttoned cassock, bow tie, mulberry-colored stockings, gold shoe buckles, and a cross-handle cane.[3]

II The Reform

Such was the theatrical scene that Ignacio de Luzán knew when he wrote the section on drama in his *Poética* (*The Art of Poetry*). Luzán was a gentleman of the world, the first of a new generation of cosmopolitan men of letters. He lived in Italy for many years, knew classical and modern European literature, and became imbued with the principles of the Italian neoclassical preceptists. In 1737 he published the *Poética* in which he developed the new criticism of the eighteenth century.

In his discussion of drama, Luzán drew the distinction between tragedy and comedy, and he developed the doctrines of imitation and verisimilitude on which the other rules of the neoclassic school rested. He emphasized the importance of the unities of action, time, and place for their contribution to verisimilitude. Likewise, he believed that dramatists should observe good taste and restraint in order not to tax the credulity of the audience. Above all, with Horace, he stressed the moral and didactic purpose of literature which, mingling *utile dulci*, should instruct as it delighted.

Some fifty years later, in 1789, Eugenio Llaguno y Amírola published a revised version of Luzán's *Poética*. During the half century that intervened between the two editions, men of letters and public officials sought to encourage literary works based on its principles. Llaguno himself translated Racine's *Athalie* (1754), which dealt with the biblical story of the widowed Athaliah, grandmother of King Joash of Judah; and Agustín de Montiano y Luyando illustrated his *Discursos sobre las tragedias españolas* (*Discourses on Spanish Tragedies*) with two examples, *Virginia* (1750) and *Ataulfo* (1753), the protagonists of which were respectively the virtuous Roman matron and the Spanish Gothic king. Montiano urged a young member of his literary circle, Nicolás Fernández de Moratín, to write "with all the rigor of art," and in 1762 Nicolás published a comedy *La Petimetra* (*The Flashy Woman*), and the following year a tragedy *Lucrecia,* which depicted the trials of another Roman woman. Years later his son Leandro described the first as lacking in comic force and the second as weak in plot and burdened with extraneous incidents.

Still, these slim beginnings began to have their effect, and in the seventies and eighties a comparatively large number of comedies and tragedies in the new style were not only written but were even produced on the stage. To be sure, the audiences who witnessed them enjoyed the *sainetes,* the short interludes presented between acts, as much or more than the plays themselves; and, if plays in the new key sorely tried their patience, they expressed their dissatisfaction violently.

Writers for the fast-developing periodical press and their readers relished the conflicts of opinion, and many a polemic was fought to a draw in pamphlets, in prologues, and in the pages of the *Diario de Madrid* (*Madrid Journal*). Futhermore, the neoclassic school had got possession of the most influential teaching job in Spain: the chair of poetry in the Reales Estudios de San Isidro, which the government operated after it expelled the Jesuits in 1767. For years Nicolás Fernández de Moratín substituted for the sickly incumbent, Ignacio López de Ayala. After Moratín's death, Santos Díez González became the substitute professor and eventually won the chair for himself. In 1793 he published his *Instituciones poéticas* (*Principles of Poetry*), the textbook for his course at the school. It is a rigorous and indeed pedantic exposition of the new criticism.[4]

Spain was ready for a man of genius capable of transforming principle into art. Nicolás Fernández de Moratín produced that man. Moratín, wrote Mesonero Romanos in his compilation of distinguished sons of Madrid, "published several poems, some of them excellent, like the epic song on *The Ships of Cortés,* two tragedies and a comedy which imitated the French classical style, and several other works; but the best of all his works was . . . his son Don Leandro."[5]

The case of the literary father who begat a literary son is not unique in Spanish letters, but the careers of Nicolás Fernández de Moratín and of his son Leandro present an unusual trajectory. Don Nicolás carefully schooled his son in the precepts of literary art which represented the new criticism of his day so that his own aspirations might be realized through his son. The literary creation of Leandro, indeed, represents a continuation and a refinement of efforts initiated by his father.

Don Nicolás was born in 1737, the year that Ignacio de Luzán published his *Poética,* that the *Diario de los Literatos de España* (*Journal of Spanish Writers*) began a brief but significant run—the year that may be said to mark the beginning of the neoclassic movement in Spain. Nicolás started his career in Madrid in the 1760's just as neoclassicism was gaining official support. In 1780 his life was cut short at the age of forty-two. Behind him he left a twenty-year-old son, who inherited his name, his friends, and his literary papers. Leandro lived to the age of sixty-eight, and when he died in 1828 José Gómez Hermosilla's rigorously classical *Arte de escribir en prosa y verso* (*Art of Writing in Prose and Verse*) with its appendix of poems by Don Leandro had become and was to remain for many years the officially adopted composition text in Spanish schools. The lives of father and son thus spanned the beginning, the development, and the triumph—unstable but real—of classicism in Spain.

An analysis of their achievement requires first an inquiry into the nature of the genius of the two men. The botanist Casimiro Gómez Ortega, a member of the coterie at the Fonda de San Sebastián, in an account of the life of Giambattista Conti, told how this Italian gentleman encouraged Don Nicolás to follow the classical precepts of art, "to the rules of which," he says, "Moratín with difficulty subjected his highly fertile genius."[6]

Nicolás Fernández de Moratín was indeed famous in his day for the fecundity of his wit and the facility with which he wrote. When the Italian extemporizer Angelo Talassi came to Spain in the 1770's, the Duke of Medina-Sidonia selected Don Nicolás to challenge him. With a boost from the admittedly partial Spanish judges, Don Nicolás' facile wit won him victory over the professional improviser who had astonished every court in Europe.[7]

On another occasion, Don Nicolás wrote a full-length play in a manner reminiscent of the composition of many a Golden Age *comedia*. In 1775 the Spanish commander at Melilla in Africa brilliantly defended the enclave against an attack by the Moroccan emperor, who was obliged to sue for peace. Public rejoicing in Madrid demanded a play, and spurred on by actors and other friends, Don Nicolás agreed to attempt one.

"I am committing folly," he told the Duke of Medina-Sidonia, who was among those encouraging him; "but I shall do so quickly since Your Excellency has declared himself the chief of this conspiracy."

"Only you can commit such follies," the Duke replied. "I can tell you right now what your play will be like. It will be a monster of art, in which we shall detect the fantasy, the diction, the sonority of Lope de Vega, even though it may be impossible to find in it the regularity of Racine."

Two hours a night for three nights—a total of six hours—composing before a group of friends, Don Nicolás dictated the play *La defensa de Melilla (The Defense of Melilla)* to a secretary and turned it over to the actors so that they might study their parts.[8]

The son Leandro inherited both the wit and facility of his father; in him, however, neoclassic distrust of fecundity became deeply implanted.

His intimate friend Juan Antonio Melón tells how, in his twenties, Leandro used to meet on Sunday mornings with a group of friends at a fountain in the Buen Retiro Park. Thanks to his wit and his jokes, his friends spent the morning convulsed with laughter. He was expert at imitating people, even those he knew but slightly. He did caricatures of the polygraph Gaspar Melchor de Jovellanos, of the dramatist Vicente García de la Huerta, even of good King Carlos III. "These jokes," Melón wrote, "issued so spontaneously from his mouth that he himself did not [at first] recognize the wit they held. . . ."[9]

When Leandro told about the wedding of his uncle Miguel, who at an advanced age married a young woman from Segovia whom he had not met until the day of the ceremony, Melón

died of mirth. In Paris in 1787, Leandro kept him up all night
rocking with laughter at one joke after another.

Leandro could direct his genius into literary channels with
notable ease. In bad weather the friends who met in the Buen
Retiro gathered in the convent cell of Pedro Estala and his fellow Piarist, Father Navarrete. Melón tells how Leandro arranged
for them to write a play: "One Sunday he declared that that
morning we would compose a play and a *sainete,* dividing the
three acts and the *sainete* by lot among the four of us. . . . I got
the *sainete*. . . . Navarrete got the first act, Estala the second, and
Leandro the third. Each one took up his pen, and when we read
the work it turned out that Estala had left all the actors dead on
the stage [at the end of the second act] so that Leandro was
obliged to redo his act."[10]

The ease with which Leandro composed endured until his
last years. He was in his sixties when he lived with the Silvela
family in Bordeaux. The son, Francisco Agustín Silvela, in a
note appended to the manuscript of a humorous improvisation,
tells how it happened to be written and was saved:

> In his conversation [Don Leandro] was an inexhaustible mine of
> jokes and witticisms that were as keen as they were innocent. My
> mother or my sister used to take a pen and encourage him to dictate
> some preposterous composition in imitation of those that are silly
> although their authors don't think they are. On one of these occasions
> he dictated the following ballad so fast that my mother scarcely had
> time to write down one verse when the next was already finished. I
> forgot to say that whenever Don Leandro let one of the women take
> her pen to write down the tragicomedy or the ballad that he was
> dictating, it was on the condition, *sine qua,* that after we had had
> our fun out of it, it would be handed over to him so that he might
> burn it in the fireplace or tear it into tiny pieces. Indeed this always
> happened. I don't know how this particular composition was saved.[11]

The paucity of Moratín's literary works is a fact, however, and
a well publicized one. Manuel Silvela explains the paradox
between his fecundity and the small number of his creative
works. "Two hundred plays and ten or twelve volumes of verse
would scarcely have sufficed to exhaust Moratín's copious wit
had not the austerity of his principles repressed and almost ex-
tinguished the fecundity of his imagination. . . . I appeal to the
testimony of his intimate friends. How often . . . would he start
to imitate some poet or other, or, sketching the plot of a play,

would he begin to act out the roles of the characters, making them talk, and never at a loss for ideas or verses or even jokes, until we were so exhausted by the violence of our laughter that we had to capitulate and ask him for an intermission."[12]

Leandro de Moratín absorbed the neoclassic lesson to which his father's genius had been recalcitrant. He grew up deeply distrustful of his own facility and that of others. Like Don Nicolás, who made sure that Pietro Napoli Signorelli appreciated Lope de Vega's art and included him in his history of the theater, Leandro warmly admired Lope. Like his father, he esteemed the intricate artistry of Calderón. He was agog at the opportunity to meet Goldoni, who was living in Paris in 1787 when Moratín first went there. But he cannot think of these men without lamenting their "overly abundant genius." "To write a lot," he affirms, "is to write badly." For he has accepted Luzán's tenet: "Good poets have composed very few dramatic works, and into them they have put much study and effort. . . ."[13]

Leandro Fernández de Moratín left behind five original comedies, several translations, a short and beautifully written history of the Spanish theater before Lope with a catalogue, a respectable quantity of verse, some travel works, and a superb collection of letters. He never attempted tragedy.

Although his original comedies are few, Moratín is, next to Lope de Vega, the most influential dramatist in Spanish literature. The combined achievement of father and son was the reform of the Spanish theater—the most absorbing aesthetic concern of the eighteenth century. Don Nicolás' comedy *La Petimetra* never got nearer the stage than being sold at a bookshop across the street from the Teatro de la Cruz. But no one who saw or read his son's *La comedia nueva* could view with the same eyes the degenerate form of heroic comedy which it mocked. And after the resounding success of *El sí de las niñas* (*When a Girl Says Yes*) proved that a simple problem about ordinary people could absorb an audience and move it to laughter and to tears, the Spanish theater took a new direction from which it was not turned either by the War of Independence or the Romantic interlude of the 1830's.

III *Moratín's Theory of Comedy*

Moratín's formula was a simple one. He defined comedy in the tradition of Aristotelian and Horatian dramatic theory with strong influence from such eighteenth-century writers as Diderot and Beaumarchais: "An imitation in dialogue (written in prose or verse) of an event occurring in one place and within a few hours among middle-class people, by means of which and through the appropriate expression of emotions and characters, the vices and errors common to society are ridiculed, and truth and virtue are accordingly recommended."[14]

Imitation is a prime tenet of Moratín's neoclassicism. The poet, in seeking verisimilitude, is the observer of nature, especially human nature. From his observation he selects, distributes, embellishes, creating a fictitious whole that is true to life. Nature presents the originals; artifice selects and combines. The dramatist, unlike authors of other genres, conceals himself behind the dialogue. He writes poems in action, for he puts his characters on the stage and lets them talk for themselves. Thus he creates in the spectator the illusion that what he sees is truly happening. Costume, scenery, movement, gesture, voice complete this delightful deception.

In his definition as in his practice, Moratín permitted either prose or verse. Prose, he wrote, imitates nature and thus is appropriate for comedy. But it is not easy to make characters speak in prose as Melibea and Areusa or Guzmán de Alfarache or Sancho Panza and his wife Teresa speak; nor can the artist easily embellish ordinary conversation without falling into exaggeration. The choice of verse presents difficulties also. Moratín rejects the more complicated verse forms—*quintillas, décimas, liras,* sonnets, and hendecasyllables—as unnatural to comedy. Only the octosyllable and *redondillas* possess suitable simplicity; and the poet must tax his skill to impart facility, energy, grace, and purity to his language.[15]

Moratín favored the famed, and defamed, unities of action, time, and place because they imparted verisimilitude to a play, making it believable. One plot with one denouement permits the dramatist to focus the attention of the public on his principal object, to lay the way for each situation, and to develop his characters. If he further limits the time and place of the action, the circumstances he depicts will appear natural and the illusion will be convincing to the audience.

Comedy, he believed, should concern itself with middle-class people. It should not usurp the great personages or the grand emotions of tragedy. Nor should it stoop to depicting the customs of the rabble; other agencies will correct the sins of the lower classes; the poet cannot. The characters in comedy should be individuals rather than types—a fault of Spain's *comedia*—for imitation requires that personages in a play, like people in real life, express the emotions and display the character which distinguish one from another.

Finally, comedy should possess a moral aim, a purpose, which is to ridicule the vices and errors common to society. Good comedy avoids emphasis on physical defects which are not susceptible to correction; rather, it focuses on moral wrongs which the spectator can recognize in himself or in his acquaintances. In censuring them, the playwright recommends to the public virtue and truth.

Leandro Fernández de Moratín's approach to playwriting was simple and direct. He sought verisimilitude, which is the key to an understanding of his theater. His search for a truthful expression breathed life into his characters, who spring from dialogue into the living reality of flesh and blood. The cult of verisimilitude resulted in a theater in which the naturalness of every entrance, every exit, every movement, every reaction conceals the deft art of the structure. The search for truth drew Moratín to the study of the Spanish language in both its popular and its elegant manifestations so that he remains today what the Spanish Academy calls an "authority on the language." It led him to a penetrating comprehension of Spanish customs and of the national psychology. "The Spanish play," he wrote, "should be clothed in a mantilla and a basquine skirt." The result was a satisfying national theater that lay, nevertheless, in the cosmopolitan mainstream of European theatrical currents.

CHAPTER 2

December Matched with May

I Mingled Laughter and Tears

GOSSIPS at the Madrid court spoke of the affair with relish. The Count of Aranda, former minister of Carlos III and at the time Spanish ambassador to Louis XVI of France, became a widower on Christmas eve of 1783. Three months later, at the age of sixty-five, the Count married the grandniece of his deceased wife, a girl who was not yet sixteen years old. The *Memorial Literario* (*Literary Digest*) for April, 1784, published an epithalamium by the attorney Miguel García Asensio in which Madrid's paltry but poetic River Manzanares, personified, relates the meeting of the distinguished gentleman and the beautiful Doña María del Pilar Silva y Palafox:

> This noble warrior, lashed by the anger of Mars,
> Feared not the tremulant hand of Fate
> Nor yet the specter of dread Discord.
> Before so sweet an image, though, he stood agape;
> He quivered, and uttered to himself, "I have been vanquished."

García Asensio's verses breathed no hint of the satire which witty Madrilenians abundantly bestowed upon a situation that richly deserved it.

It must not be supposed, however, that Leandro Fernández de Moratín's first play, *El viejo y la niña* (*The Old Man and the Girl*), owed its inception especially to the Count of Aranda's autumnal passion. To be sure, the theme was in the air and Moratín was writing his comedy about this time; but his best friend, Juan Antonio Melón, records that Moratín's play had an intimate, personal basis. When Moratín read scenes to Melón and to another friend the Piarist Pedro Estala, he also showed them letters that he had received from a young lady, whom he called Licoris, in which she declared her love for him. Melón thought he guessed her name, but Moratín refused to confess it, and Melón did not record his conjecture. Licoris married an old man, according to Melón, and Moratín was the real-life participant in a scene which he recorded in the first act of *El viejo y la niña*. Don Roque, the suspicious elderly husband, tells his servant how he surprised his wife with Don Juan; but she was busily sewing ribbons on her husband's dressing gown while the young man was apparently looking at some paintings and maps.[1]

There is reason to suspect that the object of Moratín's passion was Sabina Conti y Bernascone, daughter of Antonio Conti and Isabel Bernascone. She lived in Madrid with her parents and her maternal uncle Ignacio Bernascone on the second floor of the house in the Calle de la Puebla (today Fomento), the first floor of which was occupied by Nicolás Fernández de Moratín and his family. Leandro has testified to the intimate friendship of the two households, so close indeed that they seemed to form a single family. Leandro and Sabina knew each other well. That the two formed a romantic attachment is a supposition, albeit a well-founded one.

While Don Nicolás was still alive, the nephew of Antonio Conti, Giambattista Conti, came from Italy for a visit, and he too lived in the house in the Calle de la Puebla. He was a literary man, and he and Don Nicolás became quite friendly. He was a bachelor in his late thirties, and it was he who married the young Sabina, his cousin.[2] To Leandro, who was not yet twenty, Giambattista Conti doubtless seemed an old man. If indeed the situation resulted in the play *El viejo y la niña*, Moratín made of him a much older man. This is the revenge or perhaps the catharsis of the creative writer. We may even conjecture that writing the play healed his wounds, for a dozen years later, when Moratín went to Italy, whither Conti had borne his bride, the dramatist visited his old acquaintances at Lendinara, had a jolly time, and composed a sonnet to the local Virgin.

Moratín's first play reflects a concern that preoccupied this lifelong bachelor all his days: the upbringing of women, and their right to seek a satisfying emotional and spiritual life. His was an anxiety of the age in which he lived, and that part of Moratín's work which deals with this matter may even be regarded as a chapter in the history of women's rights. Indeed, the theme is a persistent one in modern Spanish literature. It was endemic in the Romantic theater: Doña Elvira in Larra's *Macías,* Doña Leonor in the Duke of Rivas' *Don Alvaro,* Doña Inés in Zorrilla's *Don Juan Tenorio.* It runs like an undercurrent in novels such as Valera's *Pepita Jiménez* or Pérez Galdós' *Doña Perfecta.* In the twentieth century it is a motive for comedy in Benavente's *Los intereses creados* (*The Bonds of Interest*), or for tragedy in Lorca's *La casa de Bernarda Alba* (*The House of Bernarda Alba*).

El viejo y la niña begins with a situation that precludes a happy ending. Don Roque, a widower of seventy, has recently married Doña Isabel, a girl of nineteen. An orphan, Isabel was pushed into marriage by a guardian anxious to be rid of her. He overcame the attachment which the girl had formed for her childhood sweetheart, Don Juan, only by deceiving her into believing that the youth's uncle—alas, Don Juan too is an orphan —had obliged his charge to marry another. When Don Juan, still a bachelor, comes to Cadiz on business, the two young people discover that they have been duped.

Because Don Juan's uncle had business connections for many years with Don Roque, this old gentleman finds himself actually lodging a rival in his own house. He gets no help from his widowed sister Beatriz whose sympathies are all for young Isabel. In desperation, he invokes the aid of his aging servant Muñoz to clear his house of both Don Juan and Doña Beatriz. The servant's outspoken attitude toward his master and the comic situations that result from his reluctance to be of much help provide the fun of the play.

The young people themselves realize that their love is impossible. Don Juan makes preparations to go to America on the next ship, and Doña Isabel resigns herself to her lot. But Don Roque's jealousy dominates him, and he causes his own ruin. He plots to spy on his wife. When Isabel discovers the scheme, she resolves to betake herself to a convent. Don Roque's entreaties cannot prevail against her determination, and the curtain falls as tears are shed in the *cazuela*, the section of the theater reserved for women.

II   *The Tribulations of a Novice Playwright*

So innocent and touching a theme would not seem likely to have caused its author the problems which he did indeed face.

In 1786 Moratín read the play to one of the two theatrical companies that were performing in Madrid, that of Manuel Martínez. He had already paved the way, for he had dedicated an ode to the leading lady, the charming María del Rosario Fernández, better known as La Tirana (because she was the wife of El Tirano, the actor Francisco Castellanos who specialized in the roles of tyrants). Moratín avowed to her:

> Oh, happy fortune mine
> If by your coral lips
> My verses might deserve
> To be pronounced.

> (*Feliz la suerte mía*
> *si merecer pudiese*
> *que en sus labios de rosa*
> *mis números resuenen.*)[3]

In the discussion that followed, the leading men expressed doubts that a play with so simple a plot could be successful on the stage, but the company decided, so Moratín says, that it was high time they presented some works written in accordance with the rules of art, and the actors started learning their lines.[4]

A play had to pass two censors before it could be performed, the ecclesiastical censor and the government censor. Whether both government and church favored amorous old men and frowned on romantic young love is a matter of conjecture. What is certain is that the censors so mutilated the play that scenes were truncated, dialogue became meaningless, and the whole work was quite ruined.

Another complication arose within the company. The second lady, Francisca Martínez, daughter of the impresario, was close to forty years old, but she roundly refused to play the role of Doña Beatriz, the widowed sister of old Don Roque in the play, "in order," writes Moratín, "to preserve, at least in the theater, her inalterable youth."

At this point, Moratín beat an honorable retreat. He withdrew the play and made a trip to Paris.

Back in Madrid in 1788, he read his play to the other theatrical company headed by Eusebio Ribera, and again it was a woman who intervened to dispel the dreams of the young playwright. María Bermejo, the idol and hope of the neoclassicists, protégée of the great Jovellanos, was supernumerary for the leading ladies in both the Madrid companies. Her forte was tragedy. According to Mariano Luis de Urquijo, translator of Voltaire's *La Mort de César* (*The Death of Caesar*), who exaggerated and even concealed at least one scandalous event, "she has brought such distinction to tragedies by her performances that she has won the admiration of the public when they hear something so marvelous, so that the audiences want to see only such dramas as these performed. . . ." The tragedienne, eager to win the plaudits of the court, also wanted to play comic roles. In the theatrical season 1788-1789 she did the part of the mother in Tomás de Iriarte's *El señorito mimado* (*The Spoiled Young Man*). She even won the praise of so splenetic a critic as Juan Pablo Forner, who, to be sure, praised the performance of the actress excessively in order to disparage the author.

María Bermejo read Moratín's play and, wishing to run the gamut of ages in a single season, determined that she would do the part of the girl Isabel. "That estimable actress," wrote Moratín, "could very well play the roles of Semiramis, Athaliah, Clytemnestra and Hecuba; but it was quite impossible for her to do a nineteen-year-old girl without evoking the mockery of the public for her temerity. . . . The Martínez company did not put on the play because an actress refused to play the role of a mature woman; and the Ribera Company did not produce it because another actress could not control her unfortunate desire to look like a girl."

Moratín was saved from his predicament by the ecclesiastical vicar who refused permission for the play's performance.

III *First First Night*

The year 1790 offered the playwright a better opportunity to take his first step into the kingdom of Thalia. Moratín had got to know a member of the King's Bodyguard, Don Francisco Bernabeu, who presented him to Don Luis Godoy. Don Luis in turn recommended Moratín to his brother Don Manuel Godoy, who was later to be the favorite of both the king and the queen, and whose star was on the rise at this very time. Moratín's friends believed that Don Manuel ironed out difficulties and that the license to perform was obtained through his influence.

At the same time the Ribera company had a group of actors well-suited to the parts. Since 1785 Manuel de la Torre had been leading *barba* (the name given to those who specialized in the roles of old men, because they wore a beard). Torre possessed a sonorous voice, a beautiful manner of reciting, and a true comic spark. He was capable of performing equally well the roles of a wise philosopher or a coarse jokester. In *El viejo y la niña* he did the part of Don Roque. In 1789 the actor who was to play the servant Muñoz, Mariano Querol, had been

---

El viejo y la niña
Príncipe Theater, Madrid, May 22, 1790

Don Roque, an elderly gentleman	Manuel de la Torre
Doña Isabel, his wife	Juana García
Doña Beatriz, his sister	
Don Juan, a former sweetheart of Isabel	
Blasa, maid	
Muñoz, Don Roque's manservant	Mariano Querol
Ginés, Don Juan's manservant	

---

promoted to first gracioso, or comic. Although he embittered his personal life by his vicious addiction to gambling and the consequent suffering of his numerous family, he performed cleverly and had the reputation of being unique in caricature roles. The first lady, who was to do the part of the young wife Isabel, was Juana García Ugalde. Her physical qualities were superior to her artistic talent. She had large eyes and a sweet, round face; but her soul, people said, was icy. The drama critic Santos Díez González prepared a report on her: "I find no merits in this actress except her youth and a pretty face.... Her gestures, her movements, her recitation, her insufferable singsong make her unworthy to be a leading lady on the Madrid stage."[5] But, in reality, her limited artistic gifts were not out of accord with the somewhat colorless character of Moratín's heroine.

The young dramatist attended rehearsals himself and offered the actors his opinion on the interpretation of his own characters. An actor's copy of a manuscript with Moratín's autograph revisions suggests that he made textual changes on the spot for the company.[6] The experience that he gained contributed to the proverbial fame that he had in later years for the meticulous staging of his plays.

After years of ups and downs, the play was at last ready for the public. On the day of its première, May 22, 1790, the *Diario de Madrid* carried the following notice: "At the theater in Príncipe Street, the Ribera company will perform the play entitled *El viejo y la niña*, or *El casamiento disigual* [*The Unequal Marriage*], in three successive acts; an original composition, it has only one stage setting. . . ."

The staging of the three acts successively represented a triumph for Moratín's refined taste. Normally, the acts of a play were preceded, interspersed, and followed by skits, one-act plays, dancing, and singing. It was all very jolly, but the fun completely shattered the tone and unity of the play. To be sure, the spectators were not to be deprived entirely of diversions which they heartily relished. A *sainete* and a *fin de fiesta* followed Moratín's play. The *fin de fiesta* was *Las gallegas celosas* (*The Jealous Galician Girls*) by the exceptionally popular Ramón de la Cruz. Since it was one of his weakest pieces, however, the success of *El viejo y la niña* can be attributed only to Moratín and to the actors.

The author, more indulgent than was Díez González with the leading lady, recorded these impressions of the actors: "Juana García, in the role of Doña Isabel, joined to her youth her pleasing appearance and voice, the modest expression of her face, and the grace of her movements. . . . Manuel de la Torre, one of the best comedians who flourished at the time, pleased the public extraordinarily in the role of Don Roque; and Mariano Querol played the part of Muñoz with such skill that the most presumptuous actor would not have dared compete with him."[7] Indeed, Querol made this character so popular with the public that Moratín usually referred to the comedy by the title of *Muñoz*.

In some private notes Moratín recorded with pecuniary delectation the box-office receipts, which amounted to 5,690 reales the first day, rose to 6,711 on the fourth, and then declined, as was to be expected, on the next six days that the play was performed.[8] The success was not clamorous, but it was highly respectable. The comedy was performed twice again in 1790, and it remained in the repertory of the company, always producing box-office receipts that were ample if not colossal.

IV *Tearful Comedy and the Critics*

Moratín called his play a *comedia* but the word cannot be interpreted either in the strict neoclassic sense, as it can be when applied to his other plays, nor even in the more ample meaning of the Golden Age *comedia*. *El viejo y la niña* is related in tone to what Moratín's contemporary Beaumarchais described as *le genre dramatique sérieux* and to the tearful comedy which Denis Diderot so much admired. Furthermore, its attenuated emotions are in perfect accord with the bourgeois commercialism of the Cadiz setting.

The cultivated critic of the eighteenth century was justifiably concerned if a drama had too much action, for the mediocre writers of the day had carried the exciting developments of the Golden Age to an extreme in which a violently moving plot concealed an emptiness devoid of every other dramatic element. Nevertheless, the practical playwright who wanted to see his play on the stage knew that his play must possess that *vis comica,* the lack of which Julius Caesar criticized in the Roman dramatist Terence. Moratín kept constantly before him the need for comic strength, for a drama that moved. A dramatist, he knew, cannot fool the public on this point.

In his notes to *El viejo y la niña* he writes: "In order to judge whether a play has too much action, the opinion of the experts should be sought; to judge whether it has sufficient, only the decision of the audience ought to be consulted. In the theater there is no defect more intolerable than that coldness which is the inevitable result of a weak plot. If the curiosity of the public is not aroused, if it does not increase as the audience experiences suspense, fear, and doubt, then people are distracted and bored; they fall asleep, they leave the theater, or they condemn with cries of indignation the sterile wit who enticed them into the theater only to deceive them." Like Aristotle, Moratín gives primacy to plot: "Let no one say that fine language, sonorous versification, or a graceful and lively style can oblige the public to applaud a play in which there is insufficient action, because this is not true."[9]

El viejo y la niña is an excellently constructed play. In view
of the prevailing aesthetic dogma, Moratín followed the unities
of time, place, and action. The exposition is rapid and fun. Don
Roque confides in Muñoz his concern over the presence of a
rival in his own house. Age and years of service make Muñoz an
unwilling accomplice in Don Roque's design to rid himself of
Don Juan. As the action develops, as Don Juan and Doña
Isabel realize that their situation is hopeless, the audience is on
the verge of tears. The distant cannon shot which announces
the departure of Don Juan's ship for America sounds the most
poignant note in eighteenth-century Spanish theater. Yet Don
Roque's bungling and Muñoz' grumbling counteract the inher-
ent sentimentality of the action. The farcical scene in which Don
Roque obliges his servant to hide under a sofa in order to spy on
the lovers is famous in the history of the Spanish stage.

In assessing the denouement of his play, Moratín observed
that the ordinary reader or theatergoer "will see that the plot of
this story required the author to express with all the energy
that technique provides the lamentable results of a violent and
unequal marriage, and that for this purpose the ridiculous did
not suffice if to it were not added emotional involvement. He
will see that if the situations in which Don Roque and Muñoz
enliven the stage with merriment are necessary and true-to-
life, the scenes between Don Juan and Doña Isabel are no less
so. The denouement, sad to be sure, is no less suitable, for it is
contained within the bounds of comic moderation and is designed
to show the fate of those who, joined by the indissoluble bonds
of matrimony, recognize too late the precipice to which their
lack of prudence or their innocent timidity has led them."[10]

Moratín wrote *El viejo y la niña* in verse. This was the fashion
in Spain, and he was not yet ready to break with tradition. Still,
he chose the *romance* meter, that is, eight-syllable verses with
assonant rhyme in alternate lines. The form contrasts with the
rich and varied versification of the Golden Age *comedia* or of
the Romantic theater. The simplicity of the verse corresponds
to the doctrine of verisimilitude. Dialogue must sound natural,
and verse, to appear natural, should sound like prose.[11] In Spanish the verse form closest to prose in Moratín's day was assonant
rhyme in *á-a*. Eventually, Moratín had to ask himself the ques-

tion, Why verse at all? And his answer was to write the finest prose dialogue in the Spanish theater.

In a century that was characterized by bitter literary feuds, a success, no matter how modest it might be, could not fail to arouse caustic criticism. In the *Correo* (*Mail*), the *Diario,* and the *Memorial Literario,* articles and letters, sonnets and rondelets were published for and against *El viejo y la niña.* The Aragonese cleric Don Alvaro Guerrero gave an account of the attacks in his rondelet:

> Because it's a play
> Perfect and correct,
> Harsh remarks are made
> About *The Old Man and the Girl.*

> (*Por ser una pieza*
> *perfecta y cumplida*
> *mil cosas se dicen*
> *del* Viejo y la niña.)

And he went on to explain that it had no proud kings, lascivious queens, assaults on castles, women defending fortresses; that the stage technicians had created no oceans, pinnacles, chasms, no lightning, rain showers, snowfalls nor windstorms; and since the play resembled not at all the common theatrical fare of the day, some people were speaking out against it.[12]

On the other hand, an especially pompous attack came from a writer who chose to make a rigorous application of all the rules of art. He signed himself Don Fulgencio de Soto. He may well have been Don Cristóbal Cladera, later supposed to be the model for the pedant Don Hermógenes in Moratín's *La comedia nueva* (*The New Play*). Pretending that he is citing the judgment of a friend, he indulges in a string of wordy concepts: "[My friend] says that the play is the least defective modern comedy that has come to his attention; but that in the protasis of the first act the author ought to give only an inkling of the plot, while the epitasis should belong to the second act and part of the third. In this play, however, two thirds of the whole are bunched up into the first act, since most of the plot is already revealed in it."[13]

Moratín defended himself against this criticism in a long, elegant letter, characterized by moderation, which he published in the *Correo*.[14] With less moderation, the pugilistic Don Juan Pablo Forner leaped into the combat, preferring to attack the enemy rather than confine himself to a defense of his friend Leandro. "I don't know whether I may be deceived, but I would dare to assert without much likelihood of being contradicted that the letter is the work of one of our poetasters who darn and mend up what pass for comedies, whom *El viejo y la niña* felled with a mortal blow," declared Juan Pablo who thence proceeded to assail ham actors as well: "They saw (and it gave them a big bellyache) that a simple plot sustained only by the charm and warmth of the dialogue... drew from the audience repeated applause and continuing approval. They saw that it isn't necessary for the actors to rave, gesticulate, and dislocate their joints while reciting long tirades of ridiculous and irrelevant verses. They saw that it isn't necessary for armies, encampments, castles and besieged cities to be shown on the stage, nor need battles be unleashed in order to keep the public agape and thus disguise through pageantry the sterility of their genius...."[15]

Moratín printed the play the same year it was produced, and sent off copies to some of the famous literary lights of the day. The French fabulist and dramatist Claris de Florian wrote congratulating the young Spaniard on his observation of the proprieties: "Your talent found the means to evoke lively concern for this unfortunate wife, to depict in colors both tender and strong the rapture of her first love, to place her on the stage in the absence of her husband face to face with the man she adores without for a moment offending the strictest sense of modesty, decency and morality."[16]

The distinguished Jesuit Esteban de Arteaga wrote to Forner from his exile in Italy: "... although [the play] is not strong in what Julius Caesar, speaking of Terence and Menander, called *vis comica*, nevertheless its author seems to be to be a man of taste, with a good foundation, who is following the right path. I like his style—simple, balanced, pure—enriched with certain idioms peculiar to Madrid if I recall correctly."[17]

Pedro Napoli Signorelli, historian of the ancient and modern theater, translated *El viejo y la niña* into Italian and saw it applauded on the Neapolitan stage. But the Italian ladies found the denouement melancholy, preferring, contrary to Spanish women, a happy ending. "With an excess of docility," commented

Moratín, "the translator surrendered to the powerful wishes of that sex which by weeping rules and tyrannizes. He changed the ending—if he were going to do that, he ought to have revised the whole plot—and by thus offending verisimilitude, he so manifestly contradicted the principles of art that there is no excuse for what he did."[18]

El viejo y la niña quickly attracted the attention of amateur actors so that it was necessary to make a second edition. Jovellanos in his *Diary* relates that a group in Gijón put on the play.[19] Naturally, there were imitations, including the opposite situation, *La vieja y el niño* (*The Old Woman and the Boy*), which must have been a farce.[20] In the middle of the nineteenth century Manuel Tamayo y Baus recreated the plot in *Un drama nuevo* (*A New Drama*), and gave the public one of the most theatrically exciting plays of the age. However, the theme, a lifelong preoccupation for Moratín, closely resembled that of *El sí de las niñas,* which not only had more sparkle and wit but also a happy ending. *El viejo y la niña,* Moratín's first comedy, took second place to his last original play, *El sí de las niñas.*

CHAPTER 3

A Play About Playwrights

THE critic Menéndez y Pelayo described *La comedia nueva*
(*The New Play*) as "the most astonishing satire that I know
in any language."[1] Plays about actors and the play within a play
have successfully illuminated the art of the theater; in *La
comedia nueva* Moratín presents dramatic criticism dramatized.
From the vantage point of Pastrana, a village in the Alcarria
northeast of Madrid, where he went after the success of *El viejo
y la niña*, Moratín measured the small progress of the theater
in the thirty years since his father had composed *La petimetra*
and *Lucrecia*.

I   The Madrid Stage in 1792

In 1792, Madrid still had only three public theaters. The
newest was Los Caños del Peral, built in 1708 and reconstructed
in 1758. It was devoted principally to opera. The Cruz and the
Príncipe, where plays were performed, were by now almost fifty
years old, and such was their condition that the public wore
old clothes to performances. The companies were formed during
Lent, the period in which they rehearsed their new plays. Thus
the theatrical season began at Easter and ended the next year
with Carnival. In a modified way this tradition persists in the
contemporary theater, for today many plays close in the last
days of Lent while *Sábado de Gloria* and the days immediately
following are the occasion for many premières. Madrid had first
choice of actors and actresses, but there was a flourishing pro-
vincial theater despite the efforts, frequently successful, of Fray
Diego de Cádiz and others to persuade cities, by local option,
to forbid theatrical performances.

Madrid did not succumb to the blandishments of the persuasive
friar, but it did take seriously the problem of controlling the
theaters. The Mayor of the city was also Judge Protector of the
theaters. His authority extended to everything that concerned

the actors, the plays, and the stage. He oversaw the formation of the companies; he was responsible for the equipment and maintenance of the theaters; he supervised the pay and even the conduct of the actors, being charged with seeing to it that they lived decently and did not scandalize the public in their private lives.

He was also required to examine, censor, and either approve or reject all plays. Plays were supposed to be presented to him before any action was taken, but reality was different than the law. Usually an author submitted and read his play to the company of actors. If they liked it, the actors might distribute the parts, begin studying their roles and go into rehearsal. Just before the performance, they would get around to sending the play to the Judge Protector for his approval.[2]

The Judge Protector exercised jurisdiction over the stage and the actors; a Burgess from the Bench of Burgesses presided over the pit. Although authority was divided, the two must have cooperated for the common good. For example, actresses were wont to travel between their homes and the theater in sedan chairs. The slow pace of the Galician bearers gave young blades the opportunity to exchange banter with these women who were sharp of wit and tongue. The resulting disorders led the municipal government to provide the actresses with carriages in which they went swiftly to and from the theater.[3]

The Bench of Burgesses particularly had to contend with the companies' impassioned supporters who were bent on bringing success to their favorites and failure to the competing company. The claques had begun two generations before Moratín's day. One was the Chorizos (Sausages), originally supporters of the troupe at the Teatro del Príncipe. In 1742, we are told, the property manager failed to put on stage some sausages which the gracioso Francisco Rubert was supposed to eat. So amusing were the remarks that he ad-libbed to cover the contretemps that thenceforth the Príncipe company and its fans were called Chorizos. The adherents of the Cruz were called Polacos (Poles) from the name, or more likely the nickname, of a certain Father Polaco, a Trinitarian and frequent and vocal spectator of the company that played there. Still a third group, the Panduros (Hardbread) favored the company at the Caños del Peral. When the Count of Aranda shifted the companies from one theater to another, the fans were no longer associated with a particular theater but with a company.[4]

In 1768 the Count of Aranda founded the Teatro de los Sitios Reales, a court theater that played at the various royal estates and aspired to present a more refined fare than that available at the public theaters. The director was the journalist José Clavijo y Fajardo, whose affair with the sister of Pierre-Augustin Beaumarchais inspired the Frenchman's sentimental comedy *Eugénie* as well as Goethe's *Clavigo*. A school of declamation was established as adjunct to the Teatro de los Sitios.

The next two decades did not, however, witness the theatrical reforms that the Moratíns, father and son, and their friends expected and hoped for. *La comedia nueva* thus represents a criticism and an aspiration. A would-be playwright, his family, and his friends become flesh and blood before our eyes, make foolish blunders and learn a lesson in the best comic tradition.

II *The Play Within the Play*

Moratín illustrated what he was criticizing in the drama of his day by *El gran cerco de Viena* (*The Great Siege of Vienna*), the play that his young protagonist Don Eleuterio Crispín de Andorra composed at the instigation of his wife and his friend Don Hermógenes. This play within a play is not actually performed, but the characters of *La comedia nueva* recite and describe many scenes so that we end up knowing a great deal about it. It is indeed monstrous.

The play begins in the grand manner: "Enter the Emperor Leopold, the King of Poland and the Seneschal Frederick, in full dress, accompanied by ladies and magnates and a brigade of hussars mounted on horseback." The Emperor plunges at once and without subtlety into the exposition:

> As you know, my vassals,
> some two and half months ago
> the Turk to Vienna laid
> siege with his troops.
> In order to resist him
> we mustered our courage,
> and in repeated clashes
> our noble determination
> has given ample proof
> of our unconquered hearts.

> Well do I know that lack
> of needed sustenance
> has been such that, overcome
> by the power of hunger,
> we have eaten rats,
> toads and filthy insects.

A playgoer of even moderate sophistication could readily recognize that Moratín's playwright Don Eleuterio had fathered one of those pieces in which pageantry and bathos substituted for the grandeur and the emotion of an earlier theater.

But Don Eleuterio gives us more: Act II begins pathetically. A lady falls dead of hunger after heaping imprecations on the Vizier who starved her for six days because she refused to become his concubine. At the end of the act, this rash and lascivious Turk, dark and ugly of face, squint-eyed, with large moustache, participates in a trio with the Emperor and the Seneschal. Don Eleuterio explains that each man is preoccupied with his own thoughts: "The Emperor is fearful because of a note he has found on the floor, without either signature or addressee, in which his own death is plotted. The Vizier is dying to possess the beautiful Margarita, daughter of the Count of Strambangaum, who is the traitor.... The Seneschal, who is an honorable man if there ever was one, is out of his mind because he knows that the Count is trying to get his job away from him and is always carrying tales against him to the Emperor; so each one of these characters is preoccupied with his own concern and he talks about it, and it's the most natural thing."

The trio intones:

EMPEROR. And while I my distrust . . .
VIZIER. And whilst I my hopes . . .
SENESCHAL. And until my enemies . . .
EMPEROR. Do verify . . .
VIZIER. Do achieve . . .
SENESCHAL. Do fall . . .
EMPEROR. Rancor, give me your favor . . .
VIZIER. Fail me not, oh, tolerance . . .
SENESCHAL. Courage, attend my arm . . .
ALL. That my fatherland may admire
my artifice most brave,
my most tremendous deed.

Between the heartrending first scene and the thickening plot of this last scene, the dramatist expected to treat his public to a series of melodramatic episodes: an exchange of daggers, the Emperor's dream, a prayer by the Vizier to his idols, a storm, a council of war, a dance, and a funeral; and there was more to come. But the public never got to see them. When a mother and her child came on stage crying with hunger, the child wailing, "Mama, give me some bread," and the mother invoking Demogorgon and Cerberus, the pit could take no more, raising such a racket that the curtain had to be rung down; and that was the end of *El gran cerco de Viena*.

III   *Action and Character*

La comedia nueva itself enjoyed real success on the stage, and its action is as simple as that of *El gran cerco de Viena* is complex. The playwright, his family, and friends have lunch at a café (presumably the famed Fonda de San Sebastián) near the Príncipe Theater before the première of his first play. It is 3:30, still half an hour before the 4:00 o'clock curtain, by the watch of the pedantic Don Hermógenes: "Here is my watch, which is always quite exact. Three-thirty precisely." Much later, after we hear an account of all the illusions that the characters have built up on the success of the play, the question of time comes up again. "I've got it here," says Don Hermógenes, "three-thirty precisely." All rush to the theater, having missed the first act and the *tonadilla*—the musical interlude—arriving barely in time for the debacle. The characters return to the café where the playwright's wife recovers from her fainting spell, and all of them resign themselves to the loss of their illusions.

The action of a play could hardly be simpler. Indeed, most of it hinges on the assuredness with which Don Hermógenes informs his friends of the time—by a watch which has stopped. The plot springs in the most natural way from the personality of the characters in the play.

The pedant, Don Hermógenes, became proverbial in Spain because, after saying a thing in Latin, he explained it in Greek —for greater clarity. Although he is not the principal character in the play, he may be thought of as a protagonist. He encouraged Don Eleuterio to write for the theater. He praised his friend's wit, exaggerated the merit of *El gran cerco de Viena*, and urged him to complete several other plays that he had begun. To Don Eleuterio he appeared qualified to give him good counsel: Don Hermógenes wrote for the newspapers, he translated from the French, and he gave public lectures. He was famous for the rigor and scrupulosity with which he criticized the works of other writers. Self-interest possibly blinded

---

La comedia nueva
Príncipe Theater, Madrid, February 7, 1792

Don Eleuterio, a playwright	Manuel García Parra
Doña Agustina, his wife	Polonia Rochel
Doña Mariquita, his sister	Juana García
Don Hermógenes, a pedant	Mariano Querol
Don Pedro	Manuel de la Torre
Don Antonio	Félix de Cubas
Don Serapio, a theatrical fan	Francisco López
Pipí, a waiter	José García

Don Hermógenes to the defects of the play, for, if it was successful, he expected Don Eleuterio to pay off his debts and award him the hand of his sister. When the play failed, Don Hermógenes maintained he knew it was bad all along, and he abandoned his protégé as well as the young lady.

Don Eleuterio Crispín de Andorra is a young man with no job and a large family to support: a wife, four children under five years old, and a sister. He had gone to school to the Piarist fathers and had learned to do sums and write tolerably well. With these skills he had got a job as a clerk with the government lottery, but he had left it to become a page and majordomo in the household of a man who had got rich in the New World. There he met his wife Agustina, a maid in the household. When his master died, he began to write plays, and, persuaded by Don Hermógenes that they were good, he was living from hand to mouth and deeply in debt until a success in the theater would make his fortune.

To assure the success of his play, he not only was on good terms with the actors at the theater that was to produce it, but also cultivated the friendship of the actors and fans of the other theater so that they would not turn on him. Indeed, he went regularly to the house of the leading lady of the rival company; he did a bit of shopping for her, fed birdseed to her canary, and even lent a hand in the kitchen. For all this effort he was to receive for his play fifteen doubloons, reduced from the usual twenty-five, the price that the companies paid in the winter season. As one character remarked, plays, like fish, were worth more as soon as the weather turned cool.

His wife Agustina was a bluestocking, who delighted in assisting her husband in the composition of his plays. "Fecundity," she laments to Don Hermógenes, "is a torment for educated women." Feeding, diapering, and caring for her wailing brood are painful distractions from her preferred occupation: discussing with her husband whether a scene is too long or too short, counting syllables on her fingers, deciding whether the episode played on a dark stage should take place before the battle or after the poisoning, searching the foreign section of the *Gazette* and the *Mercury* for strange surnames ending in *-of* or *-graf*. Doña Agustina—the former maid—can improvise verse, but she cannot bring herself to clean house, sew, wash, or even cook.

Mariquita, Eleuterio's sister, plays Martha to Agustina's Mary, although she was foolishly persuaded to give up marriage to a pharmacist for Don Hermógenes. She can cook, iron, sew, and darn; she knows how to write and do sums; and she can keep a house and rear a family. She is sixteen and unmarried, and this worries her. Since she gave up her pharmacist, she devotes herself to making herself agreeable to Don Hermógenes by such girlish wiles as tossing bread crumbs at his wig. When he walks out on her, she is desolate but accepts Don Pedro's counsel that if she will quit being so obvious, a young man will come along.

Don Serapio is a theater buff, a busybody and a gossip. He followed the actresses' sedan chairs to the theater, tossing them sweets; from the audience he waved at them on stage. He had breakfast with the hairdressers and lunch with the prompters, and between times he collected and spread stories of the plays that were to be produced and of the actors' personal and professional affairs. Don Serapio encouraged Don Eleuterio in his writing, and it was he who arranged the marriage between Mariquita and Don Hermógenes.

Pipí the waiter, a protatic character, serves to emphasize the theme, for even he is so infected with theatrical madness that he is about to start writing dramatic verse himself.

The antagonists to this world of delusion are Don Antonio and Don Pedro de Aguilar. Don Antonio is a kind-hearted man who plays Philinte to Don Pedro's Misanthrope. He is a cultivated man of taste. He recognizes and praises the merits of a good work of art; yet he will applaud an absurdity rather than subject its creator to cruel disillusionment. His real thoughts come through only as veiled irony.

Don Pedro is rich, generous, and honorable, but by nature serious and indeed harsh in judging his fellow man. He cannot dissimulate. If the truth will hurt, he must be silent or leave the gathering in which he finds himself. However, so incensed is he by the defects of *El gran cerco de Viena* that he disillusions Don Eleuterio when the young man seeks excuses for the failure of his play, and makes him recognize his own mediocrity. But when he learns that Don Eleuterio has family responsibilities, Don Pedro generously offers him a job as assistant to his majordomo.

Don Pedro does not carry alone the burden of teaching Eleuterio his lesson. It was the angry theater public which gave the wretched dramatist his comeuppance. The rumbling began in the first act; but at the beginning of the second act, when the starving mother appeared with her child crying for bread, the accumulation of nonsense was more than the audience could take. In the pit there was a rising surge of audible yawns, coughing, sneezing, and catcalls, followed by bellows, clapping, and stamping until it seemed as if the house was coming down. The curtain was drawn, the doors were opened, and the crowd poured into the street.

Doña Agustina arrives fainting at the café with her husband and his sister. After Don Hermógenes abandons them, and Don Pedro drives home the lesson, Don Eleuterio declares that he will burn his manuscripts before he takes up his new job, and his wife and sister offer to help him.

IV *Imitation and Reality*

Public malice, Moratín wrote, insisted on pointing to the models from real life that he had presumably used in writing *La comedia nueva*. In his prologue to the first edition (1792), he denied that he had represented any particular person: "This play gives a faithful picture of the current state of our theater;

but neither in its characters nor in allusions to people, is anyone portrayed in such a manner that the original may be identified from the copy." He imitated nature, he maintained, forming out of the traits of many people one individual character.[5]

Nevertheless, both his contemporaries and posterity have persisted in identifying the models. Don Hermógenes, it was said, was that very Don Cristóbal Cladera, who, under the pseudonym of Don Fulgencio de Soto, had attacked El viejo y la niña with a display of pedantic Latinisms. Cladera was a priest, born in Mallorca the same year as Moratín; he had taken a doctorate in civil and canon law at Valencia. He had established himself at court and edited a periodical, a digest of articles from European reviews entitled Espíritu de los mejores diarios literarios que se publican en Europa (Digest of the Best Literary Journals Published in Europe), until in 1791 the government, alarmed at events in France, suspended all publications except the Diario (Daily). In 1800, Cladera published a tract attacking Moratín's translation of Hamlet; but in later years, as a friend of Moratín's best friend, Juan Antonio Melón, he proudly recognized himself to be the model of Don Hermógenes.[6]

Even before La comedia nueva was produced or published, the prolific dramatist Luciano Francisco Comella suspected from reports he heard that he and his family were the objects of its satire, and he attempted to have it suppressed.

Comella was a native of the Catalan town of Vich, near Barcelona. He was nine years Moratín's senior, and in 1792 was already in his forties. In the 1780's he lived in Madrid under the protection of the Marquess of Mortara, who had been a comrade-in-arms of his father and who had taken in the boy when he was orphaned. One of Comella's plays, Cecilia, was performed at the noble's home, and the Marquess and the Marchioness as well as Comella and his wife took roles in it. Comella had married María Teresa Beyermón, a lady-in-waiting to the Marchioness of Mortara. They had four children, two girls and two boys. The eldest, Joaquina, inherited her father's talent for facile versification, and she helped him in writing plays. The wife died in 1792, shortly after the production of La comedia nueva, and Joaquina preceded her father in death in 1800.[7]

In a lifetime of writing (he died at the age of sixty-one), Comella composed more than a hundred plays. They were favorites among the actors of his day, and the public liked them too, although the economics of the theater were such that he never reaped the rewards of his popularity.

An article in a British magazine, written probably by the Mexican dramatist Eduardo Gorostiza, gave a more unbiased evaluation of his work than can be found among his Spanish critics:

Comella, with all his faults, his paltry style and corrupt taste, had certain qualities that may be held sufficient to have brought him into vogue. He wrote with rapidity and copiousness, and was thus easily enabled to satisfy the daily cravings of the players, ever restless after novelty. He well understood the mechanical portion of his art, whether in the distribution of scenes or the gradual development of the plot. Endued with some share of sensibility, he occasionally, and perhaps unconsciously, presented situations allied to genuine emotion, and optical exhibitions that might affect for a moment those who care but to gratify their eyes. Honourable in his private character, he always rendered homage, as a writer, to misfortune and to virtue. Accordingly, in every subject he selected we meet with a spotless victim, persecuted by a vicious potentate, suffering with exemplary patience throughout the play, and recompensed precisely at the last lines of the last act.[8]

Comella essayed all genres, denominating his plays as tragedy, tragic scene, tragic drama, drama, heroic drama, comedy, heroic comedy, musical comedy, and opera; and he also composed short pieces: the introduction, *sainete, fin de fiesta,* and *loa.* By 1792, when Moratin had seen only *El viejo y la niña* produced on the stage, Comella was already known for numerous works. His lachrymose *Cecilia* (1786) and *Cecilia viuda* (*Cecilia Widowed*), 1787, attracted the women to the theater for a good cry. *La Jacoba* (1789) enthralled audiences with the tribulations of a married woman (English, to be sure) who is involved in a love triangle worthy of a twentieth-century soap opera. He owed his greatest fame to his three *Federicos: Federico II, Rey de Prusia*(*Frederick II, King of Prussia*), drama (1788); *Federico II en el campo de Torgau* (*Frederick II on the Field of Torgau*), comedy—in the broad sense (1789); and *Federico II en Glatz* (1792), heroic drama. These plays and his many others like them were characterized by a complicated plot, frequent changes of scene, many characters, especially soldiers, much sounding of drums—and slight literary merit. They were absurd when read, but in the theater they were entertaining.

In 1790 Comella staged *El sitio de Calés* (*The Siege of Calais*). There can be little doubt that it was the model for Moratín's fictitious *El gran cerco de Viena*. The spectator is treated to the trials that the inhabitants of that port suffered when Edward III of England besieged it in 1346. In the first scene the leading lady describes to the sufferers themselves what they have been going through:

> For three months now
> your only food has been
> tasteless horse meat,
> dogs, and filthy bugs,
> and for two days past
> you have lacked even that succor.

If Comella failed to write drama of literary merit, he did create plays of undeniable theatrical appeal. If he was at fault in plot, character, thought, and style, he treated the public to an enriched fare of music and spectacle. He began his dramatic career as the author of *tonadillas*, or musical skits, and he also wrote zarzuelas. As he composed his plays he planned musical background for them. The words were not sung, but the words and actions were accompanied by appropriate music in the same way that the cinema employs music to work on the emotions of the audience. The most popular musicians of his day composed for his works: Blas Laserna, Pablo del Moral, Pablo Esteve, and Bernardo Álvarez Acero. Comella is, indeed, the outstanding eighteenth-century Spanish writer of melodrama in its original sense of a romantic or sensational play interspersed with songs and orchestral music.

An example of what he attempted may be found in his two-act melodrama *Sofonisba* (1795), the story of how the sister of the Carthaginian general Hasdrubal was ordered by her husband Masinissa to kill herself rather than fall into the hands of the Roman Scipio Africanus. In the directions, Comella described the nature of the accompanying music: "A long musical period which first indicates Galusa's surprise and afterward his desire to find out what Masinissa is doing. ... Galusa is frightened, and the orchestra indicates his terror in three musical bars ... Interlude music which shows the caution with which Masinissa is examining the entrance to the palace. ... Sophonisba appears seated and revealing the greatest dejection. After a pause marked by interlude music, she speaks with the greatest languor. ... A musical bar which imitates a sigh. ... A brief musical period which shows Masinissa's wish to free Sophonisba."

In a different vein, and among his grandest creations, was *Cristóbal Colón* (*Christopher Columbus*), 1790, with music by Bernardo Álvarez Acero. The *Correo de Madrid* (*Madrid Mail*) gave him an unmerciful drubbing in its review, but the public loved it.

To the appeal of music Comella added the attraction of spectacle which, since the seventeenth century, the Spanish stage had been developing in the *autos sacramentales*, in plays for court theaters, in the Italian opera imported by Farinelli, in the *comedia de magia* which made stage effects of supreme importance, and in the heroic drama, tragedy, or comedy which emphasized the grandiose. In *La esclava del Negro Ponto* (*The Slave of the Black Sea*), changes of scene present the public with a throne room, a palace gallery, a garden with wrought-iron fence, a grand stairway, a glass-enclosed porch, a wall with towers and merlons; and beyond the wall, Comella says in his stage directions, may be seen a part of the city which "will begin to burn with the greatest possible realism." One of the stage directions for *Asdrúbal,* a tragic drama in one act on the fall of Carthage to the Romans, states: "Battle is joined and the Romans drive off the Carthaginians. The scene changes. In the background the great temple of Aesculapius with a portico in front. All the upper part of it should be practicable. Before the portico a palisade, and in front of it a wall which at the proper moment will be knocked down with battering rams. Also, the temple will burn up at the proper time." The second scene of the *sainete* entitled *El menestral sofocado* (*The Artisan Quenched*) takes place just outside the gate from which dead animals are dragged from the bull ring. A stage direction reads: "The gate opens and two soldiers ride out on horseback followed by the mules with the dead bull."

In *La buena esposa* (*The Good Wife*), Comella provided a sort of striptease for the delectation of the audience. When the Arab Zafir of Alexandria determines to test the humility of his wife Zara by pretending to cast her out, she accepts his decision with resignation, and prepares to abandon the palace for a lowly hut, casting off even the jewels and clothes that she is wearing. "She keeps taking off the clothes that she has on," reads Comella's direction. The role was played by the great Rita Luna, a favorite of the male public. How far she went is not recorded, but she ended by donning a humble shepherdess's dress of skins which just happened to be in a drawer in the palace room.

One of Comella's virtues from the point of view of the actor was that he created great roles. *La esclava del Negro Ponto* is as preposterous a play as the eighteenth-century stage offered: the slave girl survives the assault and burning of the city, the amorous rapture of the sultan, the furious jealousy of the sultaness, the revolt of the janissaries, and ends up marrying the victorious general Solimán, who is converted to Christianity. Yet the title role was one of Rita Luna's greatest triumphs, and she had her portrait painted in the costume of the slave.

Such was the antagonist that Moratín provoked in his parody of the theater of his day. Even though he stoutly maintains that Comella was not his specific model, Comella himself clearly believed that Moratín was satirizing him. On January 27, 1792, less than a fortnight before the première, Comella had sufficient information about the play to lodge a protest with the Count of Cifuentes, President of the Council of Castile. In his letter he stated that Moratín portrayed him, his wife María Teresa Beyermón, and his daughter (under the guise of his sister) in the play *La comedia nueva*, citing as proof of the specific application that the poet in the play married a servant of his former master, that he had four children, that the play that he has written is for sale at the newsstands of the *Diario*, that the sister (that is, daughter) is sixteen years old, that the poet teaches her grammar and she writes verse, that he is a Catalan and Moratín makes fun of Catalan food. Besides these direct allusions to himself, Comella stated, Moratín invented injurious calumnies: he says the daughter (sister) was tossing bread crumbs at Don Hermógenes and he supposes that the poet is on intimate terms with an actress. Appealing to the laws which prohibit such direct satires, Comella begs the president to suppress the play. The Count of Cifuentes, on the next day, turned the matter over to Don José Antonio Armona, Mayor of Madrid and Judge Protector of the theaters. Armona in turn sought the opinion of his censors, Don Santos Díez González and Don Miguel

de Manuel. From that moment Comella had lost his cause. Both men were professors at the Reales Estudios de San Isidro, formerly a Jesuit school, now secularized and in the control of the neoclassicists. Both were friendly with Moratín, especially Don Santos. Their supposedly independent reports made fun of Comella and completely vindicated Moratín.

In the meantime the ecclesiastical Vicar, ill informed, Moratín tells us, by advisers sympathetic to Comella, was refusing to approve. Even he gave in, and then the Mayor gave his approval on February 5, just two days before the first performance, with one concession to the critics of the play: a single word was suppressed. What it was has not been reported.

So Comella lost, and *La comedia nueva* was played in February. Five months later, on July 12, his comedy of manners, *El indolente* (*The Lazy Man*), was produced. It was as if Comella had learned a lesson from *La comedia nueva*. *El indolente* studies character and presents certain defects of current society. It has a simple but adequate plot with good comic scenes presented in natural language with amusing jokes. It is not a great play, but it is a good one. In September, a musical comedy by Comella was performed with the title *El abuelo y la nieta* (*Grandfather and Granddaughter*). The pattern of the title cannot but recall *El viejo y la niña* although the theme is different: a father has gone to America, leaving his orphaned daughter to be reared by her grandfather. His permissiveness turns the girl into a haughty, willful, headstrong young woman who falls in love with her tutor, a scheming young abbé. When the father returns from America, he reestablishes order in the household and punishes the tutor. This intriguing abbé bears some resemblance to Moratín, and there are enough references scattered through the three acts to give credence to the suspicion that Comella intentionally represented Moratín. Don Santos Díez González was away and the censorship was entrusted to Friar Pedro de Centeno. Centeno did not detect the allusions to Moratín. He liked the play both for its adherence to the rules of art, and for its message concerning the proper upbringing of women, and hence approved it for performance.

Don Santos was on hand the next year when Comella presented for approval a *fin de fiesta* entitled *El violeto universal, o El café* (*The Universal Violet, or the Café*).[9] The second half

of the title could only be a reference to *La comedia nueva, o El café*. The *fin de fiesta* takes place in a café, and the author produces several characters each with his own mania. The "universal violet" refers to the scholar or literary man whom José Cadalso satirized in his book *Los eruditos a la violeta* (*Violet-Water Scholars*), 1772; the literary man acts as if he possessed vast knowledge, but in reality he is an ignoramus. Among the "violets" in the skit was a literary critic, Don Rufino, with a project for reforming the theaters.

> "I'm putting in a general director." [He tells another character.]
> "Doubtless you want the job."
> "Why do you say that?"
> "Because the primary purpose of anyone who makes up projects is to get the job with the highest salary."

Don Santos, who had seen no personal reference to Comella in *La comedia nueva,* detected clearly the satire directed at Moratín in *El violeto universal,* and he cut the whole section out, although he permitted the performance of the skit after its revision.

If Comella learned a lesson from *La comedia nueva,* it did not last long. *Los hijos de Nadasti* (*The Sons of Nadasti*) is a heroic comedy in three acts, performed in 1795. It is in the style of *El sitio de Calés* or of Moratín's fictitious *El gran cerco de Viena.* The Turks besiege Buda. Nadisti, governor of the city, determines not to surrender until the last drop of blood has been shed. The Turks kidnap his daughter. Traitors imprison him in a dungeon; and so on and on. Don Santos approved it for want of anything better to please the crowds during the celebration of the Queen's birthday, but he forbade the use of horses and riders since the effect, he declared, would be absurd on a small stage.

In the years that followed, Comella continued to be a popular dramatist whose works survived the momentary triumph of the reformers when they got control of the theaters in 1799. From 1806 to 1808 he was in Barcelona, which had selected him as "Director of the Company and Poet" at the municipal theater. Comella evidently did not bear grudges for while there he produced the Barcelona première of Moratín's *El barón* (January 22, 1807).

Nevertheless, the antagonism of Don Santos and the satire of Moratín pursued Comella to the grave, and his fame was obscured by ridicule. Even his death was portrayed as grotesque. In the terrible winter of 1812-1813, when the French invasion had brought Madrid to the point of starvation, Comella used to go to the Manzanares canal to fish, more for sustenance than for relaxation. There José Barbieri, the director at the Cruz Theater, went to seek him to ask him to write a play on the battle of Arapiles, the plain near Salamanca where Spanish patriots had just defeated the French. Barbieri invited the hungry Comella to have a snack at a wretched little roadhouse nearby, and they were served rancid herring. Such was Comella's hunger that, ironically, he satisfied his appetite on food not unlike that which he had provided the characters in his plays about besieged cities. He took ill from the spoiled fish, and died on the last day of December of 1812.

V *The Première*

The première of *La comedia nueva* took place on February 7, 1792, with the company of Eusebio Ribera, which was then at the Príncipe. Some of the actors had had parts in *El viejo y la niña*. Juana García, leading lady of the company, who had played Doña Isabel in Moratín's first play, did the part of Doña Mariquita with her usual charm. Mariano Querol, first gracioso, who had been so successful as Muñoz, took the role of Don Hermógenes, creating the complete pendant. Manuel de la Torre, the *barba,* brought to the part of Don Pedro the skill that had made his portrayal of the aged Don Roque so excellent.

Manuel García Parra, leading man in the company since 1788, played Don Eleuterio. He belonged to a large theatrical family and was a cousin of Juana García. Moratín admired his treatment of the role and especially his use of voice and gesture. In Polonia Rochel the play had a superb Doña Agustina. She had been on the Madrid stage for twenty-two years. During fifteen of those years she had been a graciosa and a favorite singer, and she became a leading character actor. She had got to be plump—some people called her fat—and in 1792 was third lady in the company, but she was said never to have done a role poorly. Moratín commented that "she portrayed the foolish presumption of Doña Agustina with all the intelligence that was to be expected from that famous actress."

Félix de Cubas, second man in the company, took the part of Don Antonio. José García, brother of the leading lady and second gracioso in the company, played Pipí the waiter. Since a third gracioso was required, Francisco López, supernumerary for both the companies, performed the role of Don Serapio.

Moratín wrote to his friend Forner about the audience's reaction:

The rabble of Sausages, pedants, streetcorner critics, and the hungry scribblers and their partisans occupied most of the patio and the ends of the tiers. Everything went well and the public applauded where they were supposed to. But in the second act when Don Serapio talks about the pimentos in vinegar, the disturbance among the Sausages and the racket they began to make was such that I was afraid that they would consign the play and me to hell. But the people who don't eat pimentos made them shut up and put up; and the performance ended with general applause that repaid me for all the troubles I have had. Nevertheless, since those devils unleashed their tongues against the play in every nook and cranny of the city, its fortune was still in doubt after the first performance; but its success on the second day and on the seven that it lasted was so great that it exceeded all our hopes and certainly was superior to that of Don Roque.

The performance was pretty good, and Juana—the stiff and frigid Juana—performed marvels. Everybody who heard her was amazed and the audience interrupted her frequently with applause.

This is all I need say now about the play, since the delirious non-sense that is heard around here from the mouth of the stinking Nifo, the pale Higuera, Concha, Zabala and the rest of the mob of fools is amusing to the ear but boresome to write. The rest of the public has received it enthusiastically. Well-intentioned people think that a work like this will result in the reform of the theater, but I think that the stage will go on as it has in the past and that Comella will enjoy his dramatic crown in peace.[10]

In deference perhaps to Moratín's antipathy toward the *tonadilla*, the entr'acte was a musical duet entitled *El premio de la constancia* (*The Reward for Constancy*). The closing piece was Ramón de la Cruz's *sainete El muñuelo: tragedia por mal nombre* (*The Doughnut: By Misnomer a Tragedy*).[11] The talkative Mudo (Dummy) declares that he is a nephew of Manolo, the hero of Cruz's popular parody of a tragedy. In this

piece, after two women have forgotten their quarrel over the
largest doughnut on a tray, Mudo and his friend Zaque sow
discord between the women's sweethearts by their report of the
affair. However, a duel is narrowly averted and the *sainete* ends
as a comedy rather than a tragedy.

The show at the Príncipe had a good box office. In the seven
days of its run the Cruz put on three plays: *Magdalena cautiva*
(*Magdalene Captive*), *Hechos heroicos y nobles del valor godo
español* (*Heroic and Noble Deeds of Spanish Gothic Valor*), and
El asombro de Salerno (*The Wonder of Salerno*). The Caños
del Peral also put on three musicals: *La Fedra* (*Phaedra*), *Las
aventuras del galanteo* (*Adventures in Wooing*), and *La Cifra*
(*The Enigma*). The following figures, in reales, suggest that the
public was receptive to Moratín's brand of comedy but that
they also enjoyed seeing the kind of theater which he satirized:

		Príncipe	Cruz	Caños
Tuesday February	7	6546	4009	4305
Wednesday	8	5007	2917	3868
Thursday	9	4495	4568	6480
Friday	10	3296	2593	4307
Saturday	11	3668	2437	4804
Sunday	12	4004	4635	5925
Monday	13	4503	6435	4094

The critics of the day reviewed the play favorably. The *Diario*,
which was in the hands of the neoclassicists, published its review
on February 21:

Everything about this play is estimable. The artifice is true to
life and the events are substantially real. Its didactic purpose is
excellent, for it encourages the theater to be what it ought to be:
a school for good manners and a temple of good taste. Its situations
are most natural, its episodes opportune and linked to the main
action, its language spontaneous, clear and suitable to the nature
of each character. The unities and other precepts are observed without
in any way hampering the genius of the author or lessening the
pleasing refinements that are found throughout the play.[12]

A couple of years later the *Memorial Literario* commented:

This play has been performed several times in the past two years.
In the case of other kinds of plays, that fact alone would not prove
its worth, but this one is exceptional. The public has recognized that
La comedia nueva provides it with a lesson, teaching it to discern

good plays and to distinguish them from the bad. This very fact
has delighted the public because it has learned from the comedy what
it could have known only after long and difficult study of the
theater.[13]

VI *Language and Spectacle*

Whereas Moratín wrote *El viejo y la niña* in the verse that
was traditional in the sentimental play, he used prose for *La
comedia nueva*. The play is comic, but because of its lesson it
may also be thought of as belonging to the category of serious
drame or what Beaumarchais called *le genre dramatique sérieux*.
In France, prose had been commonly used in the theater for
many years: Monsieur Jourdain of Molière's *Le Bourgeois gentilhomme* was delighted to speak in the language of prose, for
example. The Spanish stage was reluctant to abandon verse,
but one-act plays had long been composed in prose, and in the
eighteenth century various writers essayed prose in full-length
plays. Moratín's contribution lies not in novelty, then, but rather
in the quality of his language. In *La comedia nueva* and later in
El sí de las niñas, he set a standard of dramatic prose which
served as a model to nineteenth- and even twentieth-century
dramatists in Spain.

Language teachers abroad appreciated *La comedia nueva* for
what their students could learn from it. A certain Manuel
Ramajo, who used the anagram Ojamar as a pseudonym, published *Das neue Lustspiel, oder Das Kaffeehaus* in Dresden in
1800, printing the Spanish and German texts parallel.[14] The
anonymous author of *Les Elémens de la conversation espagnole
et française* (*Elements of Spanish and French Conversation*),
added to his dialogues the Spanish and French texts of Moratín's
La Nouvelle comédie, ou Le Café.[15]

The play also had translators for its own sake. In Italy Pietro
Napoli Signorelli, an old friend of Moratín's father, and secretary
of the Academy of Sciences in Naples, published an Italian
translation. It was not produced; indeed Moratín said that it
would first be necessary to accommodate it to the situation in
Italy, a step that would mean rewriting it entirely.[16] Many
years later, the French Romantic Gérard de Nerval was attracted
to the play and began an adaptation. His friend Arthus Fleury
finished *Le Nouveau genre, ou le Café d'un théâtre* which he

published in 1860, dedicating it to Victoria Silvela de Figuera, daughter of Moratín's good friend Manuel Silvela.[17]

Moratín intervened actively in the rehearsals of both *El viejo y la niña* and *La comedia nueva*. Neither play required much in the way of spectacle, but he was eager to see that the productions were well done and that the actors interpreted their roles as he saw them. Improvement in this area was one of the aims of the theatrical reformers, and the Spanish stage was in need of attention. One writer recalls the great Antonio Robles in the role of the protagonist in *El Maestro de Alejandro* by the seventeenth-century dramatist Fernando de Zárate:

In the play entitled *The Preceptor of Alexander,* the comedian Robles performed the part of Aristotle in an embroidered coat, silk stockings, a well-powdered wig, a sword, and a gilt-headed rattan. Yet Robles was the Roscius of the Spanish stage scarcely thirty years ago, and was said to have occasionally displayed talent productive of striking impressions on his audience, though, for our own part, we never saw him open his mouth to make an exordium without first coughing five or six times, or using his handkerchief unreservedly, or spitting, and then donning his hat with white feathers, and his knitted thread gloves, besides shifting the cane from his right hand to his left, to give himself freer scope for beating time.[18]

A few years later Moratín, better known and with powerful friends, achieved a real coup. The year was 1799 when the tide of theatrical reform reached its highest point. The actors of the Luis Navarro company were getting ready to perform *La comedia nueva*. Moratín wished to impose certain requirements and the company agreed to them, but he also wanted the backing of the Judge Protector before he went ahead. Accordingly, on June 14, 1799, he wrote to Don Juan de Morales Guzmán y Tovar, enclosing a list of seven requisites which he demanded:

1. He would have the right to review and change the text of any play of his before the roles were assigned.
2. He would select the actors and actresses from both companies and they would then study their roles "without any excuse or rejoinder at all."
3. Each actor and actress would heed his directions, and would rehearse both individually and together in front of him.
4. There would be as many general rehearsals in the theater as he judged necessary.

5. Until he considered the production ready, the date of the performance should not be set.

6. The last two general rehearsals were to be made with complete sets, costumes, and properties.

7. Sets and costumes should be presented for his approval one week in advance so that there would be time for changes.

Moratín must already have been in touch with Morales, for the Judge Protector acted with exceptional promptness. The next day, June 15, he wrote Moratín that he was granting his request. On June 24 he approved the list of actors and conveyed his decision to the manager of the company.[19] Moratín read the play to the actors on June 29, and he records in his diary that in the month following he went to fourteen rehearsals, eight partial or individual, and six general. Four of the actors played the same roles that they had in 1792: Manuel García Parra as Don Eleuterio; Mariano Querol as Don Hermógenes, Francisco López as Don Serapio, and José García Hugalde as Pipí. For the women Moratín chose María Ribera, who was fourth lady in the company, as Doña Agustina; and for the role of Doña Mariquita he went to the very bottom of the list to the young Coleta Paz, extra in both companies, who in future years was to be a superb actress.

The play was performed from July 27 to August 4. The daily receipts were not quite as good as they had been for the 1792 production, but they were exceptional for a midsummer show, ranging from a high of 5499 reales to a low of 2308.

Moratín's insistence on high standards, and indeed his ingenuity in being able to impose his will on the actors paid off in the quality of their performances. "This species of ingenuity," one commentator reported, "has grown into a proverb in Spain, where the players often say of a piece that has been well acted, 'one would think that Moratín had managed the rehearsal.'"[20]

Moratín was not optimistic about the effect that *La comedia nueva* would have in uplifting the level of theatrical art, for he was aware that in any epoch the number of good plays is less than the demand for plays of any sort on the part of actors and public. In the years after its première, *La comedia nueva* appeared regularly in Madrid, often preceded or followed by the very plays that it satirized. Moratín himself was not sanguine concerning its enduring appeal. "The day will come," he wrote, "when it will disappear from the stage, for comedy only permits the depiction of current vices and errors; but it will be a monument of literary history, unique of its kind, and not unworthy perhaps of the esteem of the learned."[21]

In 1829 it was among dozens of dramatic works which the Archbishop of Valencia, on a rampage, prohibited. Yet it was again being played during the Romantic period. An actor's copy of the time gives a cast of the best performers of the day: Matilde Díez, Josefa Palma, Carlos Latorre, Julián Romea, Antonio Guzmán, Francisco Romea, Vicente Hermosa, and José Pla. One of them wrote on the inside back cover:

> However much may be said
> by learned scholars,
> the world will always have
> outlandish poets
> and plebs who applaud
> witless shows.

> (*Por mucho que digan*
> *sabios escritores,*
> *siempre habrá en el mundo*
> *poetas ramplones*
> *y pueblo que aplauda*
> *necias producciones.*)[22]

CHAPTER 4

An Impostor

AFTER the première of *La comedia nueva*, Moratín did not have a new play in Madrid for eleven years. In the interval he traveled in France, spent a year in England, and three years in Italy. He recorded his observations in letters, in his diary, and in two works which he did not publish in his lifetime, but which appeared posthumously: *Apuntaciones sueltas de Inglaterra* (*Rough Notes on England*) and *Viaje de Italia* (*Italian Journey*). Back in Madrid in 1797, he was active in theatrical affairs, but he waited until 1803 to stage his play *El barón* (*The Baron*).

Moratín's contemporaries compared him to the Greek Menander and called him the Spanish Terence or the Spanish Molière. The action and characters of *El barón* support these assertations. The French critic Vézinet devoted a long essay to showing that Moratín's characters and plots were taken from Molière. For him, *El barón* is partly *Le Bourgeois gentilhomme* (*The Middle-class Gentleman*), with the difference that M. Jourdain has changed sex and has become Aunt Mónica; much as Dorante plays upon the foibles of M. Jourdain, the Baron exploits Aunt Mónica by catering to her illusions of grandeur. The play is partly *Le Mariage forcé* (*The Forced Marriage*), except that Moratín contrives to prevent the marriage. Vézinet even finds something of *L'Avare* (*The Miser*) in the scene in which the maid Fermina tells Aunt Mónica what the townspeople think of her, for it reminds him of a similar scene between Harpagon and Maître Jacques.[1]

An equally good case can be made to prove that Moratín followed a tradition established in the Spanish theater by Juan Ruiz de Alarcón (1581?-1639), which was imitated by the French, especially by Pierre Corneille (1606-1684), and was affirmed by Augustín Moreto (1618-1669).

The truth lies, no doubt, in the similarity of point of view and method of all these dramatists, both classical and modern. They

60

hold a mirror up to human nature, of which they are acute observers. What they see they view with humor or with irony. They portray convincingly and amusingly, and they teach a lesson to their middleclass audience.

I   *The Elements of Comedy in* El barón

El barón Cruz Theater, Madrid, January 28, 1803	
Aunt Mónica, a widow of Illescas	María Ribera
Isabel, her daughter	Rita Luna
Don Pedro, her brother	Antonio Pinto
Leonardo, a young man of the village	Manuel García Parra
Baron Montepino, the imposter	Antonio Ponce
Fermina, maid in Aunt Mónica's house	Coleta Paz
Pascual, manservant	Mariano Querol

Aunt Mónica, widow, lives in Illescas, a village on the road between Madrid and Toledo. The title *tía,* "aunt," is one of respect which in small towns is given to married or mature women. It is similar to *doña,* that untranslatable title of respect that Spanish employs with given names, which in the eighteenth century was supposed to be restricted to upper-class women. This is the key to the problem of the play, for Aunt Mónica would like to be better than she is, to be able to lift her head above the other women in the village. She is ambitious, a victim of the sins of pride and envy. When the Baron Montepino shows up in Illescas, she is taken in by his, to others, patently false tales, and, deaf to the remonstrances of her brother Don Pedro, she takes the impostor into her household. She swallows the Baron's explanations of why he, a nobleman, is obliged to be in a poor town like Illescas, without the money, servants, and equipage that people expect of a man of his rank. More than that, she determines to marry her daughter Isabel to the Baron instead of to the handsome, well-to-do villager Leonardo who is in love with the girl.

This is a simple plot of the sort that has amused audiences for centuries. Can the willful, foolish mother have her way? Will the fraudulent Baron get her money and her daughter? Or will

love and right triumph? Will the handsome, wholesome Leonardo marry pretty Isabel? Naturally, the impostor is unmasked,
the common sense of Don Pedro and the maidservant Fermina
prevails, the village lovers will marry, and Aunt Mónica realizes that envy and pride have made her the victim of fraud.

As befits comedy, the tone is light. Aunt Mónica's fault of
character puts things out of joint, it causes tension and even
tears, but her frailties do not provoke the darkness of tragedy.
She merely wants to toss her head at some of the other women
of the town by allying her family with a man of noble blood.
Like Teresa Panza, when she receives from Sancho the news that
Don Quijote has fulfilled his promise to make him governor of
an island, Aunt Mónica imagines how she will look down her
nose at some of the townswomen who have behaved haughtily
towards her. When she realizes her mistake, the tension eases,
and the ending is joyous.

The Baron is neither wicked, as he might be in tragedy, nor
sinister as in melodrama, although he may appear so to Isabel
and Leonardo. He seems rather to be a rascal who has escaped
from a picaresque novel to strut for a moment in the theater.
To Don Pedro and Fermina he is a nuisance to be got rid of;
to the audience he is preposterous. Indeed, he verges on caricature, the *figurón* which Rojas Zorrilla and Augustín Moreto
had popularized in the seventeenth century. His foolishness
is his own undoing, for his stratagems are so ridiculous that
everyone—even Aunt Mónica in time—sees through them.

The lovers Isabel and Leonardo are beloved by sentimental
audiences: she is pretty, sweet, and pure; he is handsome, up-
right, and honorable. Their colors are pastel. Don Pedro is the
man of good sense that every family and every comedy requires.
Fermina is the maidservant, smarter and even wiser than her
mistress, and too intelligent really for her calling. She is of a
kind with dozens like her in the Spanish *comedia,* in the Italian
commedia dell'arte, or in the plays of Molière and Goldoni. The
audience takes delight in her wit. Bumbling Pascual, who is very
forgetful and must always carry messages, provides the element
of farce that broadens the appeal of comedy.

Moratín wrote the first draft of *El barón* shortly after he completed his first version of *El viejo y la niña,* and long before
either of them was performed. His mind was on the unequal

marriage, the forced marriage. In *El viejo y la niña*, the problem was one of inequality in age; in *El barón*, inequality in station. To gratify her illusions, Aunt Mónica is willing to force an unequal marriage on her daughter, a marriage with a presumably noble stranger. This is not right; such is the simple lesson that Moratín teaches, *utile dulci*. His theme, stated on the back of the title page, he took from the admonition of the Latin fabulist Phaedrus who tells the tale of the peacock that complained to Juno about his poor voice; the goddess counsels the vain fowl:

> Strive not for what has not been given you,
> Lest, your hope deluded, you fall into self-pity.

> (*Noli adfectare quod tibi non est datum,*
> *Delusa ne spes ad querelam reccidat.*)[2]

As in *El viejo y la niña*, Moratín wrote an assonant rhyme, preferring the vowels *é-a* or *á-a*. He is on the verge of rhythmic prose, and but a step from the brilliant prose dialogue of *La comedia nueva* or *El sí de las niñas*.

In the setting, he avoids spectacle. The tragedian lays the scene in a hall in a palace; Moratín sets his in a room in a bourgeois household, nothing more. His emphasis was on character, on dialogue, on the message, and on bringing pleasure to his public.

II *The Musical Version of* El barón

The play that figures in Moratín's works as *El barón* was first performed and published in 1803; but sixteen years before, while he was in Paris in 1787, he completed a musical play, a zarzuela, that bore the same title and was very much the same. In Spain the zarzuela (operetta or musical comedy) originated in the second half of the seventeenth century, its most important exponent being the great Calderón de la Barca himself. These musical plays were first staged at the Palace of the Zarzuela, so called because it was constructed in a zarzuela, or bramble patch, near the Royal Seat of the Pardo, a winter residence of the kings of Spain just north of Madrid. Very soon the palace gave its name to the musical plays.[3]

At the urging of his employer, the banker Francisco, Count of Cabarrús, and evidently against his own will, Moratín wrote the book and lyrics of a zarzuela to be performed by amateurs at the home of the Dowager Countess of Benavente, Doña Faustina, the patroness of Ramón de la Cruz. The Countess's friends did not get around to putting it on, but it fell into the hands of the musician José Lidón, organist at the Royal Chapel, who composed music for the songs. With and without music, it was played by amateurs and in the public theater of Cadiz. On his return to Spain, Moratín persuaded Lidón to forego his effort so that he might rework *El barón* as a straight play.[4]

The most apparent difference between the zarzuela and the play is that Moratín has suppressed all the songs. This task cost him no pain, for he really did not care for the zarzuela form. To Jovellanos he had written in 1787 that he only composed it to please his employer and that he found it a "hard and repugnant task forced upon me by your great and good friend in the same way that he obliged me to plow through the snowdrifts of Almazán [in northern Spain in midwinter]."[5] Still, it is curious to observe just how Moratín employed the songs. He is not very adept at the zarzuela, which, to be sure, had not yet progressed far in uniting the music and the action. For the most part, the songs simply conclude a scene or interrupt one; they do not carry the action forward. They impart, as it is to be expected, a lyric and emotional quality, but they are not integrated into the total work. In another letter to Jovellanos of the same year he wrote: "It's a genre that I don't like. I don't know who can be so bold as to defend the continual lack of verisimilitude that it necessarily entails. Speaking frankly, my opinion is that no one has yet discovered the art of enhancing the forcefulness and beauty of speech by adding music to it without thereby affecting the quality of verisimilitude."[6]

Most of the zarzuela is in spoken dialogue, which is interrupted when one of the characters bursts into song, often at the end of a scene or monologue. Thus as Leonardo and Fermina conclude the first scene of the zarzuela, which is much like the one in the play, the young lover sings before he exits:

> Tell her that from love I'm dying,
>   Wounded by her cold disdain.
> Tell her from her lips I'm sighing
>   For blest deliverance from my pain.
> Tell her that those hearts, so faithless

> They forget when they incline,
> Ne'er can hope to know the sweetness
> And the bliss of love divine.
>
> *(Dila que amando muero*
> *a su desdén rendido,*
> *que de su labio espero*
> *alivio a mi dolor;*
>
> *Que un pecho fementido*
> *que olvida cuando quiere*
> *nunca lograr espere*
> *las dichas del amor.)*

Even although he requests the maid to deliver his message and his words affirm that he is not going to give up the girl easily, so that the song does indeed bear a relation to the action, it adds nothing to what he has just been saying in the dialogue. On the other hand, at the end of the zarzuela, song and action are integrated as the Baron confesses his deception:

> I confess the deceit.
>   I deserve to be caned,
>   To be fettered and chained.
>
> I've been a cheat;
>   Now I entreat
>   Your compassion.
>
> *(Confieso el delito,*
> *merezco grillete,*
> *azotes y brete,*
> *que he sido maldito;*
> *pero ya contrito*
> *pido compasión.)*

The assembled company respond individually and in chorus: "Scalawag! Scalawag!" (*¡Picarón! ¡Picarón!*) But they have no pity for him; the bailiffs march him off to jail.

The songs themselves are typical of the day, and indeed as banal as the songs of musical comedy have been in modern times. Moratín wrote them in verses of from four to seven syllables and he used consonantal rhyme, so that they contrast with the simple assonance of the dialogue, which is in eight-syllable verse.

In telling how he revised the zarzuela, Moratín, writing of himself in the third person, said: "He expunged everything that other people had added, and deleted the songs; he made the plot more interesting and true-to-life; into the characters he infused greater vigor; and by making some changes in the first act and recasting completely the second, out of a defective zarzuela, he created a satisfactory comedy."[7]

In the first act, besides suppressing the songs, Moratín shortened the speeches of the characters so that the dialogue is more vivacious. He also updated it; for example, the amounts of money mentioned by the characters reflect an increase in the cost of living. The significant changes, however, were made in the second act, and the turning point was the second scene. In the zarzuela, the scene is between Don Pedro and the Baron and lays the ground for some complicated plot developments that depend on chance. After the two have left, Antón, a journeyman tailor summoned by Aunt Mónica, shows Fermina a ring which he would like to sell to her mistress. It is the very ring that Aunt Mónica had given the Baron to send to his distinguished sister— fictitious, of course— and which the scoundrel pawned. Antón has not yet seen the Baron, however; but when he does, he recognizes him as a young scalawag he met in Segovia, there known as Luquillas. The rascal had ingratiated himself with a priest and made off with a sum of money. The anagnorisis takes place in front of the other characters and the public; the mayor of Illescas and his bailiffs arrive to arrest the impostor; everyone sings about the situation, the mother recognizes her mistake, and the lovers are united.

In the play, the second scene of the second act offers the inevitable dialogue between Leonardo and the Baron. Leonardo shows himself to be a spirited and determined young man who is firmly prepared to defend his threatened happiness. He challenges the Baron to a duel. From that point on, the development of the plot depends on the character of the two young men, for the Baron is cowardly, and he chooses to abandon his scheme rather than fight a duel. Furthermore, Don Pedro's knowledge of human nature, and Fermina's native astuteness, instead of the concrete evidence of the ring or Antón's reports from Segovia, lead them to the certainty that the Baron is an impostor. As a result, Moratín threw out all the complications of plot, and he no longer required the character of Antón, whom he eliminated. It was sufficient for the Baron to run away without being brought back on the stage; since Moratín had also eliminated the songs, he no longer needed the mayor and the bailiffs, and he also omitted them.

In his revision, Moratín changed the impact of the drama. In Act II, Scene ii of the zarzuela, Don Pedro expresses concern about the decorum of his niece: if word has been bruited about that she is to marry a noble, no one in the village will then want to marry her. In the play, the scene between Don Pedro and the Baron occurs after the obligatory scene between Leonardo and the Baron. The uncle is concerned in the play about the unequal marriage: the couple ought to be of the same social status. The best husband for Isabel is the honest youth from her home town, not the depraved noble from the city. Apart from making a variation on the old theme in praise of the simple life, Moratín was also catering to the anti-aristocratic spirit of the ordinary people in the pit who both envied and criticized the privileged classes. It is important to remember that the French Revolution occurred between 1787, when he wrote the zarzuela, and 1803, when the play was published and staged. Furthermore, he wrote the zarzuela to be performed privately in an aristocrat's palace; the comedy he intended for the public playhouse.

In the play Don Pedro informs his sister, who romantically imagines that passion can move a noble to marry a village girl, that among aristocrats a marriage is a calculated business arrangement. Moratín is telling the audience that love, a natural emotion, makes the villagers superior to the aristocrats, and Aunt Mónica's fault is that she opposes the natural inclination of the young lovers. In this sense, the play reflects a point of view that is firmly rooted in eighteenth-century ideas. Viewed from another aspect, the play makes propaganda in support of class distinctions in the face of the class struggle unloosed by the French Revolution. Plain people are honored and are shown to be esteemed within their own milieu while a certain type of hereditary nobility is ridiculed. Plain people are informed of the dignity and happiness that are attached to their estate.

The difference between the closing scenes is significant. At the end of the zarzuela, Aunt Mónica, who has put herself in a

ridiculous position, throws herself at her brother's feet. In the
play, after Aunt Mónica acknowledges with dignity the error
of her ambition, the young people, with filial respect, kneel at
her feet to receive her blessing as the curtain falls on a scene
of familial piety.

III   A *Rival Show*: La lugareña orgullosa

Moratín dedicated *El barón* to the Prime Minister Manuel
Godoy, Príncipe de la Paz—Prince of the Peace, so called because of a famous peace treaty that he concluded with the
revolutionary government of France—to whom he owed financial
support during his long sojourn abroad, and the job that he
got on his return to Spain, Secretary of the Office of the Interpretation of Languages. Less than three weeks before the première of *El barón*, in January, 1803, another play was performed
for the first time which in its printed version was dedicated to
the prime minister's brother Don Diego Godoy in his capacity
as Inspector of Cavalry. The author was Andrés de Mendoza,
a cavalry officer. The play, which bore a remarkable resemblance
to *El barón*, was entitled *La lugareña orgullosa* (*The Proud
Village Girl*).

On the title page, Mendoza claimed that his was an "original
comedy." In his own prologue, however, he states that in 1798
the manuscript of a zarzuela called *El barón* fell into his hands.
It was so defective in every way that he could hardly believe
it was by the author of *El viejo y la niña*. Nevertheless, he liked
its theme. "My first intention," Mendoza wrote, "was to purge
that despicable embryo of its many errors in order to read it in a
tertulia of friends; but once I settled down to work I realized
that that was improper and that it would be simpler for me to
write a new play on the same theme, the object of which would
be to satirize the urge that many parents have to sacrifice their
children for the sake of their ridiculous vanity without taking
into account the children's inclinations or their best interests."[8]

The plays of Mendoza and Moratín are obviously very near in
theme. Furthermore, the plot of *La lugareña orgullosa* follows
closely that of Moratín's zarzuela, although there are differences
of detail. Mendoza, rather arbitrarily, used three acts instead of
Moratín's two. The setting is in the patio rather than in a room
of the house, and Mendoza describes it in some detail. Although

Mendoza's version is a play and not a zarzuela, Faustina sings seguidillas, and at one point the orchestra plays background music, a practice current in melodrama of the time.[9]

The cast of characters is also very nearly identical with Moratín's musical play but, of course, different from his revised comedy. The two works diverge chiefly in characterization, and hence the dialogue and the tone are sufficiently different that Mendoza no doubt felt justified in claiming that he had written an original comedy. Except for Basilio, who had no name in the zarzuela, and Pepito, the names of the characters are the same or begin with the same letter (and Pepito's boss, who does not appear on stage, is named Antón). Probably on purpose, Mendoza changed Leonardo to Leandro, which was Moratín's given name. Moratín's Aunt Mónica has become Doña Mónica; that is, she has already put on airs by assuming the title of *doña*, although no special point of this is made in the play.

La lugareña orgullosa
Caños del Peral Theater, Madrid, January 8, 1803

Doña Mónica, a widow	Joaquina Briones
Isabel, her daughter	Antonia Prado
Don Pedro, her brother	Vicente García
Leandro, a young man of the village	Isidoro Máiquez
The Marquess, an imposter	Eugenio Cristiani
Faustina, maid in Doña Mónica's house	Gertrudis Torre
Perico, manservant	Joaquín Suárez
Basilio, mayor of the village	Joaquín Caprara
Pepito, a journeyman tailor	José Infantes
A bailiff	Francisco Ronda

Isabel seems to live up to the title of the play, for at the beginning she appears proud and haughty, characteristics that are out of keeping with her status as a village girl. In showing her to be willful and assertive, Mendoza was undermining his theme; therefore, he does not sustain this note, and toward the end she resembles Moratín's ingenue. The quality of moderation is the key to the distinction between Moratín's characters and those of Mendoza. The personages of the cavalry officer turned playwright are extremists: they are explosive, they shout

at each other, they gesticulate, they react violently to one another and to the situations of the play. Their emotions are near
the surface; they do not run deep. The actors may have liked
the play better than *El barón*, for it enabled them to show off
their histrionic pyrotechnics and did not require them to penetrate the studied subtlety of Moratín's characters.

The Marquess appears on stage earlier in the play than does
the Baron. The fifth scene takes place between him and Isabel,
and it resembles the sixth scene in Moratín's play between the
Baron and Aunt Mónica. The Marquess shows himself to be a
currutaco, a man who is very affected in following the latest
extremes in fashion; he appears ridiculous and hence is more
of a caricature than is the Baron. The scene also establishes
Isabel's haughtiness vis-à-vis the Marquess, and justifies the
title of the play.

The character of Doña Mónica is poorly conceived. Despite
her tempestuous temperament, she vacillates in the course of
the play. While Aunt Mónica was completely taken in by the
Baron, and was assailed by no doubts, Doña Mónica wonders
whether or not she should force the will of her daughter. Yet,
in the end she is unrepentant. "Don't sermonize me," she tells
her brother Pedro. "You got what you wanted, which was to
order us around. All right. Marry the girl to anybody you want
to. I don't want to know about it or approve it." And she stalks
off stage having learned no lesson at all. Thus, while Mendoza's
play is neither very good nor very bad, it is weak because the
characters are inconsistent with themselves and with the theme.

The performance of *La lugareña orgullosa* such a short time
before the première of *El barón* smacks of a conspiracy, and
Moratín's friend Melón says that Don Dámaso Gutiérrez de la
Torre was back of it. In later years, he was mayor of Madrid
during the French occupation, and he and Moratín became
friends. In the 1802-1803 season, however, he was associated
with the Caños del Peral theater which sheltered both an opera
company and a drama company, and was the only rival of the
Cruz after the Príncipe burned in July, 1802. Moratín was at the
time associated with the official effort of the government to
impose theatrical reform. The venture upset theatrical traditions
of long standing and ended in a fiasco. It was to be expected
that the people associated with it should incur the hostility of

many actors and theatrical people. These foes encouraged Andrés de Mendoza, and at the end of December he was to read the play to the drama company at the Caños.

Mendoza invited Moratín to come hear his play: "Sir: Tomorrow, Monday the 27th, at ten in the morning, I shall read my play to the actors in the business office of the Caños theater. I am informing you in case you would like to hear it. If you will take the trouble to attend, it will be clear to you that our plays have in common only the basic plot and that not a single verse nor a single idea have I taken from yours. The gossip continues, and neither you nor I can avoid it. What we ought to do is scorn it, and that is what your humble servant is doing.[10] Although there is a note of insolence in Mendoza's words, he may have deceived himself into believing that he had indeed created an original work. The reading had to be postponed and Moratín did not hear it although he even went to Mendoza's house, only to find him out. However, he did attend the Caños theater on the first night, January 8, 1803.

Mendoza had an excellent cast for his play. The leading man of the company, who did the role of Leandro, was Isidoro Máiquez. Máiquez had just spent more than a year in Paris studying with the great Talma, and on his return he had triumphed in the title role of *Otelo* (*Othello*), in the version which Teodoro de la Calle translated from the French adaptation that Jean-François Ducis made of Shakespeare. Antonia Prado, Máiquez' wife, played the role of Isabel. She may not have been well cast as a village girl, for she was in her late thirties and she was especially noted for her fashionable dress, but she had been pleasing Madrid audiences for twenty years while at the same time she advanced the career of Máiquez, who was three years her junior. By contrast, the role of Doña Mónica was played by Joaquina Briones; she was little more than twenty years old although she was already a widow. She usually played comic roles, and she sang well. Eugenio Cristiani, an Italian who possessed a good voice, good Spanish, and an excellent comic talent, was the Marquess. For Vicente García, who had earned a fine reputation as a *barba*, Don Pedro was one of his last roles, for he retired at the end of the season.

The critics of the time assessed Mendoza's effort justly. The article in *El Regañón General* (*The General Scold*) recognized that the play was adequate and that the performance pleased the public. But it took Mendoza to task for so boldly calling his work original, when it was obvious that he had made a servile imitation of the zarzuela *El barón*.[11] Financially, the play was satisfactory for the company but it was not a great success at the box office. In the following season it was given six times and produced 23,571 reales. By comparison, *El Cid*, a translation by Tomás García Suelto of Corneille's play about the Spanish national hero, produced 38,372 reales in six performances; an *Otelo* took in 29,366 reales in only four playings.[12]

IV   *The Première of* El barón

The company at the Caños possessed much talent, and they staged their plays and operas with care. Hence, Moratín and the company at the Cruz took pains to create a good production of *El barón*. Although the setting was a very simple one, they spent some 4,800 reales on it, a sum equal to the total ticket sales for a performance of many plays.[13]

The Cruz had a good company of actors, too, and they were tried and true friends of the author. Mariano Querol, who had been Muñoz in *El viejo y la niña* and Don Hermógenes in *La comedia nueva*, played the manservant Pascual. It was undoubtedly for his benefit that Moratín wrote into the play a scene of pure slapstick in which Pascual tries on Aunt Mónica's dressing gown. María Ribera, who did the role of Aunt Mónica, was the daughter of the impresario Eusebio Ribera, who had first staged *El viejo y la niña*, and the wife of Dionisio Solís, a prompter, and adapter and translator of plays. It is likely that Moratín made the role more sympathetic than it had been in the zarzuela because of the actress who was to play it. Rita Luna, one of the great actresses of the time, took the part of Isabel. Manuel García Parra, of the famed theatrical family, played opposite her as Leonardo. Antonio Ponce, who was renowned for his gallants in Golden Age *comedias*, gave his talents to the role of the Baron; and Antonio Pinto, an excellent *barba*, played Don Pedro. The vivacious Coleta Paz, a rising young actress, portrayed the maid Fermina.

The company spent more than 1,000 reales to send one of their number to Aranjuez especially to invite the Prince of the Peace to come to the opening night, which was scheduled for

January 28, 1803; and they paid out another 815 reales to put new wallpaper in the two boxes that were reserved for the Prince and his party.

In the meantime, Moratín's adversaries were at work and on opening night they had a full representation in the theater. The author describes that famous evening:

It was understood beforehand that [the play] was going to be booed. The leader of the expedition was well known and redoubtable, the mob that he had at his command numerous and intrepid. More than once during the performance the vociferators opened the attack, but the audience succeeded in containing them. When but a few verses remained to conclude the play, they found it urgent that they make one last effort to satisfy the obligation which they had contracted. They had recourse to hoots, yells and hisses—a frightful hubbub; and that part of the audience that had liked the play contributed to the uproar and confusion by clapping. Some of them asked that a performance be given for them the next day while others cried that the show should go on.

Above the tumult which reverberated pertinaciously from one part of the house to another, the actor Antonio Pinto, a friend of the author, managed with difficulty to make himself heard, saying: "The actors have been of the opinion that the play they have just performed is one of those few pieces which do most credit to the Spanish theater. A part of the audience vigorously supports this judgment and expresses it in a manner that is not to be questioned; another part of the public appears to abominate the play and asks that a different one be announced for tomorrow. The actors want to make the right decision, and we would like to know whether the comedy *El barón* should be performed tomorrow or not. What the public decides, we shall do. Our obligation is to please you." This speech, far from calming the disorder or conciliating the divergent views, only served to augment the clamor and to divide the adversaries. The discord would have continued longer had not the conspirators, taking their victory as assured, rushed tumultuously into the street to publish the news among those who were waiting outside.

Word spread through streets and thoroughfares, taverns, cafés, and gatherings of friends that Moratín's comedy had been booed—a report that filled with joy those people who continually lament that nothing good is ever done in Spain and yet who disparage an honest effort when on occasion something good is done—those people who trample under foot men of merit with whom they cannot compete. Many a wiseacre, male and female, went to bed late that night, for they were busy until the wee hours writing vapid, spiteful couplets to celebrate the victory which ignorance and bias had won over talent and exemplary diligence. The next day these opuscules circulated from hand to hand, and within a few hours they perished, despised and forgotten. At the second performance only the sound of applause was to be heard. The conspirators did not attend, for wine had brought them together and wine is expensive in Madrid. An impartial public avenged previous insults by extending its approbation. It retained many phrases of the play as proverbial expressions, and since that time it has listened appreciatively to this simple, comic, instructive and true-to-life story in which the author observed, as he did in his other plays, the precepts of art and good taste.[14]

The conspiracy, contrary to the design of its instigators, had a beneficial effect on the box-office receipts at the Cruz. The first night produced 9,112 reales, more than any performance in January or February except one night of *La más ilustre fregona* (*The Most Illustrious Kitchen Maid*), a play by Cañizares based in turn on one that Lope de Vega took from a novelette by Cervantes. *El barón* ran eight nights consecutively, a very good run for those days. *La lugareña orgullosa* had had a seven-day run and had taken in 30,636 reales; by comparison, in its first seven days *El barón* produced 46,416 reales.

An anonymous critic—Moratín kept the statement among his papers—wrote that the work lacked "all the principal qualifications that might characterize it as dramatic. There is no action, no movement, no plot. At most, it is a rustic tale of an event that one can listen to with interest but without surprise." The writer conceded the play some merit if it was read, but predicted that the actors would not get rich with it: "it does not belong to the dramatic genre," he stated categorically.[15] The lively and capricious scribbler José Mor de Fuentes, who, if he was not among the vituperators at the première of *El barón,* was of their ilk, wrote of Moratín's plays in general and of this one in particular: "For my taste, his comedies, and especially *El barón,* are absolutely lacking in imagination. They are little more than long *sainetes* sprinkled with cute remarks that are more or less opportune, which he used to gather from the mouths of fishwives, as I myself have witnessed. And this is our Molière!"[16]

Other critics found much to praise in the play. The *Memorial Literario,* at the time under the editorship of the poet and playwright Manuel José Quintana—who was not a special friend of Moratín—admired the achievement: "Joining true comic talent to a profound knowledge of the art, he makes Thalia speak in

our tongue. . . . His plays are models that young men who devote themselves to this career ought to study if they wish to
make progress in it. . . . Joined to his eminent wit, they will observe ample adroitness, refined taste, excellently portrayed
characters, and the choicest diction admirably adjusted to the
persons depicted." The writer thought the dialogue in Act II,
Scene vi—in which Don Pedro tells Aunt Mónica a few truths
about herself—worthy of the pen of Terence, and complimented
Moratín on the purity of the language, the proper choice of
words, the elegance of the verse, and the maxims with which
he ended the principal scenes.[17] Another friendly critic, his
father's old acquaintance Pedro Napoli Signorelli, wrote from
Italy to tell him of the delight he took in reading the play. The
characters, he pointed out, were not new to the theater, for
authors have often ridiculed ambitious or enamored old women,
"but you have told all this with a jaunty air and by means of
novel situations. . . ."[18]

The poet Alberto Lista saw a production of *El barón* almost
two decades after the première. "In this play," he wrote, "Mr.
Moratín came closer to the theater of Plautus than in any other.
The truth is that a rascal from Triana and a credulous woman
from Illescas did not give him sufficient opportunity to wield the
delicate, urbane brush of Terence. It is not surprising then that
this play has been regarded as the weakest of those by this
dramatist. But its weakness lies only in the plot and the moral
lesson, for the diction and verse are as always what we expect
from the author of *El viejo y la niña*."[19]

CHAPTER 5

A Pious Deceiver

FIFTEEN months after the first performance of *El barón,* Moratín's fourth play was produced in Madrid. He had written it, too, before his English and Italian journeys; it had circulated in manuscript, and it had been played by amateurs. It was entitled *La mojigata* (*The Pious Deceiver*).

The excessively devout woman who haunts churches has long been a feature of Spanish society. She has usually been regarded with indulgence, and to describe her Spaniards have jocosely used the team *beata* ("blessed"), the same word applied to those who are on the road to sainthood. There is not, necessarily, an implication of insincerity.

The English word "hypocrite"—cognate of the Spanish *hipócrita*—is not an exact translation, for the *mojigata* is somewhere between the *beata* and the hypocrite. *Mojigato* (the masculine form) was derived from an Arabic word meaning concealed or feigned. However, the fanciful etymology of the seventeenth-century lexicographer Sebastián de Covarrubias illuminates the connotations: "*Mogigato,* the concealed scoundrel, who is like the pussycat [*mizigato*]: when you say 'pussy' [*miz*] to him, he grovels and purrs, and then he scratches." In the sense that Moratín used it, the word may be taken to mean a dissembler, especially in a moral or religious sense, who, on occasion, feigns humility in order to achieve his end.[1] This is the modern definition in the dictionary of the Royal Spanish Academy, and since Moratín is officially recognized as an authority on the language by that body, it is apparent that the character of the protagonist in his play is responsible for the special sense in which the word is understood.

I *The Moral and the Characters*

The thought that Moratín presumably intended to convey by his play is expressed in a Latin quotation on the back of the title page of the first edition: *Malus, bonum ubi se simulat, tunc est pessimus.* ("When a bad man pretends he is good, he is then worse"). It is from the *Sententiae* (*Maxims*) of Publilius Syrus, a favorite actor of Julius Caesar and author of mimes whence his maxims were drawn and preserved. Moratín apparently intended that the axiom apply to Doña Clara, the *mojigata* of the play. Her father, Don Martín, brought her up very strictly and he was pleased with the result. In her he saw a devout, obedient daughter who had decided· to enter a convent, thus renouncing an inheritance which would then devolve upon him, a contingency that he was pleased to allow.

Don Martín's brother, Don Luis, was a permissive parent with his daughter Doña Inés, and he had reason to believe his system of education superior to that of his brother, for he observed that Martín's strictness had made Clara deceitful. She only pretended to be devout; behind her father's back she read romantic books and flirted from her window. The action of the play tells how the cunning Clara gets her deserts, how her cousin Inés shows her strength of character, and how Don Luis's method of education is vindicated. The instrument is a young man named Don Claudio. His father, who lived in the nearby town of Ocaña, had known Don Luis years before, and he sent his son to Toledo for the express purpose of courting Doña Inés.

Claudio is a grown-up delinquent. He drinks and gambles, and consorts with women of ill repute. He is abetted by his manservant Perico. As soon as the two of them find out that Clara is heiress to a considerable fortune, they drop Inés and shift their attention to her. To keep their scheme going, they cheat old Uncle Juan, a messenger from a convent, out of some money that belongs to the nuns. Claudio and Clara are indeed soulmates, who richly deserve each other. They are on the point of eloping when a reversal of circumstances occurs: the rich relative, having learned that Clara has said she intends to abandon the secular life to enter a convent, leaves his money to Inés. Inés reveals her nobility of character, for she determines that she will share her fortune with her cousin. Don Luis, however, insists that the division rest on Inés' word rather than on legal documents so that Clara will be under the obligation to please her cousin and will thus reform not only her own character, but also that of her husband.

La mojigata
Cruz Theater, Madrid, May 19, 1804

Don Luis, a gentleman of Toledo	Antonio Pinto
Doña Inés, his daughter	María García
Don Martín, Don Luis's brother	Francisco Vaca
Doña Clara, Don Martín's daughter	Josefa Virg
Lucía, maid to the two girls	Joaquina Arteaga
Don Claudio, a dissipated gallant	Antonio Ponce
Perico, his manservant	Mariano Querol
Uncle Juan, messenger for a convent	Tomás López

The cynic may be permitted to doubt that the hopes of the denouement will be fulfilled, for in both Clara and Claudio Moratín has drawn characters, whose flaws appear ingrained. In the first scene of·the play, Don Luis tells his brother Martín what Clara is like: she fasts when her father is watching her, but when he leaves she runs for the pantry and makes up for her abstinence; she recites her prayers, counts her rosary, performs her novenas, but she also closes the door to her room, opens the window, and passes the evening chatting with the corporal on color guard next door; when her father is present, she leafs through books of devotion, but alone, she reads light verse, love stories, and amusing novels that preach virtue and teach vice. Don Martín's rigorous inflexibility in bringing up Clara, Don Luis tells him, has produced dissimulation and feigned virtue; he has made her false and hypocritical; she will never profess in a convent.

In effect, Clara's words and actions bear out Don Luis's assessment. "You'll never get anywhere in this world," she tells her maid Lucía, "unless you practice to deceive." When Perico informs her that his master Don Claudio has his eye set on her, she is too pleased to conceal her interest. To Lucía she exclaims, "No more veils, no more convent doors!" With Don Claudio she at first puts on her holy air. "I live quietly at home," she tells him. "My best clothes are this simple black dress; my only distractions are prayer and the reading of devotional books." When

her father and Inés interrupt the conversation, Clara is so adept
that she not only makes her father believe that Inés was alone
with Claudio, but also convinces him that Inés is trying to put
the blame on her.

The roles of Claudio and Perico are excellent for actors. The
young man is dissipated and unscrupulous; his valet is un-
hampered by any sense of morals. Since Claudio has spent all
his money on wine, women and gambling, Perico does not
stickle to deceive Uncle Juan and Don Martín in order to re-
plenish their pockets with the nuns' money. Let it be said, however, that Claudio was already attracted to Clara before he
found out about her inheritance. She was his type. "The one
that really gets to me," he tells Perico, "is little Clara. I've been
giving her the old come-on." It takes little effort on Perico's
part to bring the two of them together. They are ready for each
other, although one can well wonder how Clara could overlook
Claudio's boorish manners. Don Luis reprimands him for his
conduct at a friend's party: he smoked when no one else was
smoking, he whistled, he interrupted others who were talking,
he scratched his legs, and he cleaned out his chocolate cup with
his fingers and licked the cup! "People ought to allow a fellow
a little freedom," Don Claudio counters.

Inés is a merry young woman who loves to dance and go
to parties—all properly supervised by oldsters, to be sure. Her
father regards her behavior as befitting her youthful exuberance, but her uncle is convinced she is bound for perdition. He
thinks she could learn humility and good sense from his daughter
Clara. Inés is not attracted one whit to Don Claudio, and she
frankly tells her father so. She does not fight back when Clara
blames her for what she did not do, but, in the end, when she
falls heir to the fortune that Clara was supposed to have received, she generously offers to share it with her cousin.

Some critics, both contemporary and subsequent, have professed to see in *La mojigata* a pallid imitation of Molière's *Le
Tartuffe, ou L'Imposteur* (*Tartuffe, or The Impostor*). Certainly,
there is nothing in the creation of Doña Clara that quite equals
the sanctimony of Tartuffe's words to his valet when he first
appears on stage and realizes that he is being observed:

> Lock up my hair shirt and my scourge,
> And pray for Heaven's lasting grace.

Should someone come to see me, pray say
I've gone to the prison to distribute alms.

(*Laurent, serrez ma haire avec ma discipline,
Et priez que toujours le Ciel vous illumine.
Si l'on vient pour me voir, je vais aux prisonniers
Des aumônes que j'ai partager les deniers.*)

Molière's play had been translated and had played in Madrid
shortly before *La mojigata*. The aims of the two dramatists, however, were different. Molière was making a frontal attack on
religious hypocrisy, in particular on the falsely devout. Moratín's
main concern is with a different problem: the upbringing of
children.

The subject of the proper rearing of children has a long tradition in the theater, which began with Menander's *Adelphi*
(*The Brothers*), known to us in Terence's version of 160 B.C.
More than most Roman comedies, *The Brothers* had a purpose:
to set forth two opposing systems of education—kindness and
generosity versus harshness and restraint—and to show the results of each. The problem of the father who must deal with
his offspring—and variants on the theme that extend to other
family relationships—have preoccupied and appealed to many
generations of playgoers if we are to judge by the descendants
of Terence's play in modern times: in Italy, Giovanni Cecchi's
I Dissimili (*Different by Upbringing*); in France, Molière's
L'Ecole des Maris (*School for Husbands*), 1661, which Moratín
himself later adapted into Spanish as *La escuela de los maridos*
(1812); Michel Baron's *L'Ecole des Pères* (*School for Fathers*);
and Denis Diderot's *Le Père de famille* (*Father of a Family*),
1758; and in England, where the subject was exceptionally popular, John Marston's *Parisitaster, or The Fawn* (1606); Beaumont and Fletcher's *The Scornful Lady* (*ca.* 1609); Thomas
Shadwell's *The Squire of Alsatia* (1688); Sir Richard Steele's
The Tender Husband (1705); David Garrick's *The Guardian;*
George Colman's *The Jealous Wife* (1761); Richard Cumberland's *The Choleric Man* (1774); and Henry Fielding's *The
Fathers* (1778).

In Spain there were two important precedents for Moratín's
play: Tirso de Molina's *Marta la piadosa* (*Pious Martha*), *ca.*
1615, and Calderón de la Barca's *Guárdate del agua mansa*

(*Still Waters Run Deep*), 1649. Both belong to the *comedia* of the seventeenth century. Tirso's play, while it has something of the nature of a comedy of manners, and presents in Marta one of the most interesting characters of the Spanish stage, is especially a comedy of intrigue in which chance and the unforeseen relationship influence the course of events more importantly than do the characters. Marta's duplicity is not ingrained by her upbringing. She feigns piety and expresses her intention of entering a convent only when her father forces her toward marriage with an old man. She wants to marry the youth on whom her heart has fixed, and she has recourse to pretending a religious vocation which she does not feel, only as a temporary expedient. In *Marta la piadosa* the severest tax on the public's credulity is that the youth whom Marta and her sister both love is the murderer of their brother, and they know it. That the father accepts him for a son-in-law, if it little concerned Tirso's public, was too much an affront to verisimilitude to suppose that Moratín was greatly influenced by the Tirso play.

The two sisters of *Guárdate del agua mansa* are Clara and Eugenia, and there are four suitors. One of them is a cousin, a nephew of their father. He is Don Toribio Caudrilleros, an oaf from Asturias. In his boorishness he resembles Moratín's Don Claudio, but he is a fool rather than a rake, and his role in the play, though not the principal one, imparts to it the nature of a *comedia de figurón,* of caricature instead of character. Calderón's Clara is shy rather than devout, but her shyness conceals burning passions. This explains the proverbial title: Still waters run deep. Although her father at first thought of Don Toribio as a possible husband for one of his daughters, he does not try to force the ridiculous boob upon either of them. Clara has her heart set on one of the other three suitors, and in the game of love she is double-dealing, underhanded and deceitful with her sister, her father, and the suitors. There is no hint of her being falsely devout, nor is there any note of religious hypocrisy.

Indeed, in the characterization of both Tirso's pious Marta and Calderón's shy Clara, it is clear that their outward appearance is a part of the game of love, assumed in one case and belied in the other. Furthermore, their upbringing—whether it was suitable or not—is not brought into the question.

Moratín's *La mojigata* lies clearly within the tradition of Ter-

ence's play, although there are echoes of the Spanish *comedias*
by Tirso and Calderón. In this work he has for the moment abandoned the question of the unequal marriage that preoccupied
him in *El viejo y la niña* and in *El barón*, to concentrate on the
proper education of women—a subject on which he had already touched. In his next play, *El sí de las niñas*, he was to fuse
the two themes in the best comedy of the neoclassic period in
Spain.

Moratín wrote the first version of *La mojigata* in 1791, after
El viejo y la niña and the zarzuela *El barón*, which were in verse,
and before *La comedia nueva*, which was in prose. In *La mojigata* he used the simple ballad meter of the other two plays. In
the first act he employed assonant or vowel rhyme in *é-a*; in the
second *é-o*; in the third, in *á-a*. The diction could hardly have
been simpler in its form. Yet already his contemporaries observed
both the elegance of his language and his superb ability to
capture the popular flavor of the spoken tongue. Without making
an issue of it—for he was exceptionally skillful and indeed tal-
ented in the employment of a wide variety of meters—he was
on the verge of abandoning verse to seek the freedom of expression which prose gave him. He took the step immediately when
he wrote *La comedia nueva*, and he employed prose again in
El sí de las niñas.

II   *The Madrid Première of* La Mojigata

It took *La mojigata* thirteen years, from 1791 to 1804, to reach
the public stage in Madrid. Moratín had composed a version of
it even earlier, for Pietro Napoli Signorelli wrote him from Naples
in 1788: "I await your *Mojigata*, but I should like to know why
it has been condemned to be neither printed nor performed."[2]
It began to circulate in manuscript after 1791, and while Moratín
was in Italy Melón gave him news of it which incensed the author.
"As long as I don't print it, I won't claim it as mine," he wrote.
Moratín himself read it to friends at the Spanish College in
Bologna in 1794; and Jovellanos obtained a copy which he
read in 1796.[3] Amateurs in Madrid got hold of it and performed
it—well, according to reports—at the home of a Madrid attorney
named Pérez de Castro and at the palace of the Marchioness
of Santiago. Professional actors performed it in the provinces,

but, out of respect for the author, the Madrid actors did not play it. Moratín systematically destroyed the manuscripts of his plays after they were printed, but there were too many of *La mojigata,* so that it is the only one that is known in several manuscript versions, one of which is holograph.

Three of the male actors who had taken parts in *El barón* were in the première of *La mojigata.* The *barba* Antonio Pinto, who had played Don Pedro in *El barón* and had attempted to quell the tumult in the audience at the end of the first performance, again took the role of the sage man of reason as Don Luis, the gentleman of Toledo and father of Doña Inés. During rehearsals he came often to Moratín's house. Antonio Ponce, the Baron Montepino two seasons before, was now the leading man at the Cruz, and created the role of Don Claudio. His lackey Perico was done by Mariano Querol, who had played the parts of graciosos in Madrid since 1783 and had maintained his position as first gracioso since 1789. The cast of characters required that all three *barbas* of the company take part, so that Francisco Vaca played the strict father, Don Martín; and Tomás López did the cameo role of Uncle Juan. Moratín, who liked to see small things well done, wrote that López made people regret that his role as messenger for the convent was not longer, for he excellently portrayed a little old man as pusillanimous, inept, timid, apathetic, simple, and whiny as the author had imagined the character to be.

The women's roles were not taken by the two leading ladies of the Cruz company, but by the understudies for that season: María García played Doña Inés and Josefa Virg did the part of Doña Clara. María García was an excellent actress, but she never quite made it to the top until the French occupation. Then she became the friend, and later the wife, of Manuel García de la Prada, a banker and Mayor of Madrid, so that her elevation to the first lady was understandable. Moratín's friendship with her began with the rehearsals for a revival of *El viejo y la niña* which the Cruz company put on several times in the 1804-1805 season. He was at the theater almost every night, either in his box or backstage at the Cruz or at the Caños del Peral. In April and May he went to the homes of both María García and Josefa Virg to rehearse them in their parts in *La mojigata.* Moratín's friendship with Marquita García blossomed

though it did not flower. He kissed her in a carriage he tells us
in his diary, and he rechristened her Clori in his poems. He came
to associate her with carriages. In a ballad he writes that he was
on the way to visit her when he was accosted by an importunate
acquaintance determined to sell him a coupé with two mules;
as a result, he never got to her house. In a sonnet he sees his
Clori in a hired carriage drawn by tired beasts and driven by
a wine-drunk coachman, but to him she is transformed into Venus
in the half-shell pulled by white swans, encircled by the Graces
and the Muses, while round her Cupids hover and sigh. Years
later, in 1812, when he fled Madrid on foot to take refuge in
Valencia as Wellington's forces were entering the city, Mariquita García and Manuel García de la Prada stopped their carriage to pick him up and carried him to Valencia with them.

During rehearsals he took Mariquita and Josefa Virg out to
a dinner of ham slices, and they discussed their roles in the
play. Josefa Virg had gone on the Madrid stage in 1790 at the
age of fourteen as tenth lady in the company. Her appearance
was not unusually attractive; she was of medium height, dark
of complexion and flat-nosed, but, while her voice was monot-
onous, she was jovial of character, vivacious in movement, and
she possessed bright, mischievous eyes which she used to good
effect. She must have been just right for the part of the deceitful
Doña Clara, which required her to change character according
to the person with whom she was talking. Moratín wrote of
her performance: "She successfully imitated the impatient desire
for freedom, the effrontery, the astuteness, and the false piety
of Doña Clara."[4]

The part of the maid Lucía was taken by Joaquina Arteaga,
leading graciosa of the company. She had got her start on the
stage singing *tonadillas* in the 1780's, and she was as fortunate
in her stage career as she was unfortunate in her many love
affairs. To the role she brought one of the great comic talents
of the Spanish stage.

The first performance took place on May 19, 1804, at the
Cruz. Compared with the tumult that accompanied *El barón*,
it was a quiet affair. The attacks were to come later in the
press and in papers that circulated from hand to hand. *La
mojigata* ran through May 29, for eleven consecutive performances. It brought in a total of 61,288 reales. At the Caños del

Peral, which put on both operas and plays, and changed bills daily or every other day, the box office took in less than half that amount, 29,631 reales, in the same eleven days.

III   *The Gleeful Critics*

The theater authorities were not disposed to tolerate a repetition of the scandalous uproar that took place at the première of *El barón* in 1803. Furthermore, Moratín had powerful protection, for he was one of that group of writers who enjoyed the favor of Manuel Godoy, Prince of the Peace, then at the peak of his power as favorite and prime minister. Before his fall in 1808, Moratín accepted his protection with dignity and good humor; afterward, he remained loyal to a man who could no longer do anything for him. He wrote a simple prose dedication to him for *El barón*, and when he also dedicated the first edition of *La mojigata* to Godoy, he composed, in unrhymed hendecasyllables, a confession of his devotion to Thalia, the muse of comedy, and a simple statement of thanks for Godoy's patronage.

While the prime minister's influence prevented an overt manifestation at the première, it did not stay the hand of the scribblers. They attacked with gusto. Moratín had resolved after *El viejo y la niña* not to answer criticism, but to take it for what it was worth to him. He almost forgot his resolve when he wrote a prologue for the first edition of *La mojigata*. He thought better of it before the book was printed, and published the play without an introduction, but he kept the manuscript.

In his commentary Moratín distinguishes three types of critics who irk him: the ignorant young dilettante, the learned pedant, and the amateur café critic. He focuses first on the

vain, scatterbrained youth who escaped full speed from school, fleeing from the nominative cases of Latin nouns, who learned a little French from an emigrant from Limoges, and who carries on his person a brush, a mirror and a pocket dictionary in order to extricate himself from whatever difficulties he may encounter. Burning with a thirst for knowledge he has read the prologue to Bayle's *Dictionary* and one fascicle of a universal history. He went to a chemistry laboratory for two weeks, spent one Friday at the Academy of Civil Law and two afternoons in a botany lecture hall, and he has witnessed, without fainting, an anatomical dissection. He knows three cavatinas and four rondeaux by heart; he weaves and knits; and in his spare time he has begun to translate one of Young's *Night Thoughts* and one of Dorat's *Baisers,* "Kisses." Would it not be a shame for so studious and enlightened a youth to confess ingenuously to his darling viscountess that even although he occupies his orchestra seat every day he has not the least notion what the theater is, that it is difficult to speak about the subject without uttering stupidities, that although the money he paid at the door gave him the right to sit in the first row and use his eyeglass, it did not give him the right to pronounce judgment on the merits of the play, because it is one thing for the play to appear good or bad to him and quite another for it to be excellent or detestable![5]

Moratín's description of the pedant—ridiculous and dogmatic, bristling with citations, swollen with pride—is mindful of his own brilliant creation, Don Hermógenes. His lips, Moratín says, "never open but to discredit the achievement of another man, to recommend his own merit, and to applaud his own extraordinary wisdom. He bewails the misery of his fatherland, condemned to ineptitude and stupidity until the government shall deign to recall *his* existence and, elevating him to conspicuous rank, shall command him to illuminate the literary horizon and to disseminate his portentous erudition for the benefit of a destitute and impoverished humanity."[6] His own learned works are in manuscript, but he prefers picking to pieces the books of others to publishing his own. He finds insufferable whatever appears in print. At dinner parties he displays his recondite erudition; without missing a bite, he points out the absurd defects of a dramatist, mouthing with his food remarks about the protatic character, the nexus, the catastasis, and the unity of interest. At his *tertulia,* as he arranges the jack of diamonds and the ace of clubs in his hand, he rearranges the distribution of scenes in the play.

The amateur also holds forth in the café where cigars burn and discord flares. For every bowl of punch drunk, an orator declaims, with the authority of the Abbé d'Aubignac's *Pratique du Théâtre* (*How to Write for the Theater*), that the public has no right to applaud what it likes, and that it ought not to be amused by plays that teach and also make it laugh. Gathered at the bookstores, these same critics discredit the author, and moved by their spirit of charity—which bears a greater resemblance to envy—they pick his work to pieces, polishing his verses, adding characters and situations, improving the plan, changing ideas; and then decide that the play is worth nothing after all, that they are the only true scholars because they dare to censure what they do not know how to read.[7]

When two decades later Moratín wrote the prologue to *La mojigata* for the 1825 Paris edition of his works, he recalled that there were in 1804 a few critics who wrote with urbanity and moderation, qualities rare in any period. He was likely thinking especially of the article which Manuel José Quintana wrote for *Variedades de Ciencias, Literatura y Artes* (*Variety: A Journal of Science, Literature and the Arts*), of which he was editor.[8] Twelve years Moratín's junior, Quintana and his literary friends formed a group that was not friendly toward those writers who were protected by the Prince of the Peace. Quintana was not, however, an antagonistic man, and he possessed a good measure of classic moderation. Furthermore, while he was better known in his time and to posterity as a patriotic and humanitarian poet, he was versed in the theory and practice of the drama. In 1791 he had written *Las reglas del drama* (*Rules of the Drama*). In 1801, the company at the Príncipe theater had performed his tragedy *El duque de Viseo* (*The Duke of Viseo*), derived from Matthew "Monk" Lewis's *The Castle Spectre* (1798); and he had already written another, *Pelayo,* on the first hero of the Reconquest, which was to be produced the following year.

Quintana found much to praise in the plot and characters of *La mojigata,* and little to censure. He did criticize the introduction of the character of Uncle Juan, the messenger from the convent, as having little connection with the principal action of the play, and Quintana was right except that he overlooked the practical side of the theater: Uncle Juan had to be created in order to give Mariano Querol in the part of Perico the opportunity to perform the antics which the public so much loved in him.

Quintana also opened a discussion that has never been satisfactorily closed. It concerned the way in which Moratín conceived his principal character, Doña Clara. Taking his cue from the axiom of Publilius Syrus at the beginning and paraphrasing the closing lines of the play, Quintana wrote:

The object of this work is to encourage men not to trust to outward appearances and to learn to distinguish true virtue from false.

Such is the moral dictum that ends the play. The depiction of hypocrisy is the means chosen to attain this object, and it must be confessed that it was both right and obvious. But is hypocrisy shown in
its true light in La mojigata? Here lies the doubt. The author realizes
—and the axiom he uses at the beginning of his work proves it—that
the evil man who pretends to be good is all the more evil. Now if
the character of Doña Clara is analyzed, it will be evident that she
is not the worst personage in the play. Pressured and harassed by her
father, she has pretended to be a little saint in order to free herself
of her father's meddlesome intrusions.[9]

Quintana then observes that Don Claudio and Perico are morally
worse than Doña Clara and that her sins are not such as to
stress the perversity of the vice that the author intends to correct.

In a subsequent issue of Variedades, Quintana printed a reply
to his critical review. Although the answer appeared anony-
mously, the author was Juan Tineo, the nephew of Jovellanos
and one of Moratín's circle of friends at the time. Tineo refuted
each of Quintana's points, and Quintana in turn replied in a
series of footnotes to Tineo's rejoinder. The significant part of
Tineo's statement lies in his concept of the object of the play
and the distinction that he draws between hypocrisy and dissimulation. Moratín's purpose, he says, was to teach parents a
lesson in the rearing of their children. Wise and loving parents
discover the reward for their efforts in the true rather than the
feigned virtue which they observe in their children. Harsh and
capricious parents who abuse their authority suffer the conse-
quences of forcing deceitful practices upon their children.

The principal object, as we have seen [Tineo writes] was to demon-
strate the effects of a poorly conceived upbringing; and therefore,
Doña Clara must appear vicious not because vice is characteristic of
her but because the rigor and harshness with which her father has
brought her up have forced her to pretend to be what she is not.
Thus she is a mojigata and not a hypocrite, because the vice of
hypocrisy is ingrained in a person, as it is in Tartuffe, while the
quality of mojigatez may be found, as in this case, in a person
naturally inclined to candor and sincerity. These two vices are essen-
tially different although, because they reveal themselves in the same
ways, their appearance and effects are similar. The hypocrite is always
a mojigato; the mojigato is not always a hypocrite. To draw and fix
this line, not to confuse these two vices, was the great difficulty that
had to be overcome; and it seems to us that the author of La mojigata
surmounted it skillfully and delicately.[10]

Since Tineo was close to Moratín, it may be safely assumed that he was privy to the dramatist's intention in writing the play, and the distinctions he draws merit the attention of the critic. On the other hand, Quintana rightly indicates in his notes equivocal points: not only the axiom of Publilius Syrus and the concluding words of the play, but also actions and statements of Doña Clara such as "You'll never get anywhere in this world unless you practice to deceive."

Those critics who see in *La mojigata* but a pallid imitation of Molière's *Tartuffe* overlook Moratín's primary interest in the theme of Terence's *Adelphi* rather than in the vice of hypocrisy, and they ignore the semantic distinction between hypocrite and *mojigata*. Moratín had a different theme and focused on a lesser vice than did Molière. Yet he himself later seems uncertain of his aim, as if critics had brought him around to their point of view. In the foreword to the 1825 Paris edition, he speaks of the *falsos devotos*, the "falsely devout," which can only be a translation of the *faux dévots* whom Molière attacked in *Le Tartuffe*. Furthermore, the record of the American literary historian George Ticknor's interview with Moratín in Paris in 1818 suggests that the dramatist had come to think of Doña Clara as a female Tartuffe. Ticknor left with Moratín a questionnaire on *La mojigata* which the Spaniard answered in his own hand. Some questions, to be sure, were slanted, but Moratín did not take the opportunity to rectify them. Ticknor's first query was: "What is the moral aim of *La mojigata*?" Moratín answered: "To show that true virtue lies in actions and not in words since under the guise of piety and devotion the greatest vices are often concealed." To the slanted question, "Why are there so many hypocrites and *mojigatos* in Spain?" Moratín replied: "There have been many hypocrites in Spain because Catholic practice favors this vice, because the priests have always supported the outward appearance of virtue, because in human conduct they have required words, gestures, exterior trappings, much faith and very little charity."[11] On the basis of these replies, Ticknor understandably rendered the title of the play into English as "The Female Hypocrite." The conclusion is inescapable that Moratín himself adopted the critics' point of view, but it must be affirmed that the play loses merit if it is considered predominantly as a treatment of the vice of hypocrisy.

The Spanish Inquisition turned its baleful gaze on Moratín's play. By the first decade of the nineteenth century, the Holy Office was moribund but not extinct. Having done its job so effectively in the past, it no longer provided the public with spectacular *autos de fe,* although during the rehearsals of *La mojigata* Moratín wrote in his diary that he had observed a woman in the street wearing the *coroza,* the cardboard cone decorated with allusions to the crime which the Inquisition obliged a delinquent to wear. In its decadence the Inquisition had devoted itself to the policing of literature and books, and in the eighteenth century, the ideas of the French philosophes and later the revolutionaries had given it much business. Still, nothing happened to Moratín in 1804. Ticknor inquired about the matter in 1818 and Moratín answered: "The Inquisition would have harassed [the author] had not the distinction with which the Prince of the Peace favored him among all the writers of that period convinced the tribunal that persecution of Moratín would bring down upon it the displeasure of that powerful minister."

The Inquisition bided its time. Then it all but disappeared, for the French conquerors of 1808 and their Spanish sympathizers during the reign of Joseph Bonaparte and many—though by no means all—of the Spanish patriots at the Cortes of Cadiz wanted to rid the country of the tribunal. In the meantime, *La mojigata* was often revived in the Madrid theaters. The *Gaceta* for February 9, 1810, reported: "*La mojigata* has been performed these days to general applause. The sound and refined sense of ethics which pervades this play is so easily within the grasp of all the spectators who attend the theater, our customs are portrayed so truly and with such brilliant force, and the dialogue is so natural, amusing and agreeable that everyone leaves satisfied, edified and cheerful."

Such was not the view of another sector of the public which was represented by this opinion directed to the editor of *El Procurador General del Rey y de la Nación* (*The General Solicitor for King and Country*), and published on December 7, 1814:

I wonder whether you have observed recently that the street corners of our city have been plastered with posters announcing in letters as big as Aragonese peaches the performance of *La mojigata*? I need not tell you that this play is the product of the talent of one of the biggest . . . . . . who in the late disturbances made public profession of his irreligion and his Francophilism. Even if one overlooks its immorality—and one ought not to overlook it—should not this circumstance suffice to justify the prohibition of this play at a time when everyone of influence in the government ought to be exerting every effort to discredit the ideas and the authors that have corrupted us?[12]

The writer realized his desire. When Fernando VII returned to Spain in 1814, he announced in a decree of July 21 that he considered it fitting that the Inquisition resume the exercise of its powers. With the ponderous lentor that befitted its age, the Holy Office turned its attention to the censorship that had principally concerned it in recent decades. More than a year later, in August, 1815, the Suprema in Madrid ordered the examination, among other plays, of *La mojigata,* which was withdrawn from circulation while it was under consideration. On May 16, 1818— just a week before George Ticknor arrived in Madrid—the tribunal formally forbade the comedy.

During the constitutional triennium of 1820-1823, when freedom from censorship prevailed, *La mojigata* was played in Madrid. But the Duke of Angoulême with French troops restored the absolute rule of Fernando VII for another decade, and the play disappeared again from the Madrid stage. The bishop of Valencia included it among a great many other printed plays which he prohibited in 1829. With the death of Fernando, it was back in the theater in 1834. Mariano José de Larra saw it then and reviewed it for *La Revista Española* (*The Spanish Review*). He lamented that the play should have been suppressed so long that dramatists had not learned from it, for it was superior, he thought, to comedies of its kind that were written subsequently.[13]

Like all of Moratín's plays, *La mojigata* was revived several times in the 1830's and 1840's so that Doña Clara and Don Claudio, Don Roque and Muñoz, Don Eleuterio and Don Hermógenes, Aunt Mónica and the Baron Montepino trod the same boards as the famed characters of the Romantic stage: Macías, Don Alvaro, the Trovador and Azucena, the lovers of Teruel, and Don Juan Tenorio and Doña Inés.

CHAPTER 6

School for Parents and Guardians

IN 1794 Moratín's friend Pedro Estala published a translation
of Aristophanes' *Plutus* with an introduction in which he
gave a history of the theater including the Spanish Golden Age
comedia and the eighteenth-century drama in Spain. He praised
Moratín and described each of his plays including one entitled
El tutor (*The Guardian*), of which he wrote: "*El tutor* is far
superior to *El viejo y la niña*. The action is more lively and
interesting, and the characters are more varied and better con-
trasted."[1] Moratín had indeed written such a play, and in Rome
on October 22, 1793, he read it to the exiled Jesuit Esteban
Arteaga, a distinguished literary and music critic. In his diary
Moratín recorded the Jesuit's reaction: "*Non placuit*. He did not
like it." When Moratín read Estala's words, he wrote to Melón,
in 1796: "Why does he speak of *El tutor*, which does not exist?"

Moratín destroyed the play *El tutor*, but some scholars have
supposed that *El sí de las niñas* may represent a reworking of it.
The title itself, *El tutor*, suggests that it must have been close
in theme to *El viejo y la niña* and to *El sí de las niñas*. Moratín
had completed a versión of *El sí*—he was accustomed to use
the abbreviated title—as early as 1801. In July he read it to
friends: Melón, Juan Tineo, the Arabist José Antonio Conde. In
September, when he was at his country house in Pastrana—
east of Alcalá de Henares—he gave a reading of it to his circle
of intimates there, including the local priest. Again in January,
1802, and in December, 1803, he read it to his Madrid friends.
Each time he wrote in his diary that the play pleased those who
heard it. On October 24, 25, and 26, 1804, he read the play, one
act each day, in the home of the Prince of the Peace, where it
was again favorably received. On February 27, 1805, he read it
at the home of the Marchioness of Villafranca. The fame of the
play was spreading, and it was time that it was produced on the
stage. On November 15, he went to Antonio Pinto's house and
92

read it to the actors of the company at the Cruz Theater. They too liked it.

I A Lesson in Dramatic Craftsmanship

El sí de las niñas provided the general public with moral instruction in parenthood and guardianship, and it gave several generations of playwrights a lesson in dramatic craftsmanship. It is an excellently constructed play. The dramatic conflict is simple: Doña Irene, a widow of modest means, wants to marry her daughter Francisca, who is sixteen years old, to Don Diego, a wealthy gentleman of fifty-nine. However, although Doña Francisca has led a sheltered life at a convent school in Guadalajara, she has met a handsome young army officer whom she knows by the name of Don Félix. Her heart belongs to him, and, while she is an obedient daughter, she is hardly enthusiastic about her mother's plan.

El sí de las niñas
Cruz Theater, Madrid, January 24, 1806

Don Diego, a wealthy gentleman	Andrés Prieto
Don Carlos, his nephew	
Doña Irene, an impoverished widow	María Ribera
Doña Francisca, her daughter	Josefa Virg
Rita, maid to Doña Irene	
Simón, manservant to Don Diego	
Calamocha, manservant to Don Carlos	

The setting is a common room on the second floor of an inn in Alcalá de Henares, a university town twenty miles east of Madrid on the road to Guadalajara and Zaragoza. The first act, divided into nine scenes, consists of five sequences.[2] The first scene and the first sequence coincide. Don Diego is complaining to his servant Simón about the prolonged stop in Alcalá de Henares. He and Simón had accompanied Doña Irene to Guadalajara to pick up Francisca and her maid Rita at a convent school where one of her aunts was a nun. They have stopped at Alcalá on the way back so that the young lady may visit another aunt, also a nun. In the first lines of the scene, the curiosity of the audience is piqued: Don Diego has refused to

leave the inn for two days because he does not want to be seen
in Alcalá where he has many acquaintances. He unburdens his
thoughts to Simón, and the point of attack in the play begins
with Simón's misunderstanding of his master's intentions. Simón
thinks that Don Diego plans for his nephew Don Carlos, a
dashing young officer who is stationed in Zaragoza, to marry
Doña Francisca. Simón, who knows Don Carlos and has just
met Doña Francisca, thoroughly approves of the idea. When
Don Diego suggests that people will gossip and will say that
there is too great a dfference in ages, Simón says: "Why, I don't
think the difference is so great. Seven or eight years at the
most." Don Diego is astonished: "Why, man! What do you
mean seven or eight years? She was sixteen just a few months
ago. ... And I, while thank goodness I'm healthy and ... even
so, I'll not see fifty-nine again." It is Simón's turn to be surprised
as he realizes that Don Dego expects to marry the girl himself.
"Well, that's a good one on me!" he exclaims, telling his master
he thought the plan was to have Francisca marry Don Carlos.
Don Diego is disgusted with his servant: "What an idea indeed!
To think I was going to marry her to my nephew! No, sir! Let
him study his mathematics." The equilibrium that existed has
been disturbed, and the play is underway. A foreshadowing of
the plot occurs when Don Diego tells Simón that although Carlos
left Madrid on July 3, he still had not joined his regiment in
Zaragoza at the end of September. The uncle supposes his
susceptible nephew was having a love affair somewhere along
the road. "If he meets a pair of black eyes, he's a lost man."

In the next sequence (Scenes ii-iv), after Doña Irene, Doña
Francisca and Rita have returned from their visit to the aunt
in the convent, Don Diego attempts to discover the true senti-
ments of Doña Francisca. The girl is quiet and seems naïve, but
the mother chatters loquaciously. Francisca takes leave of them
by displaying the French curtsy she has learned, saying almost
pointedly: "For you a curtsy and for mama a kiss."

When Don Diego and Doña Irene are alone, he remarks that
the girl has shown no sign of affection for him. Doña Irene
assures him that she and her daughter talk about him constantly
when they are together. "Why last night after you went to bed,
she was speaking so intelligently! I'd have given anything for
you to have been able to hear her. ... And she is so right to
think that it is better for a girl her age to have a husband who

is along in years, experienced, mature, whose conduct ..." Don Diego interrupts: "You don't say! She was saying that?" Doña Irene answers: "Oh, no, *I* was saying that, and she was listening to me as attentively as if she were a woman of forty, really!" With her remarkable flow of words, Doña Irene calms Don Diego's concern as she chatters of her own three marriages, the twenty-two children she bore of which Francisca is the only survivor, and her family relations. The sequence ends harmoniously as an equilibrium is established between the two elderly people, the future son-in-law and mother-in-law.

The third sequence (Scenes v-vi) is transitional as one set of characters leaves the stage and another set is brought on. In it, however, a fact is established which frames or limits the action of the play. Don Diego and Doña Irene fix the time of their departure for six o'clock the next morning. This creates an underlying tension, for the public realizes that whatever is to happen must be resolved before the party leaves for Madrid, where the projected marriage will take place. Also, in the short scene between Rita and Doña Irene, the piquant saucy character of the maid is revealed; and Doña Irene's pet thrush, which figures later in the action, is introduced.

The exposition continues and the complication begins in the fourth sequence (Scenes vii-viii). Calamocha, Don Félix' man-servant, arrives at the inn with their baggage, and a simple recognition scene occurs between him and Rita. Only the most dim-witted member of the audience would fail to suppose that Don Félix and Don Carlos are the same person, although none of the characters is yet aware that the rivals are uncle and nephew. Having been made privy to the plans of Don Diego and Doña Irene, and having observed the equivocal attitude of Francisca, the public now discovers the antagonistic action of the play. As soon as Doña Irene and Don Diego arrived at the convent in Guadalajara, Francisca and Rita wrote to Don Félix in Zaragoza in the hope that "he would not allow his darling Paquita to end up in the arms of a stranger or permit the many caresses, tears and sighs which they shared by the garden wall to be forever lost." Calamocha tells Rita that they no sooner received the letter than they left at a gallop for Madrid and have only paused in Alcalá because the horses are exhausted. This combination of exposition and complication is told in the jocular, lighthearted tone characteristic of the graciosos in Spanish plays with just a trace of spice. Rita points out to Calamocha the rooms occupied by the members of the party including the one that she and Francisca share: "And that one is ours." "What do you mean, ours?" Calamocha asks with a jaunty leer. "Yours and mine?" And at the end of the scene he cannot refrain from returning to the subject: "So that is *our* room, eh?"

In the final sequence of Act I (Scene ix) Rita and Doña Francisca complete the exposition. The young woman's distress as she unburdens her worries to Rita is moderated by the poetic quality of her memories of the courtship: her acquaintance with Don Félix at the country home of a government official, their discreet meetings at the garden wall of the convent, the three claps that he gave to call her attention, his strumming on the guitar. As Francisca's melancholy deepens, Rita tells her that Don Félix has heeded their call of distress. He is in Alcalá. Paquita's spirits revive, and as the evening shadows fall, she says to Rita: "Do you remember how he told me he could never forget me, that no danger would detain him, that he would stop at no difficulty for me? ... Well, you see, he told me the truth."

Rita foreshadows the crisis when she says: "With all of us here, there could be the very dickens of a scene among the mother, the daughter, the fiancé and the sweetheart. If we don't rehearse this dance well, we may get lost in it." Yet the act ends on a note of moderation. By contrast, we might think of the end of Act I of a Romantic play, the Duke of Rivas' *Don Alvaro*: the hero has accidentally shot the father of his beloved Leonor and exclaims in horror, "My God! Fatal weapon! Terrible night!" Leonor cries, "Father, father!" and, as the dying man gasps, "I curse you!" she faints and Don Alvaro drags her inert body to the balcony. In Moratín's play, Don Diego the agonist has laid his plans. Somewhere in the background, for we have not seen him yet, his antagonist Don Félix is at work. The conflict is clear, the complication is simple, the frailties are human, the emotions are honest and deep.

In the first sequence of Act II (Scenes i-iv), the action progresses little, but the tone of the play is reaffirmed. In the conversations between Doña Irene, Rita and Francisca, the mother complains of her ailments, praises Don Diego, insists on the good fortune that the nuns' prayers for Francisca have brought them. Francisca is secretly worried that there is no word from Don Félix yet, and Doña Irene is concerned that her daughter does not say more about the projected marriage. She thinks Francisca wants to be a nun, and she causes a certain uneasiness in the audience when she says: "You can serve God in every walk of life, Frasquita; but pleasing your mother, helping her, being with her and consoling her in her troubles, that is the first obligation of an obedient daughter." The audience feels that the cause of Don Diego may be gaining ground in the conflict when Francisca answers: "Believe me, mother, I shall never leave you nor cause you concern."

In the next sequence (Scene v), Don Diego is determined to talk the problem over with Francisca. He is mature, understanding, indeed fatherly toward her. He is courteous, but he firmly makes Doña Irene keep quiet so that he and Francisca can talk. He will not force the girl's will, he says, if she wishes to become a nun or if she is in love with someone else. Doña Irene cannot contain herself at the idea that her daughter has another love affair. She becomes almost hysterical as the scene reaches a crisis: "Just tell him about the sweethearts," she cries ironically to Francisca, "that you left in Madrid at the age of twelve, and the boyfriends you made in the convent when you were with that saintly woman!" Francisca disarms them both, "I don't know what to say if the two of you are going to get angry." She reassures her mother that she is an obedient daughter, and the scene dissolves into sentimentality as Don Diego suggests that they should go to their rooms: "Come. Let's go before someone comes and finds the three of us crying like children."

The third sequence (Scenes vi-viii) contains the obligatory scene between Francisca and Don Carlos, for Rita has arranged for the sweethearts to meet. "How's it going, beautiful, how's it going?" Don Carlos greets her. The scene is not passionate but is infused with tenderness, a quality rare in the Spanish theater before Moratín.[3] Don Carlos' rival is in the next room with Doña Irene, but the young man is reasonable. "He must be an honorable man and it would not be right to insult him because he is in love with a woman so worthy of being loved." There is dramatic irony in the solution which Don Carlos sees to the problem. He will go to Madrid too the next day, and his uncle will come to his aid. "There," he tells Francisca, "I can count on the help of a respectable and virtuous old gentleman whom

I ought to call a friend and a father rather than an uncle. I am his closest relative and the one he loves best. He is a very rich man. ..." The sequence ends in a tender exchange that has charmed audiences:

"Good night, Paquita."
"Go to bed and rest."
"Rest when I am jealous?"
"Of whom?"
"Good night. Sleep well, Paquita."
"Sleep when I am in love?"

And the public now feels that just possibly Don Carlos might win out.

The fourth sequence (Scenes ix-x) contains a simple recognition as does the fifth (Scenes xi-xiii): Don Carlos and Calamocha are as astonished to see Simón at the inn as he is to see them; then Don Diego comes out of Doña Irene's room and discovers his nephew. Because of the twilight, he does not at first recognize Carlos, and the suspense is heightened. In the obligatory scene between the uncle and nephew, that is, between the two rivals, Don Carlos immediately comprehends the situation, but Don Diego does not. Don Diego is at first upset and vexed that Carlos should turn up so inopportunely; then he is concerned that his nephew may be in trouble. Reassured that Carlos is all right, Don Diego peremptorily orders his nephew to return to Zaragoza and gives him money so that he may quickly be on his way. The young man is not even to spend the night in Alcalá but at an inn outside town. Carlos is obedient, and there is virile sentiment in their leave-taking. Carlos' parting aside seems definitively to give the victory to Don Diego: "(And I am abandoning her! And I am losing her forever!)" When his newhew has gone, Don Diego reflects: "How respectful he always is to his uncle. He's as malleable as clay."

The final sequence of the act (Scenes xiv-xvi) begins with dramatic irony. Francisca elatedly tells the maid: "Things are so different now, Rita. Don Félix has come, and I'm not afraid of anybody. With my fate in his hands, I am the most fortunate of women." When she learns from Simón that the army officer and his servant have left the inn, her dreams collapse. Carlos' action is inexplicable to her. "Did I deserve to be deceived so perfidiously? Did my love merit this reward? What has my transgression been, what has it been?" As the curtain closes on a darkened stage, it seems that Don Diego's cause is winning out.

As the first sequence of Act III begins (Scenes i-iv), it is three o'clock in the morning and Don Diego leaves his room to get some air in the common room where Simón is sleeping. They hear three handclaps in the street and the sound of a guitar. When Francisca and Rita come from their room, master and servant remain in the shadows while Francisca talks to Don Félix from the window. The young man is reticent, but he tosses a note into the room. The two are saying farewell, and before Francisca finds the note Simón stumbles on the pet thrush's cage, and the women flee to their room. Don Diego, now realizing that Francisca does in truth have a sweetheart, exclaims, "This is the end of all my illusions!" At this point, ironically, both rivals have renounced the hand of Francisca. In a brief soliloquy Don Diego voices the frustration he feels at the ridiculous situation in which he finds himself: "To be jealous at my age! It's shameful."

The play reaches a climax—the maximum disturbance in the equilibrium, the maximum point of emotion and tension—in the second sequence (Scenes v-vi). Francisca and Rita look for the note from Carlos and cannot find it. "Don't bother," Francisca says. "*They* have it. That's all I needed to make my misfortune complete." Without the letter Carlos' sudden departure remains unexplained. "It's the duplicity of a man who made promises he had no intention of keeping. He came here, he found a rival and he said to himself: 'Why should I bother anybody? Why should I come to the rescue of a woman? There are plenty of women! Let them marry her off. I've nothing to lose. My peace of mind is more important than the happiness of that poor girl.' May God forgive me, forgive me for having loved him so much!" Her dejection is complete. Rita urges her to go back to her room before Don Diego or someone else discovers her there. "If I have lost everything, what have I to fear? Do you think I have the heart to get up? Let them come. Nothing matters to me now." The emotional impact of *El sí de las niñas* has reached its most intense point, for each of the three principals in the triangle is now plunged into despair.

At the beginning of the third sequence (Scenes vii-viii), it is obvious that Don Diego has read Carlos' note and realizes who his rival is, for he sends Simón to overtake Carlos and Calamocha and bring them back to the inn. He tries to penetrate Doña Francisca's reserve, but she disconsolately affirms that she neither has another love nor wishes to enter a convent, and that she expects to obey her mother and please her. At this point, Moratín uses a simple but effective technique: the lights begin to come up as the day dawns so that by the end of the play the stage is bathed in brightness. Don Diego's discourse on the upbringing of girls fits naturally into the dialogue: "This is what people mean when they talk about rearing a daughter properly: they teach her to belie and hide the most innocent feelings with perfidious dissimulation. They think girls are proper if they are expert in the art of silence and lying." After pointing the moral, Don Diego himself shows a changed attitude toward Paquita. He speaks of himself as her friend, and he calls her child. But the suspense continues because Paquita still does not know the identity of Don Félix.

In the following sequence (Scenes ix-x), the audience is doubtful about Don Diego's attitude. In his conversation with Simón he calls his nephew a rascal and a scoundrel. With Don Carlos he is severe. He shows him the note that the young man wrote to Francisca and asks him to relate the tale of the love affair. At the conclusion, Don Diego says calmly: "Well, you see, Carlos, it is time for you to begin thinking differently. ... If you love her, I love her too. ... Not half an hour ago she herself told me that she is ready to obey her mother and give me her hand. ..." This produces Carlos' only outburst: "But not her heart! ... You may marry when you like. She will always act as virtue and propriety demand. But I was her first love; I am and shall be the only object of her affection. You will be the husband, but if once or often you surprise her with tears flooding her eyes, you will know she sheds them for me." Carlos prepares to say goodbye. There is talk of war, he says, and he will probably be gone a long time. Don Diego insists, however, that he wait a little longer and sends him into his room.

In the fifth sequence (Scenes xi-xii), Don Diego informs Doña Irene—as best he can, for she constantly interrupts—that her daughter is in love with another man. The mother becomes hysterical without reading the note or even learning who the suitor is, and calls her daughter to come out. Don Diego himself must read the note so that at last Francisca understands. The crisis comes as Doña Irene, in a frenzy, threatens to beat her daughter, and Don Carlos rushes from Don Diego's room ingenuously to defend her. The stage is prepared for the final sequence (Scene xiii), which is the denouement. Don Diego, who in the last scenes has shown that his thoughts have been changing, cedes Francisca to Carlos. "So he's your nephew?" asks Doña Irene in order to be reassured. "Yes, madam," replies Don Diego, "my nephew, who with his clapping, his guitar music and his notepaper has given me the worst night of my life." The young people have knelt in front of him for his blessing, and he acquires greater stature as he says: "The effort I am making leaves a painful impression on my soul, for I am, after all, but a weak and wretched man." He takes occasion to lecture Doña Irene: "He and your daughter were madly in love while you and her aunts were building castles in the air and filling my head with illusions that have vanished like a dream. This is the result of the abuse of parental authority, of the oppression that young people suffer." The curtain falls on a scene of balanced sentiment as Doña Irene admires Carlos' good looks and the young people express their gratitude to Don Diego.

II *The Elements of Drama*

The characters of *El sí* are conceived with the warmth of a mature understanding. If the action of the play approaches that perfection which only true craftsmanship can bring, it is because it springs naturally and with all verisimilitude from the characters themselves. The personality of Don Diego is pivotal to the action. There is no hint of caricature as Moratín conceived him; he is far removed from Don Roque of *El viejo y la niña*. Don Diego is a gentleman; he is fifty-nine years old but strong and healthy; he is well-to-do and with no family but his nephew Carlos; he wants to enjoy the comforts and pleasures that marriage can bring him; and he has let himself be deluded by Doña Irene into thinking that a young girl will be attracted to him. But he is a reasonable man, and his reason is at work from the moment he appears on stage, for he is concerned about the difference in age and what people will say. Furthermore, when he sees that Francisca is courteous but unresponsive, his reason tells him that something is amiss, and he is determined to get at the cause if Doña Irene will let him. Throughout the exposition and the complication, there are subtle indications that he is indeed, as he says at the end, a weak man, and these add to the suspense; but there is also evidence—in his gentle, fatherly conversations with Francisca and in his affection and concern about his nephew—that he is of noble character. At the denouement, his renunciation of his illusions, his abdication in his nephew of his own dreams of family life, make him one of Moratín's finest creations.

Doña Irene is Moratín's best comic character. Like Don Hermógenes, she has entered into the fabric of Spanish culture, for everybody knows someone very much like her. Self-centered, garrulous, she talks but never listens, and her chatter provides many of the laughs in the play. Widowed three times, and now aging, with drug and doctor bills and little money, she sees the only solution to her troubles in an advantageous marriage for her only surviving daughter. In Don Diego she has seen her opportunity, and she has filled his head with illusions while nursing her own. There is pathos in the situation, but Moratín avoids both the pathetic and the opportunity for ridicule, just as he eluded ridicule in his concept of the character of Aunt Mónica in the second version of *El barón*. On the other hand, he does not give us a reformed Doña Irene at the end. Doña Irene really learns nothing, but she quickly grasps the significance of Francisca's catch, for the nephew will have his uncle's money. It is doubtful that the moral lesson makes the slightest impression on her, for once her mind is at ease concerning money, she—who enjoyed three husbands and bore twenty-two children—turns her attention to the young man. "My goodness, Francisca, you've made a fine choice. He's certainly a good-looking fellow. A little dark-complexioned maybe, but he's got a very seductive look in his eyes."

The two young people are excellently conceived. Their passion is both romantic and believable. Doña Francisca is caught in a chain of events that she can resist only by being silent and unresponsive. Don Carlos' determination to keep his girl is as convincing as his renunciation of her when he discovers who his rival is, for the circumstance is indeed an unusual one. When he is given the opportunity, his moving account of the courtship and his eloquence in speaking to his uncle convince Don Diego of the depth of the young man's feeling.

The three servants fill precisely the correct bounds. They serve

the action without intruding into it. The affair between Calamocha and Rita, while it mimics as in the Golden Age *comedia*
the love affair of master and mistress, is merely sketched but
does not become central to any scene. The good sense of Simón
and the playful wit of the other two provide necessary notes
toward the total harmony of the play.

The thought that Moratín intended to express comes through
clearly: the inappropriateness of a marriage between an elderly
man and a young girl, and the criticism of the education of
women which makes them false to their inner feelings. The
play says something more, too, which has given it enduring
appeal: the eternal conflict between parents and children, the
futility of forcing upon youth the values of the elders, the idea
that love will find a way. This is the stuff that fills the columns
of advice to the lovelorn, it is the stuff that literature is made
of, it is the stuff of life.

Moratín was fully committed to prose when he wrote *El sí*.
In the original version, Don Carlos sang a song outside the inn,
a simple ditty in the style of those Moratín wrote for the zarzuela
El barón. He deleted it in later versions for the sake of verisimilitude: Don Diego overheard it and presumably might have
recognized his nephew's voice. Probably no ear has ever been
better attuned to the speech of Madrid than Moratín's. *El sí*
has been a model of dramatic prose, of language adjusted to
character, to those generations of playwrights whose modes and
themes obliged them to write in prose. It also served for over
a hundred years as a text for students learning the Spanish
language in Europe and America. And a fine text it was, for
whether the expressions were new or old in Moratín's time, his
use of them fixed them in the language, and such was his genius
that they retain to this day the sparkling wit that he observed
in them.

III *Literature and Life*

In Moratín's time and subsequently, critics have pointed to
antecedents for *El sí de las niñas*. Among Spanish authors, Lope
de Vega and Francisco de Rojas Zorrilla wrote plays with similar
situations. Lope's *La discreta enamorada* (*Love Sharpens a
Woman's Wit*) presents a widow, her daughter, and an elderly
captain who is in love with the daughter while the widow is

attracted to him, and the daughter is enamored of his son. But the action is far more complicated than anything that Moratín would have found tolerable. The daughter takes advantage of the captain's interest in her in order to charm the son; hence her claim to the quality of discretion. The son, however, is attracted to an unconventional young woman, who in turn has another admirer so that the complications become intricately involved in the best fashion of the *comedia*. In short, it is a Lope play filled with fast-moving action, but lacking motivation through characterization or the quality of verisimilitude which were so important to Moratín.

The relationship with Rojas Zorrilla's *Entre bobos anda el juego* (*Game of Fools*) is limited in two aspects. A father attempts to force his daughter into a marriage she does not want; and the scene of the second act is an inn in Illescas during the night.

Variations on Moratín's subject were very common during his day. An article in a periodical *El Corresponsal del Censor* (*The Censor's Correspondent*)—the *Censor* was another newspaper—published in 1787 by Santos Manuel Rubín, deals so clearly with the theme that we may suspect that Moratín read it. A popular one-act play in which Isidoro Máiquez played in 1802 was *El sueño,* in which a father and son are unwittingly rivals for the hand of a young widow; when the father overhears a scene between his son and the widow, he blesses their marriage.[4] The play may have been an adaptation made from the French by Félix Enciso Castrillón, and indeed the clearest antecedents are to be found in two French plays: Marivaux's *L'Ecole des mères* (*School for Mothers*), 1732, and Marsollier's *Le Traité nul* (*Broken Engagement*), 1797.

The cast of characters of Marivaux's play is remarkably similar to that of *El sí*: Madame Argante, a widow; her daughter Angélique; the maid Lisette; the young lover Eraste; his father Damis, who also is in love with Angélique; his valet Champagne. Only the other valet is different: he works for Madame Argante instead of for Eraste, for the setting is at Madame Argante's house and Eraste disguises himself as a valet in order to enter the household.[5] Besides the characters and the situation, the stress that Madame Argante gives to filial obedience resembles Doña Irene's use of the same weapon; and the obligatory scene between

Monsieur Damis and Angélique is similar to the scene between Don Diego and Francisca. That there is an echo of Marivaux in Moratín's play is undeniable. Yet the dissimilarities of detail and spirit are marked. In a one-act play Marivaux resorts to farce to resolve the action so that the tone approaches, but does not attain, the level of the comedy of manners. The rivalry of father and son, common to several of the antecedents, was unacceptable to Moratín; he decorously changed the relationship to uncle and favorite nephew. But the essential difference is one of spirit. There are two different worlds: one is French and the other Spanish. One is the never-never land where Marivaux's delightful creations play at a game of love and chance; the other is a real world with real people who are motivated by self-interest and love.

Contemporary critics commented on the resemblance to a one-act play in French by Benoît-Joseph Marsollier, *Le Traité nul*, which was produced in Paris in 1797 and appeared in Spain as *El contrato anulado* in 1802.[6] The characters are similar: a widowed mother and her daughter, an uncle and a nephew who both propose marriage to the daughter. However, the mother is a rich widow; the whole situation is early revealed; and the rest of the play is concerned with the attempts of mother and uncle to outwit one another in the financial arrangements that accompany the engagement of the daughter and the nephew. This preoccupation, central to numerous French plays since the period of Molière, is incidental to *El sí*.

The French critic, Vézinet, as he did in other plays of Moratín, detected echoes of Molière in *El sí*. The conflict brings to his mind that of Arnolphe, Agnès and Horace in *L'Ecole des femmes* (*The School for Wives*). There are situations that recall *L'Avare* (*The Miser*): the scene in which Don Diego praises Doña Francisca's virtues and Simón thinks he is planning for her to marry his nephew Carlos parallels the one in which Harpagon praises Mariane to his delighted son Cléante who supposes his father is thinking of the young woman as a daughter-in-law, and the scene in which Doña Irene exalts to Don Diego the advantages of an aging husband recalls the one in which the meddlesome Frosine of *L'Avare* embroiders this theme in order to get money out of Harpagon.[7] However, the relationship to the work of Molière is tenuous. As the critic Joaquín Casalduero has pointed out, the characters of Moratín do not attain the comic grandeur of a Tartuffe or an Harpagon. Yet his theater is not a dwarf. It is a different theater that belongs to a different time and place.[8] Its concern is close to human life and nature. Its appeal is enduring because there are always parents who domineer and youths who will have their way.

In recent years, a story has been propagated in the manuals of literature that *El sí de las niñas* is autobiographical, that Moratín, in a real-life situation, played the role of Don Diego, that there was a real Francisca named Francisca Muñoz, that Doña Irene was her mother Doña María Ortiz de Muñoz. Juan de Dios Mendoza has studied this latter-day legend and the biographical facts as best they are known; and he has concluded that there is no justification for any such statement.[9] In 1798, shortly after his return from Italy at the age of thirty-eight, Moratín began to visit the home of Don Santiago Muñoz, his wife Doña María Ortiz and their only daughter Francisca Gertrudis. The reason was that his friend, the Arabic scholar José Antonio Conde, lived at that house, apparently as a boarder. Moratín was a bachelor and, while he had relatives in Madrid, he had no immediate family. In his foreign travels and in Madrid, he had love affairs and brief, even sordid, encounters. In the years after 1798, he and the Muñoz family developed a friendship which was to continue during Moratín's self-imposed exile. At first, one may judge from Moratín's diary, he had the lightest of flirtations with Francisca, but there was no passion, and his infrequent visits to the house do not suggest the lover. In 1801 he had written *El sí de las niñas*; in January of 1806 it was staged, and the night of the fourth performance he took Doña María and Francisca to see it. At the end of that same year, well after *El sí* was written, performed and published, the possibility that Francisca might marry came up; we do not know the name of the suitor. Moratín, as a close friend of the family, was consulted. Apparently, the marriage did not take place. Years later, in 1816, after Moratín had left Madrid definitively for the rest of his life, Francisca received another marriage proposal; and Moratín was again consulted, this time by letter. Sometime that year she married a military man, Francisco Valverde.

We may conjecture that Francisca and her family at first thought of Moratín as a possible suitor, but as the confirmed and determined bachelor let time pass, the relationship became simply a family friendship. Moratín's fondness for the Muñoz family comes through clearly in his many letters to them, but he always addresses them with the formal *usted*. Francisca's affection for Moratín is confirmed by her attachment to his portrait which Francisco de Goya painted in 1799. She kept it at her house during all the years of his exile, and when, on his death, he willed it to the Royal Academy of San Fernando, she was so saddened to part with it that the executor promised to have a copy made for her.

Moratín's first biographers gave no support to the legend. Melón, who tells of the early situation in which Moratín was the youthful suitor that lost the girl to the aging man—the case that paralleled *El viejo y la niña*—makes no mention of Francisca Muñoz in connection with *El sí*, which was written and produced at the time when the two men were on the closest terms. Manuel Silvela, with whose family Moratín resided in Bordeaux and Paris over a period of years, says nothing; nor does Buenaventura Carlos Aribau in the biography which he wrote a few years after Moratín's death.[10]

The source of the legend goes back to the excerpts from the diary which Juan Eugenio Hartzenbusch published in the *Obras póstumas* in 1867-1868. Hartzenbusch selected mostly items of literary or historical interest. Guided by mid-century prudery, he omitted the many references to Moratín's amatory escapades; but he did copy the innocent passages referring to Francisca Muñoz, including the consultation in 1806 concerning her marriage. Hence, the name of Francisca looms large as one of the few women mentioned in the Hartzenbusch extracts; and it appears more frequently there than in the diary itself, in which there are weeks and months with no mention at all of her or the Muñoz family.

The novelist Patricio de la Escosura, in an article published in a popular magazine in 1877, suggested the idea that *El sí* reflected a romance between Moratín and Francisca Muñoz. In an article that appeared in another magazine in 1891, M. Ossorio y Bernard, who had seen the extracts but not the manuscript diary itself, wrote that Moratín had transferred Paquita from his heart to the stage, and he too identified the character with Francisca Muñoz. The fiction might have lain forgotten in the pages of the magazines had not Federico Ruiz Morcuende incorporated it into his introductory essay to the widely diffused Clásicos Castellanos edition of *La comedia nueva* and *El sí de las niñas* in 1924. From there it spread to the manuals of literature. The story is a fabrication, and as we have seen, Juan de Dios Mendoza has documented its falsity.

Moratín himself in his essays gave the lie to those critics who make art the literal depiction of life. A play results from mimesis: it imitates life; it does not copy it. "The poet observes nature and chooses from it only what suits his purpose. He arranges and embellishes his material; from many real parts he composes a whole that is completely fictitious, that is true to life but is not fact; fact is similar to the original but never identical. If a stenographer should copy down all the words spoken for a year in a family abounding in ridiculous characters, a comedy would not be the result of the copy. In dramaturgy, as in the other imitative arts, nature presents the originals; art selects, embellishes and combines them."[11]

Moratín's themes were very much in the air of his times. His friend, the artist Francisco Goya, saw them too in his peculiar way and put them on canvas or used them in his etchings. Whereas Moratín viewed the problem sentimentally in *El viejo y la niña*, Goya in his 1787 tapestry cartoon *La boda*, (*The Wedding*), paints a grotesque scene of an unwilling young girl and an ugly man in a wedding procession with the priest, the best man, and the musicians.[12] He employed the same grotesque treatment in etching 14 of his collection *Caprichos*, (*Caprices*). Commenting on the etching entitled "¡Qué sacrificio!" ("What a Sacrifice!"), Goya wrote: "The bridegroom is hard to look at, but he is rich. At the cost of the happiness of one poor child the security of a hungry family is bought. Such is the way of the world." Goya also takes another point of view and shows up the opportunism of some women in etching 2 of the same collection: *El sí pronuncian y la mano alargan al primero que llega* ("They Swear to Be Faithful, Yet Marry the First Man Who Proposes"). To which Goya adds the comment: "The indifference with which many women marry, hoping thereby to gain greater liberty."[13]

There is a bitterness in Goya that contrasts with the optimism of *El sí de las niñas*. Had Moratín seen the problems as Goya

did, he would have written "black comedy." He does not.
Besides his own youthful experience, besides the well publicized
example of the Count of Aranda, besides the cases that Goya
viewed dolorously, Moratín had observed a situation in his own
family. After he returned from Paris in 1788, he stayed at the
home of his Uncle Miguel. Melón writes that the uncle "had,
at an advanced age, married by proxy a young woman from
Segovia whom he had not seen. When [Leandro] told me the
scenes of his uncle's wedding, it was enough to make a person
die laughing."[14] Yet, while Moratín came close to ridicule in
El viejo y la niña—written before but produced after his uncle's
wedding—the dominant note is sentimentality. He avoids ridicule
completely in *El sí*, and he is distant from the bitter irony of
Goya. In this re-creation of reality, he concludes with the optimism of a brilliant morning and a brightly lighted stage.

III *The Première of* El sí

For the principal roles of his new play, Moratín did not
choose the leading actors of the company, but secondary ones
who better fitted the parts he had created. Josefa Virg, who had
been Doña Clara in *La mojigata,* was cast as Doña Francisca.
She pleased Moratín, made the role thoroughly her own, and
was still playing it on occasion years later. In her younger days
María Ribera had been a favorite actress of the Madrid public, but she herself had asked that she be assigned a less onerous
position in the company. Moratín had been pleased with her
interpretation of Aunt Mónica in *El barón,* and to the role of
Doña Irene she brought the experience of a quarter of a century
on the Madrid stage. It was her last big role, for she retired that
same year. In his correspondence with her husband Dionisio
Solís, Moratín called her Doña Irene.

For the part of Don Diego he chose a newcomer to the Madrid
scene, Andrés Prieto, an understudy in the company, who had
arrived from Barcelona the year before. His triumph in *El sí*
was the beginning of a fruitful career on the Madrid stage which
lasted for many years.

Rehearsals for *El sí* began early in January, and Moratín went
frequently—as he always did—to the Cruz Theater. He also went
to the actresses' houses in the mornings to rehearse them at

home. The first stage rehearsal took place on January 12, and on the 23rd and 24th Moratín attended the final morning rehearsals at the theater.

The first performance was announced for Friday, January 24, 1806, at 5:00 P.M. The play had been much talked about, and interest in it ran high. The King and Queen of Spain, in residence at San Lorenzo del Escorial thirty miles from Madrid, gave permission for all of the royal retinue who could be spared to go to the city. The Prince of the Peace himself, to whom the first printed edition of the play was dedicated, occupied the principal box together with his wife and as many ladies and gentlemen of the court as could comfortably be seated. His brother Brigadier Don Diego Godoy, Duke of Almodóvar, sat in an orchestra seat; and in a less conspicuous box was the favorite's mistress, the vivacious Andalusian Pepita Tudó. Aristocrats, government officials, foreign diplomats, actors, writers, and plain people had come to see the most talked of play of the decade. It was true that the three chandeliers with a total of only sixty oil lamps did not provide a brilliant spectacle in the cramped old Cruz Theater. But the première of *El sí de las niñas* marked a significant change in theatrical life in Madrid. Thenceforth, the theater became a social event which the bourgeoisie and the aristocracy shared with their adherents from the arts.

Influential as he had become in the theater, however, Moratín was powerless against the tradition which demanded adventitious entertainment. The performance concluded with a fandango and a *tonadilla*. But the success of the comedy itself was overwhelming. It played for twenty-six successive nights, and the run concluded only on the eve of Ash Wednesday when the theaters closed for Lent. In a period when an initial run of eight or ten performances was exceptional in Madrid, the success of *El sí* was the theatrical phenomenon of the decade.

The income was very gratifying to the actors. The first night produced 7,942 reales, and the box office reached a peak of 9,413 reales on the fourth day, which was close to the maximum that the seating capacity of the Cruz permitted at the current prices. Only once in the twenty-six days did the income fall below 6,000 reales. The competition was very painful to the drama company at the rival Caños del Peral Theater, which changed its bill ten times. On the first night of *El sí* their ticket sales amounted to only 1,662 reales; and, while they did better on succeeding nights, there was one black Monday on which they took in only 1,502 reales. Although the Caños could seat many more people than the Cruz, its total income for the twenty-six days that it competed with *El sí* was 130,000 reales compared with 194,000 at the Cruz. Income would not have reached even 100,000 had not the company prepared a really fabulous evening: a one-act play with an edifying moral entitled *Los aduladores* (*The Sycophants*); a *tonadilla* for three singers; and—the real attraction of the evening—a new *sainete* entitled *La fiesta de toros de Juan Tuerto* (*One-Eyed John's Bullfight Festival*), in which, the newspaper announcement said, "four bulls will be baited with the greatest naturalness." In February and just before Lent, Madrid aficionados could not resist such an opportunity, and the Caños box office took in more than 12,000 reales the first night and continued to garner rich rewards until the theaters closed. However, the spectacle obviously attracted a different type of public, for it had no effect on the income at the Cruz.[15]

IV   *The Attack and the Defense*

At least one member of the audience on January 24 was displeased with the play. He was a courtier named Antonio Nicolás de Solavide, whom Manuel Silvela called "the most insolent beast that the eighteenth century produced, and it produced some good ones!" On the following morning, from the Royal Seat of the Buen Retiro, he sent Moratín a gratuitously insulting note: "Yesterday I saw the performance of your play *El sí de las niñas*. My friend, it can be cited as a model of dullness, an exemplar of insubstantiality and a prototype of ineptitude. . . . I have been told that you paid a large and noisy mob to applaud it, which is as low a thing as the silliest fool would do. After two or three years you have turned out a first-class piece of nonsense. My friend, you are a real dolt."[16]

The articles which appeared in the press did not descend to the abysmal level of Solavide's letter, and since many writers for the journals were friends or admirers of Moratín there were defenders as well as denigrators. In one article which Moratín copied from a journal, the critic commented that the moral of the play was commonplace, that the scenes were long drawn out, that the denouement was obvious from the beginning. The writer

also drew attention to details which offended his sense of propriety with respect to religious matters, a subject that was later
to be thoroughly scrutinized by the censors of the Inquisition.[17]
Another critic had read and absorbed the *Lecciones sobre la retórica y las bellas letras* (*Lectures on Rhetoric and Belles Let-
tres*), translated and amplified in Spanish by José Luis Munárriz from the work by the Scottish Presbyterian clergyman Hugo
Blair. He applied its rigorous neoclassical principles to *El sí*
and found the play wanting. For example, conceiving the unity
of time literally, he observed that more time passes in *El sí*
than it takes to perform it; he would have it end at night instead
of the next morning, having failed to note the significance of the
bright light of the new day and the mood of hope and happiness
with which the play ends. But the writer liked the play for its
comicality, the superb motivation of each character, and especially the portrayal of chaste love.[18]

A lot of ink was spilled concerning Moratín's debt to *Le Traité
nul* and another one-act French play *Le Oui des couvents*. A
writer for the journal *Minerva* was among several who came to
the dramatist's defense simply by analyzing the characters of
the plays.[19] The principal result of the dispute was to provide
a good sale for the Spanish translation of the Marsollier play
which had just been published.

The published version of *El sí* was also enjoying an excellent
sale, and copies were shipped promptly to the provinces. In
May the professional company in Cadiz performed it to the same
enthusiastic applause that it had had in Madrid, and a writer
who signed himself D. J. M. de V. reported to the *Memorial
Literario* on its success.[20] He had heard of the accusations of
plagiarism which were being bruited about in Madrid by, in his
words, "small-minded critics in rompers," and he recalled the
lines of Alexander Pope from the *Essay on Criticism*:

> In search of wit these lose their common sense,
> And then turn critics in their own defence;
> . . . .
> All fools have still an itching to deride,
> And fain would be upon the laughing side.
>   (lines 28-29, 32-33)

Copies of *El sí* reached Zaragoza while it was still playing in
Madrid, and a group of aristocratic amateurs performed it even

before Lent began. Manuel de Inca Yupanqui, a descendant of
the Peruvian nobility and once a friend of Moratín's father, wrote
Leandro to tell him about the performance. The Marchioness of
Santa Coloma played the role of Doña Irene, the daughter of
the Baroness of Escriche that of Doña Francisca and the Baroness herself Rita. The Marquess of Aguilar took the part of Don
Carlos; Don José Toledano, an officer in the army accounting
office, played Simón; and the Marquess of Artasona was Calamocha. Don Manuel de Inca Yupanqui—fifty years old and with
snow-white hair—was Don Diego. The whole city was alive with
expectation, and the public, Don Manuel reported, was delighted
with the results. The actors had only five days for rehearsals.
If Moratín felt any qualms about this, he carefully hid his
thoughts and expressed to Don Manuel in his reply the great
satisfaction he enjoyed in knowing that his play had received
the plaudits of the Aragonese public. Moratín's letter was read
avidly by his fans in Zaragoza, who made copies of it to circulate
among their friends. A shipment of copies of *El sí*, Don Manuel
wrote in a second letter, was sold out in forty-eight hours, so
that those who had copies were obliged to lend them to others
who were anxious to read a play that they had enjoyed so much
on the stage.[21]

The most serious atack on Moratín came from a certain Bernardo García. García was acting for others, and the motivation
was political rather than literary, for it was directed against
Moratín as the literary protégé of the favorite Manuel Godoy.
It was also related to the recent defeat of the French and Spanish fleets by the British off Cape Trafalgar on October 21, 1805.
For Godoy, who was attempting to ward off the embrace of
Napoleon by cooperating with him, Trafalgar was a serious
political blow. His protégés in literature rallied to his side,
and several of them—Juan Bautista Arriaza, Manuel José Quintana, and Moratín—composed poems on the subject. Since the
English admiral Lord Nelson lost his life in the battle, the poets—
and the journalists, too, for that matter—seized upon this motif
with the result that Spanish readers, influenced by the fervency
of their expression, may well have believed that Spain was vic-
tor in the conflict.

Bernardo García prepared a long paper entitled "Carta crítica
de un vecino de Guadalajara sobre la comedia *El sí de las niñas*

por Inarco Celenio (Moratín) y las dos odas de Quintana y Arriaza sobre el combate naval de Cabo Trafalgar en 21 de octubre de 1805," "A Critical Letter by a Resident of Guadala-jara on the comedy *El sí de las niñas* by Inarco Celenio (Mora-tín) and the Two Odes by Quintana and Arriaza on the Naval Battle at Cape Trafalgar on October 21, 1805." Juan Antonio Melón wrote in his notes on Moratín's life that the attack did not come directly from García. Back of it were the two sons of the Count of Campo de Alange, the elder Don Manuel María Negrete y Adorno and his younger brother Monsignor Agustín María, prothonotary apostolic and archdeacon of Mora, who were in connivance with the sons of other nobles and were surreptitiously supported by the Marquess of Caballero, minister of Public Faith and Justice (Gracia y Justicia) in Godoy's own govern-ment, whose disloyalty became evident two years later when he refused to take action to quell the disturbances of March 19, 1808, disturbances that caused the fall of the Prince of the Peace.

Melón had just become chief of the newly created Office of Press Censorship (Juzgado de Imprentas), which, it was in-tended, would take over the duties of governmental press cen-sorship that had been exercised under the aegis of the Council of State. He was struggling to get the office organized at a time when the war commitments of the government drained off funds. Melón had no money, and he was obliged to ask his friends to read works for him. As a result, when Bernardo García turned his manuscript in to the Office of Press Censorship, which was headed by Moratín's friend Melón, the latter gave it to José Antonio Conde, also Moratín's good friend, for evaluation.

The resident of Guadalajara begins his letter by informing his correspondent that he had been suffering for eight months with tertian fever, so that the reader wonders whether the ill humor with which he reads *El sí* may not be caused by his sick-ness rather than by the defects he professes to observe in the play. García took his text from Horace's *Art of Poetry*:

> But if you dare to launch upon the state
> Originals that ne'er graced poet's page,
> Let them one tenor to the last pursue,
> Consist throughout and to themselves be true.

(Si quid inexpertum scenae committis et audes
Personam formare novam, servetur ad imum
Qualis ab incepto processerit et sibi constet.) [22]

He criticized *El sí* especially for a whole series of details which he considers lacking in consistency and hence in verisimilitude. For example, he cannot accept Don Diego's credulity in thinking that Doña Francisca could love a man of his age. He finds the language of Doña Irene ill bred and not believable in one who is supposed to be a lady. Furthermore, he takes Moratín to task for his use of unfinished speeches marked by suspension points.

When he turns to the moral issue, he takes an approach which was designed to attract adherents to his cause. The play is a satire, he says, directed against the convents of nuns which provide education for young women. Besides objecting to Don Diego's frontal attack on the education that Spanish women receive—the famous speech at the end of the play—García points to many barbed remarks that make jest of religious education. The writer of the letter professed to feel more keenly the injustice of these remarks because they were directed at a convent in his own town of Guadalajara where there was but one.

In his evaluation of García's manuscript, Conde began bluntly: "This paper is one of those abortions produced by the mania some people have for writing about things they do not understand; it is filled with ignorant remarks and trivial or malicious objections." He succinctly answered García's criticism point by point and concluded: "I have wasted more than enough time on this importunate and poorly conceived document, and I am of the opinion that its publication should not be allowed since it contains nothing useful, instructive or delightful."

Conde's position was a solid one in the light of the charge that governmental censorship had long been given in Spain. Furthermore, the censor, besides judging the qualities of usefulness, instruction or pleasure which printed matter was supposed to possess, was required to see that His Majesty's hot-tempered subjects did not indulge themselves in unseemly and harmful polemics.

To Conde's seven-page evaluation, García prepared a ninety-page rebuttal which he also hoped to print. He appealed his case to both the Prince of the Peace and the Marquess of Caballero.

To García's short petition Godoy answered that he had no objection to the publication. García's appeal to the Minister of Public Faith and Justice contained a confidential statement in which he accused Moratín, Quintana, Conde, Melón, and others of forming a clique which now controlled the press, permitting publication of books and papers by their friends and denying the privilege to all who opposed them.

As a result of these appeals, the García documents and the play *El sí de las niñas* were sent to the Inquisitor General, Ramón José de Arce y Reynoso, so that he might arbitrate the dispute. He entrusted the task to five censors, all ecclesiastics. They were unanimously of the opinion that the play contained no proposition or statement which was subject to theological censure or which sinned against religion or good manners. They found that publication of García's letter could serve two useful purposes: it would warn dramatists not to mingle religious matters in plays in such a way as to lead to equivocal interpretation, and it could foment advances in literature and good taste since this is the purpose of criticism. However, they concluded that the spirit of partisanship, the heated debate, and the animosity which the letter revealed made its publication imprudent, and the Inquisitor General advised against it. He also took the opportunity to counsel the King to issue a Royal Order forbidding the publication of plays or other works containing ill-considered remarks on ecclesiastical matters which could lead to malicious interpretations or to situations subversive of public order and the harmony between Altar and Throne. Eleven days later the government issued such a Royal Order. The Bernardo García affair ended there, and his "Carta crítica" remained in manuscript.[23]

V *The Inquisition Appraises* El sí, *1815-1819*

The Inquisition suffered an eclipse during the tumultuous years of the French occupation and the War of Independence.[24] Arce y Reynoso resigned as Inquisitor General on March 22, 1808, immediately after the fall of Godoy. His successor did not take possession until August of 1814. The French, propagators of eighteenth-century enlightenment, viewed the Holy Office with unconcealed aversion. The Spanish liberals who created the Constitution of Cadiz attacked it ferociously, but they did not formally suppress it; they simply declared that it was incompatible with the Constitution.

When Fernando VII returned to Spain in 1814, he decreed that the Holy Office should resume its former powers.[25] Salvaging its property and records, the Inquisition went back into business at once, turning its attention particularly to the many questionable "propositions" that had been uttered or printed during the French occupation. The Consejo de la Suprema called upon all the tribunals in Spain to notify it of objectionable books and papers published within their jurisdiction. A year later, on July 22, 1815, it issued an edict listing 183 publications which it ordered withdrawn from circulation until they could be examined. The list included *El sí de las niñas*. On August 3 three members of the Suprema and the Inquisitor General ordered the tribunals to examine all publications listed in the edict of July 22 and printed in their jurisdiction. The order singled out *El sí* and two other plays for immediate attention.[26]

A month later the Madrid tribunal sent *El sí de las niñas* to one of its censors, Fray José García y Carrillo, instructing him to follow the usual practice of conferring with another person who merited his confidence. García y Carrillo, active in inquisitorial censorship at this time, was still at work a decade later as ecclesiastical censor, plaguing a new generation of dramatists who thoroughly detested him. Antonio Gil y Zárate, one of his victims, described him: "A priest of excessive obesity, dull witted, filthy, dirty, all dusty with snuff, whose greatest pleasure consisted in attending criminals in the death house and accompanying them to the scaffold. . . . Because of some caprice or scruple he struck out the word 'poor' every place he found it in one of Bretón's comedies. He gave no quarter to the expressions 'my angel' or 'I adore you,' because, in his opinion, they were only permissible when dealing with celestial things. . . ." In one play he deleted "I hate victory" because he thought it reflected on his own Convento de la Victoria. He forbade Gil's play on King Rodrigo, explaining: "Although it is true that kings have often been fond of girls, it is not proper to show them so much in love in the theater."[27]

Carrillo's censorship of *El sí de las niñas* was characterized by the same pettiness Gil y Zárate recorded. He would not prohibit a work entirely if he could tidy it up to satisfy his scruples. He read the play several times, and he concluded that it could safely be published and performed if certain corrections and suppressions were made.

However, Carrillo refused to brook Moratín's criticism that young girls were taught, at home and in convent schools, to hide their true feelings, and were educated in hypocrisy. He took pains to show that one might be bad regardless of his education. Adam and Eve reared their sons well; yet one was good and the other evil. Christ taught the Apostles excellently; yet one denied Him and another sold Him. Doña Francisca's peccadillos were hardly in the same class with the sins of Cain or Judas, but logic was not Father Carrillo's strong point.

He was willing to believe, however, that in some cases parents reared their children poorly. He gave special attention to Don Diego's forceful expression of the theme in the speech beginning, "Here you see the fruits of education." (Act III, Scene viii) He changed the sentence to read "bad education" and revised the rest of the speech so that it could not be construed as a criticism of formal instruction in Church schools, but only of the abuse of parental authority.

Carrillo was at his eagle-eyed best when expunging objectionable trifles, and was particularly hostile to the mingling of the sacred and the profane. The details he censored were realities of Spanish life that Moratín must have taken from his own experiences. Alcalá de Henares, for example, was an overnight stop for him on his frequent trips to his country house in Pastrana. Don Diego's servant Simón describes the dirty, noisy room at the inn with its engravings of the Prodigal Son, and complains of his boredom after two days spent there. (I, i) Carrillo censored the phrase "the engravings of the Prodigal Son" not only because it mingled the sacred and the profane, but also because a person should not be bored by so edifying an example.

In the scene in which Doña Francisca shows Don Diego some farewell presents from the nuns (I, ii), Carrillo cut out the mother-of-pearl rosaries, the cypress crosses, St. Benedict's rule, and the words "blessed against thunder" which describe a clay bell. He substituted "a figurine" for the sugarpaste St. Gertrude whose head the maid breaks. He justified his excisions because the mother dismisses these objects as "trinkets."

Doña Irene's speeches often wounded the censor's sensibilities.

When she tells Don Diego about Francisca's great-great-uncle, the bishop-elect of Michoacán, Carrillo cut everything from "Why, he died in the odor of sanctity" to "At the age of eighty-two years, three months and fourteen days." (I, iii) The censored portion describes the biography of the saintly man. The nine folio volumes already completed cover the first nine years of his life, and the plan is to have a volume for each year. Carrillo was appalled at such buffoonery at the expense of the clergy.

In fact, Carrillo found that Doña Irene scarcely opens her mouth without mingling the sacred and the profane. She complains that her pet thrush kept her awake: "Why, if it didn't spend the whole blessed night reciting the Gloria Patri and the prayer of the Holy Shroud! Of course, that was edifying, to be sure; but when a person is trying to sleep . . ." (II, iii) Learning that her daughter met Don Carlos while in the convent school, Doña Irene exclaims: "So the daughter of my womb, locked in a convent, fasting every blessed Friday, in the company of those saintly nuns! . . ." (III, xi) In these words Carrillo detected satire on the fasting of the regular clergy.

Doña Irene is even guilty of expressing a "proposition." Assuming that Francisca objects to marriage with Don Diego because she wants to be a nun, Doña Irene tells her daughter that the first duty of an obedient child is to console her mother in her tribulations. (II, iv) This scandalous "proposition" offends pious ears, Carrillo said, because the first obligation of man is to serve God. He cut this and another sentence on the same theme: "I've already told her it's time for her to turn over a new leaf and just think about pleasing her mother and obeying her." (II, v)

Alert to words that might shock the devout, Carrillo cut out Calamocha's "Damn," suggesting "Curse" as an acceptable substitute. (II, x) Especially sensitive to anything lascivious, he saw what he expected to see in the love scene between Doña Francisca and Don Carlos. The maid, having arranged for the lovers to meet, admonishes her mistress just before leaving: "Get down to business . . . and be careful. . . ." (II, vi) In these words Carrillo saw an equivocal and offensive meaning. He detected lewd intent in the lovers' simple conversation. When Doña Francisca asks her suitor what he plans to do (meaning about his rival), the ardent young officer replies: "If I should give way to my passion and the feeling your eyes inspire in me, something reckless. . . . But there's time . . ." (II, vii) Carrillo deleted this and even a simple "Vamos," by which Don Carlos meant nothing more than "Well."

Having mutilated the play to his satisfaction, and having purged it of much sparkle and wit, Carrillo, together with a fellow priest in the Order of Minims, signed the report and sent it to the Madrid tribunal on November 14, 1815. The attorney in the Cámara del Secreto, Dr. Zorrilla de Velasco, kept the dossier until February 17, 1816, when he wrote his opinion that the play should either be expurgated as recommended, or, in view of how much there was to be cut, be prohibited. The tribunal decreed on February 19 that *El sí* should be prohibited.

On March 8, 1816, the dossier came before the Consejo de la Suprema, for that body jealously controlled all censorship. The eight inquisitors of the Suprema, dissatisfied with Carrillo's censoring, returned the dossier with the order that the Madrid tribunal reevaluate it, "employing for that purpose persons who, besides the necessary judgment, also possess some knowledge of plays. . . ." At this point the dossier on *El sí de las niñas,* lost in the files of the Madrid tribunal's Cámara del Secreto, was forgotten for twenty-two months.

While Moratín's play was being censored in Madrid, the Barcelona tribunal was also scrutinizing it. Don Antonio Alegret, a beneficiary of the Cathedral and author of several books on Catalan language and history, denounced it, and on September 15, 1815, the tribunal sent it to the Discalced Carmelite Manuel de los Dolores for censoring. Fray Manuel and his associate, Fray Magín de San Antonio, examined the play and held that, "although in it there are several rather outspoken expressions as far as decency is concerned," it contained nothing contrary to the Catholic religion and could be permitted. The Barcelona tribunal finally sent the dossier to the Consejo de la Suprema on July 18, 1817. The Suprema took it under consideration on August 25, recalled the other dossier, and ordered the two joined.

They sent the papers first to Father Agustín García Porrero, who excused himself, and then to Father José Tolrá, a Jesuit, who took as his associate another Jesuit, Father Francisco Xavier Bouzas.

In their report they coincided with Carrillo on some points, they overlooked others which he had stressed, and they found objections of their own. They too frowned upon Simón's bore-

dom with the prints of the Prodigal Son, Doña Francisca's assort-
ment of trinkets, the prayers of Doña Irene's thrush, and Don
Diego's condemnation of the upbringing of girls. The bishop-
elect of Michoacán could even become proverbial, they feared.
They passed over Calamocha's "Damn," Doña Irene's "proposition" on the duty of an obedient daughter, her phrase "fasting
every blessed Friday," and the love scene between Doña Francisca and Don Carlos.

They discovered new points, however, which had escaped
Carrillo. They found most offensive Doña Francisca's comment
after Doña Irene says that the nuns had a cool locutory despite
the hot weather: "Well, even so, that fat nun named Mother
Angustias used to sweat a lot. Oh, how the poor woman did
sweat!" (I, iii) They also deemed indecorous the nuns' names:
Angustias, Trinidad, Circuncisión, and Candelaria. (III, xi)
Returning late to the inn, Don Diego explains: "I had scarcely
set foot out the door when I ran into the rector from Málaga
and Doctor Padilla, and they wouldn't let me go until they had
stuffed me with chocolate and buns." (II, v) Such humor, they
declared, was at the expense of religious persons who were not
accustomed to stuff either themselves or others with chocolate
and buns.

Although these censors saw nothing out of the way in the
love scene between Doña Francisca and Don Carlos, they did
object to the talk between Doña Francisca and her maid about
the novels they secretly read, and the nocturnal visits of Don
Carlos to the convent walls. (I, ix) This conversation suggested
disorderly conduct in convent schools. They also saw an equivocal
meaning in Doña Irene's hysterical speech to her daughter when
Don Diego suggests that Francisca may be in love with someone
else: "Tell him the sweethearts ... you acquired in the convent
at the side of that saintly woman." (II, v) Doña Irene was speaking ironically, but since Francisca did have one sweetheart, the
Jesuits feared that someone might suppose that she had had
many lovers with the assent of her aunt, the nun.

Tolrá and Bouzas concluded that the comedy ridiculed ecclesiastical persons and religious practices and discredited the upbringing of girls in convents. Their decision, *salvo meliori*, was
that both its publication and performance would be prejudicial.
They sent their appraisal to the Madrid tribunal on January 30,
1818, and at the end of March, the dossier again came before

the Suprema. This body ordered the tribunal to find Moratín so that he might make his defense, but he could not be located because he had taken the precaution of going to France some time before. Accordingly, Dr. Zorrilla advised the inquisitors to appoint defense counsel to represent the author. They chose Father Rafael Muñoz, himself a censor for the Holy Office.

Muñoz was versed in the literary theories of his day and was pleased to show his erudition. He built his defense around the tenet that an author must both please and instruct his audience. He cited examples from the ancients—Homer and Vergil, and the Moderns—Tasso, Camões, and Milton. He reasoned that Moratín simply followed the practice of these writers, and that since all were famous, the former ancient, and the latter Catholic (yes, Milton, too), they could not be suspect.

Assuming that Moratín's purpose was to criticize the abuse of parental authority, Muñoz made light of the criticism of religious education which Carrillo had tried to cover up in his revisions. To carry out his aim, Muñoz said, the author created the character of Doña Irene, a foolish and fanatical mother pre-occupied with her financial well-being, whose words should be understood in that sense. Her character forced Doña Francisca to dissimulate and even to imitate her mother's way of speaking. Don Diego, too, recognized Doña Irene's stupidity and, accommodating himself to it, made foolish remarks to her. His speech on the fruits of a bad upbringing was directed not at religious education but at parents like Doña Irene, who could learn a lot from this play.

Muñoz vitiated the effect of his arguments by an accompanying letter, saying he had written the defense only because it was required of him. His true opinion was that *El sí de las niñas* was highly prejudicial and should be forbidden. Unwittingly, he paid Moratín a compliment: "This comedy is all the more harmful because the language and the witticisms in which it abounds are taken from the purest elements of the Castilian tongue and are accompanied by a charming naturalness in the characters who speak."

The Madrid tribunal sent Muñoz' defense to Fathers Tolrá and Bouzas for their rebuttal. They replied that it was not at all satisfactory. They did not dispute the elementary axiom that the object of a work of literature is to instruct and please, but they sneered at Muñoz' ostentatious display of commonplace knowledge. To their own satisfaction they demolished his points, accusing him of irrelevance, incoherence, evasion, arbitrary interpretation, and lack of logic and common sense.

The defense having been made and rebutted, the Consejo de la Suprema, on November 9, 1819, forbade *El sí de las niñas,* "because it is lacking in the respect which holy things pertaining to religious worship deserve and with which they should be treated; because it is unbecoming and offensive to the ecclesiastical estate; and because it is insulting to the Christian and pious education of girls in the convents of nuns."

VI *The History of* El sí

The greatest triumph of his career turned to ashes for Moratín. The virulent attacks of men like Solavide and Bernardo García, the suspicious eye of the Inquisition—these were more than a man of his timid character could bear. The debacle of 1808, and the collapse of the society which he knew, confirmed him in the determination not to write again for the theater. In later years his young friend Manuel Silvela teased him about his scant collection of five original comedies in a country that had produced the fecund genius of Lope de Vega and Calderón. When Silvela cited Moratín's contemporaries—Comella with eighty plays to his credit and Valladares with 113—the provocation was too much for the dramatist and he angrily answered: "If I had not been subjected to such terrible harassment, the Spanish theater would have had at least five or six more comedies of mine."[28] This was the number of uncompleted plays which he destroyed after the attacks on *El sí.*

The play itself has preserved the lustre of his name through generations of changing tastes. The Inquisition's fulmination against it did not long endure. Rafael de Riego's revolt against the despotic government of Fernando VII began near Cadiz on January 1, 1820, and spread slowly over the country. On March 9, under duress, Fernando issued a decree abolishing the Holy Office; and, after his return to absolute government in 1823, he did not choose to revive it. *El sí de las niñas* reappeared in Spanish theaters. Moratín, under the protection of the revived Constitution, came back to Barcelona in October, 1820. He wrote to his friend Melón: "Verses have been written here on my arrival and have passed from hand to hand in printed form. *El sí* was performed, and the large audience clapped and shouted and called for the author. The author was in a seat in the orchestra and would have given a lot to have been a spaniel dog on that occasion. In short, he crouched down as best he could; Andrés Prieto came out to thank the audience, and the storm was calmed."[29]

In November of 1820 *El sí de las Niñas* was performed at the Cruz Theater in Madrid. The following year a writer in *El Censor* called it "one of the few perfect dramas that exist in our language." In 1823 the French—from whom Moratín's enemies had accused him of stealing the idea—appropriated the play and converted it into a one-act musical. It required three writers to commit this villainy, as Moratín called it, and he was no little piqued that his Don Diego and Doña Irene should be singing witty and epigrammatic couplets filled with *esprit* in a Paris vaudeville.[30]

With the restoration of Fernando's absolutist power, however, the Inquisition's denunciation of the play was not forgotten. In 1825, Josefa Virg, who had played the role of Doña Francisca in 1806, was invited to perform at Aranjuez. She had to request permission from Fernando VII to put on *El sí*. She repeated the performance at the Escorial in 1826. Emboldened, she sought royal permission in 1827 to give the comedy in Madrid. Her request was denied.[31]

The publication of Moratín's works in 1830-1831 by the Academy of History gave them new currency, and *El sí* was performed at the Royal Conservatory in Madrid before Fernando VII and his fourth wife the Neapolitan María Cristina, who took great pleasure in the arts. However, in 1832, when a group of socially prominent ladies in Granada decided to act it in a benefit performance for an orphanage which they sponsored, they discovered that the prohibition apparently still applied. They appealed to the Capain General of Granada and he to Madrid, and the Queen, who was by now running the government for her failing husband, gave permission for the performance of a play which had so recently been given in her august presence.[32]

The next year the actors in Madrid sought permission to present *El sí* in a charity performance for one of their own religious organizations, the Committee of the Chapel of the Congregation of Our Lady of Almudena; and the request was granted provided the text of the Academy of History, which had been corrected was used.[33] It was only a step to performance again in the public theater, and with the liberalization that followed the death of Fernando, *El sí* again played at the Cruz in February, March, October, and December of 1834, and it was performed during the rest of the 1830's, in the hey-day of Romanticism, each year except 1836.

Mariano José de Larra, who was born two years after the 1806 première of *El sí,* saw the play in 1834 and published a review of it in *La Revista Española.* With the self-satisfaction characteristic of a man who belonged completely to the nineteenth century, he no longer saw value in the play as a corrective of old abuses. To him *El sí* belonged to a bygone period. Unlike Molière's *L'Avare* or *Tartuffe,* it presented no character as the enduring mirror of a vice or passion. Yet Larra recognized the technical excellence of the play. "The plot," he wrote, "is perfectly conceived." He also made a basic observation about the theater of Moratín: "Moratín was the first comic poet to give a tearful and sentimental tone to a genre in which his predecessors had only presented the ridiculous. . . . This is the basic difference that exists between him and Molière. The latter always speaks to the mind and he convinces us by presenting the laughable side of things. Moratín presents certain characters which satisfy the crowd's desire to laugh; but he also gives prominence to the roles of his lovers for the sake of the more sensitive spectators. On the one hand, he convinces the mind by depicting a ridiculous situation; on the other, he moves the heart. . . ."[34]

In 1848, twenty years after Moratín's death, the Madrid theaters paid homage to him by presenting his plays in March around the date of his birthday. The Príncipe put on both *La comedia nueva* and *El barón;* and a new theater, the Instituto, staged *La mojigata.* At the old Cruz, where it had had its first performances, *El sí* was played. For the occasion Ventura de la Vega composed a one-act play in imitation of Molière's *La critique de l'Ecole des femmes* (*Critique of the School for Wives*). He called it, of course, *La crítica de El sí de las niñas* (*Critique of When a Girl Says Yes*).[35]

The setting for Vega's play is the vestibule of the Cruz Theater during the intermission of the very performance of *El sí* which the audience is seeing. Among the spectators is a young woman named Paquita, whose foolish father Don Benigno wants her to marry the elderly Don Diego. Paquita, who has a boy-friend named Don Carlos, bears little resemblance to Moratín's Paquita of *El sí*. She is a wild young thing of the year 1848. She promenades in the Prado every afternoon; she goes dancing every Sunday; she takes part in amateur theatricals, and is a member of the Lyceum, the Museum, and the Institute—activities which Don Benigno considers natural for her age, sixteen years. As for the proposed marriage to Don Diego, she tells her father, "I need him like I need a dog at mass."

Don Benigno is satisfied with his handiwork as a father. He brought up Paquita—as Don Martín did Doña Clara in *La mojigata*—with complete freedom. No one ever said her nay; she has done as she jolly well pleased. There is nothing priggish about her, he is pleased to say, and she speaks whatever comes into her head. In time, he assures Don Diego, she will settle down.

The Don Carlos of 1848 is also a different man from the loyal sweetheart, the obedient nephew, and the dashing artillery officer of 1806. He is the idle *señorito* about town, and he is juggling three affairs: besides Paquita he is involved with the merry widow Casilda and a Marchioness who in her turn is carrying on with a Viscount. Carlos is not concerned with Paquita's proposed marriage to Don Diego; he thinks there will be time and opportunity for him afterward. Besides, he is keeping in reserve an actress at the Príncipe and another at the Instituto.

Also in the vestibule at intermission are the 1848 reincarnations of characters from Moratín's own *La comedia nueva*: pedantic Don Hermógenes, deluded Don Eleuterio, stagestruck Don Serapio, splenetic Don Pedro, and rational Don Antonio. Don Hermógenes and Don Serapio are convulsed with laughter because someone in the audience shouted for the author twenty years after his death. A naive young artisan named Serafín approaches them: "Come, gentlemen, such scoffing! I'm the one who asked for the author. So what? Some friends over there have already told me he is dead. I didn't know it because I am a working man and I don't keep up on such things. I don't go to the theater much. I thought the comedy was new, I came to see it, and I asked for the author because I like the play. That's all there is to it." Serafín's words are a clear note of sanity in a wave of supercilious remarks.

Don Hermógenes, although he now uses more French than Greek in his discourse, pronounces the comedy "homopathetic— a drop of action dissolved in three quarts of water," an observation which Don Serapio delightedly applauds with a "Bravísimo." When Don Hermógenes calls the theater enterprise stupid because it describes *El sí de las niñas* as "a jewel of the modern drama," Don Pedro intervenes to tell the pedant to count him among the stupid as well as two generations of playgoers who have also considered *El sí* a jewel.

Don Eleuterio is bored with the tired old works of yesteryear. He wants something up-to-date—his own play, for instance, which the theater enterprise has kept for three months without answering him. But if *El sí* must be staged, he would at least like to revise it. He would show Paquita at the convent; he would have the sinister figure of a nun, Mother Circuncisión, for example, who would discover the girl talking to Don Carlos at the wall, would fall in love with him herself, and would lock the girl up in the convent dungeon. Don Carlos would scale the convent walls, the nun would take him to her cell; but he would make his way to the dungeon aided by Calamocha; he would free his beloved, and there would be a beautiful scene in *quintillas*. Then Don Eleuterio would put in a dream sequence in which Doña Irene would see the ghost of the bishop-elect of Michoacán and the shades of her three husbands.

In his new incarnation Don Eleuterio is a drama critic. During intermission he is writing his article for the next day: "The performance of *El sí de las niñas* was wretched, worthy of the play itself. The Cruz Theater is leading a languid existence. . . ." When he is informed that the management is about to give serious consideration to his own drama, he changes the text on the spot: "The performance of *El sí de las niñas* was admirable, worthy of the play itself. While the Príncipe and the Instituto lead a languid existence, the Cruz is improving every day. . . ."

Don Hermógenes and Don Serapio call upon the women to confirm their dim view of the comedy. The merry widow Casilda finds it detestable; it made her so nervous that she has completely ruined her fan, a criticism of *El sí* from which Don Serapio thinks there is no appeal. The Marchioness is offended by the language of the characters: The wife of the Intendant is referred to as the "missus." She thinks Doña Irene vulgar to keep a lowly thrush as a pet. And the very mention of the menu at the inn—watercress salad, meat balls and roast kid—has given her indigestion. Paquita, an amateur actress herself, thinks *El sí* is a dull bore. She laments that the timid, retiring heroine should have the same name as herself. "And the scene between the two lovers! Have you ever seen anything so stupid?" she asks. "They are madly in love and they don't kiss or embrace! And they are alone!"

From his position as an observer, Don Pedro points out to Don Antonio that these are the critics of *El sí*: a pair of coquettes, a spoiled young girl, a venal critic, a stage-struck fool, and the pedant who is always with us. "Where is the Moratín of our age?" he asks. "Moratín exposed the parental tyranny and the priggish convent education of his day. Where is the dramatist who will paint for us the other side of the coin—the weakening of our social fabric—with the magic brush that no one since has wielded so well as that great poet?"

CHAPTER 7

The Foothills Of Parnassus

"HOW difficult it is," Moratín wrote, "to acquire two crowns in Parnassus." His was chiefly the realm of Thalia, but he was a man of letters in the broad sense, and he contributed to Spanish culture in a variety of fields. He would have liked to be a better poet than he was. He wrote much verse; yet the only poem that has had enduring appeal is the polished version he made of his father's "Fiesta de toros en Madrid"("Bullfight in Madrid").[1] Among his important minor contributions are his translations, an edition of a 1611 description of an *auto de fe,* and his history and catalogue of the Spanish drama.

From 1797, when he returned from Italy, until 1811 when José Bonaparte appointed him royal librarian, Moratín held the post of chief of the Secretariat for the Interpretation of Languages with the honor of being secretary to His Majesty the King. The Secretariat served the public in providing, for a fee, certified translations of any documents which a citizen required for religious, business, or legal purposes. It was a small office with only two translators and two clerks besides Moratín, for it did not do translations for the government ministries. Moratín knew Latin, French, Italian, and English, and the translators handled these and other languages while outsiders were asked to do occasional translations from or to exotic languages. The post provided Moratín with a sinecure that paid him twenty-eight thousand reales a year, and, if we are to judge from his diary, once he got the office organized, he did not spend a great amount of time there.

There was nothing literary about the translations that were done at the Secretariat, but accuracy was important, and the subjects were as boundless as the private commercial and legal relations of the day. What influence his post may have had on his literary work is difficult to judge. His artistic translations, like his own creative work, are few but choice.[2]

I *Shakespeare's* Hamlet

The Terror in Paris that drove Moratín to seek refuge in England in 1792 gave Spain her first Shakespearean scholar. The English dramatist was known to Spaniards through the prejudiced
writings of Voltaire, who saw in him a barbaric genius, and the
adaptations into French of Jean François Ducis, who recast
the plays into the neoclassic mold. Using the Ducis text, Ramón
de la Cruz wrote a Spanish version of *Hamlet* which was performed in 1772 by some of Madrid's best actors, but the play
did not enter into the Madrid repertoire and was forgotten.

While Moratín saw other Shakespearean plays in London,
he missed seeing *Hamlet*. Furthermore, he was bound to possess
the same misgivings that Voltaire felt toward Spakespeare. It
is to his credit that he rose above his prejudices. He began the
prologue to his translation by stating: "The present tragedy is
one of the best of William Shakespeare and the one that is most
frequently performed and applauded in the theaters of England."
Yet, like Voltaire, he could not quite bring himself to forgive
Shakespeare everything; on the back of the title page he adapted
a maxim from Martial: "Had he not erred, he would have
achieved less."[3]

Moratín's own accomplishment is remarkable, for his knowledge of English when he arrived in London was defective.
Wisely eschewing verse, and preferring to make a reading version rather than a stage adaptation, he chose to make an exact
rendition into prose. The result was the best translation of *Hamlet* into a Romance language that anyone had made up to that
time.

The English-speaking reader who knows Spanish will find that
this translation often illuminates the English text, for Moratín's
Spanish is, naturally, more modern than Shakespeare's English.
Occasionally, he makes an outright mistake. For example, he
translates Francisco's words "I am sick at heart" in the first scene
as *Yo estoy delicado del pecho.*[4] Such instances are, however,
rare. He achieved clarity by resort to circumlocution; a modern
English text would normally require a footnote to explain what
comes through clearly in the Spanish translation. But the English
reader is bound to be disappointed by Moratín's rendition of
those phrases which have entered into the web of our language.
"Something is rotten in the state of Denmark" becomes *Algún*

grave mal se oculta en Dinamarca. "Brevity is the soul of wit" is rendered as *La brevedad es el alma del talento.*

Once Moratín censors Shakespeare; he omits one of Hamlet's rude remarks to Ophelia, but he gives the English in a note. However, he does not censor him because he disagrees with him on the basis of artistic principles. He reserves this disagreement for the notes. To Francisco's words in the first scene, "Not a mouse stirring," Moratín makes this comment in a note: "A perfectly natural expression for a soldier and completely alien to the sublime quality of tragedy. Mr. Home, in his *Essay on Crticism,* dares to prefer it to the expression of Racine in the first act of *Iphigénie:* 'Mais tout dort, et l'armée, et les vents, et Neptune.' ('Everything sleeps: the army, the winds, and Neptune.') It requires either great ignorance or great partiality to reach that conclusion."

As an introduction to the play, Moratín wrote a brief biography of Shakespeare, the first of its kind in Spanish. He used the secondary materials provided by English scholarship of the day, and some of them proved to be more fiction than fact. Still, the Spanish reader could gain from it some notion of the Elizabethan theater which paralleled the glorious years of the Spanish stage in the time of Lope de Vega.

Moratín had completed his work by August of 1794 when he wrote to Melón from Bologna: "You should see the English tragedy entitled *Hamlet* that I have translated from beginning to end!"[5] He published it in 1798 after he returned to Spain. It produced one sharp reaction, a pamphlet entitled *Examen de la tragedia intitulada "Hamlet"* (*An Examination of the Tragedy entitled "Hamlet"*). The author hid behind his initials, but he was known to be Don Cristóbal Cladera.[6] He was suspected of being the Don Fulgencio de Soto who had written a pompous attack on *El Viejo y la niña;* and people pointed to him as the model for the pedantic Don Hermógenes of *La comedia nueva.* Cladera fancied he knew more about Shakespeare and the English language than did Moratín. Indeed he did catch some of Moratín's errors, one of them quite amusing. At the end of the first act, Hamlet cautions his friends, "And still your fingers on your lips." Moratín translated, *Poned el dedo en la boca,* which would mean "Put your finger in your mouth." Cladera gleefully asked "What for? To suck it? To bite it? No, Mr. Translator, the original does not say that; what it says is to be quiet, to keep silent. . . ."

The tone of Cladera's attack obscured some of the sounder criticisms that he had to make. This was unfortunate for Shakespearean studies in Spain, for a calm assessment would have been useful. Moratín's translation has remained in Spain the basic version on which all subsequent texts and adaptations have been based.[7]

II A Comedy from Molière

Although Moratín did not produce or publish an original comedy after *El sí de las niñas*, he made two translations from Molière. One was *L'Ecole des maris* (*The School for Husbands*), which was among the many antecedents of his own *La mojigata*. Performed for the first time at the Palais Royal in Paris on June 24, 1661, following the failure earlier in the year of a play from which Molière expected much, *L'Ecole des maris* was the French dramatist's first firm step into the realm of high comedy. It had thirty-eight successive performances and was played 333 times in the reign of Louis XIV.

The theme had a long tradition in the theater: what attitude ought a man to adopt toward his wife? Should he be suspicious and hence keep a tight rein on her actions, or should he be trusting and let her be a perfectly free agent? Molière may have found his basic intrigue partly in a Spanish play by Antonio Hurtado de Mendoza (1586-1644), *El marido hace mujer y el trato muda costumbre* (*A Man Molds His Wife, or Handling Can Change Habit*); but other plays made their contribution too, notably Terence's *Adelphi* and Dorimond's *La Femme industrieuse* (*The Hard-Working Wife*), in its turn influenced by Lope de Vega's *La discreta enamorada* (*The Clever Woman in Love*). In Hurtado de Mendoza's play, the two brothers have just become the husbands of the two women; in Molière's comedy, the brothers are the guardians of the two orphaned girls. The severe, suspicious brother fully intends to marry his ward; the mild, trusting brother expects to let his young woman choose her husband.

In the preface to the Madrid edition of his adaptation, the title of which he translated literally as *La escuela de los maridos*, Moratín expresses his admiration for Molière and his debt

La escuela de los maridos
Príncipe Theater, Madrid, March 17, 1812

Don Gregorio de Velasco	Eugenio Cristiani
Don Manuel, his elder brother	Joaquín Caprara
Doña Rosa, Don Gregorio's ward	Josefa Virg
Doña Leonor, Rosa's sister and	
Don Manuel's ward	María García
Juliana, Leonor's maid	Gertrudis Torre
Don Enrique de Cárdenas, Rosa's	
sweetheart	Isidoro Máiquez
Cosme, his servant	Joaquín Suárez
A Commissioner	Bernardo Avecilla
Don Simplicio, scrivener	Tomás Contador
A servant of the Commissioner	
Pepe, servant of Leonor's	
friend Doña Beatriz	

to him. As an inscription for the back of the title page, he took a verse from the historical poem the *Thebaid*: *Sed longe sequere, et vestigia semper adora* ("But follow him at a distance, and always honor his footsteps"). He confessed that when pedants gave him lessons in writing, when critics harassed him, he would say nothing but "would open a volume of Molière and would renew his faith in the soundest principles of dramatic art."[8]

Moratín admired what Molière did for the comic art in France. On the French stage he found a kind of comedy that imitated Italian and Spanish models, which were composed of an unbelievable tangle of circumstances, incidents, and characters: dark rooms, hidden rooms, houses without doors and doors without locks, disguises, mistaken names and mistaken identities, lost children, kidnappings, foolish old men, dissolute young women, frantic knife-wielding gallants, go-between servant girls, and scurrilous lackeys. Molière rejected all this to fix his gaze on the characters and passions of human beings, and out of his superb mimesis was born his comic strength. His enemies might rage against his comedies, but, as Boileau said of Corneille when the Academy censored *Le Cid*: *Le public revolté s'obstine à l'admirer* ("The public, in disagreement, insists on admiring him"). (Satire IX, 1. 234)

In presenting his translation of *La escuela de los maridos*, Moratín wrote, he wished to express his own admiration and to give his thanks to Molière. "The translator of this comedy owes to this great master the indulgence which the Spanish public has accorded to his own plays. Far from failing to recognize the lessons which he received from reading Molière's works, he attributes to his constant study of them such success as he has achieved in writing his own."

Whereas Moratín had aimed at exactness in his translation of *Hamlet,* he was so much at home in French and with Molière that he sought the spirit of the author and the play rather than faithfulness to the text. Speaking of himself in the third person he said, "He has translated Molière with the freedom which he believed proper in order truly to translate him and not abuse him. He is pleased to reflect in advance on the astonishment of the faultfinders when they see how inexact he has been in rendering the original French into Castilian, when they find whole pages on which there is scarcely a word that can be said to have been translated literally." To show what an exact version from the French might be like, he translated in the introduction a long speech from the first act in the manner which he says is typical of the translations that have been published in Spain. The effect, when compared with his own rendition of the same speech, is absurd.

Moratín took the further liberty of abandoning the verse of Molière's rhymed alexandrines, and adapted the play into prose. What he may have lost in poetic diction he gained in sparkle and wit that equals or transcends the original. For example, Sganarelle looks at his brother and Leonor and sneers: *Oh! que les voilà bien tous formés l'un pour l'autre.* Moratín puts these words into Don Gregorio's mouth: *Dios los cría y ellos se juntan. ¡Qué familia!* ("God creates them and they discover each other. What a family!")

In preparing his version of *La escuela de los maridos,* Moratín had in mind, of course, its performance on the stage in Madrid, and hence he made not an exact translation, but an adaptation. He began by changing the setting. The scene is no longer a street in Paris; it is in the Plazuela de los Afligidos on the outskirts of Madrid. He chose this out-of-the-way square, named for the convent of Our Lady of the Afflicted, in order to make it credible that the action could take place in the street without passersby mingling with the principal actors.

He changed the characters into Spaniards with Spanish names:

L'Ecole des maris	*La escuela de los maridos*
Sganarelle	Don Gregorio
Ariste	Don Manuel
Isabelle	Doña Rosa
Léonor	Doña Leonor
Lisette	Juliana
Valère	Don Enrique
Ergaste	Cosme

He omitted the digressions in the original that dealt with the fashions in France in 1661. He motivated the entrances and exits of the characters—an area in which Molière was notably weak. To Isabelle's web of fiction he added circumstantial details which made her tale believable and mitigated the stupid credulity of Sganarelle. He suppressed words and phrases which were permitted on Molière's stage, but which were indecorous in Spain in 1812. He also changed the brazen character of Isabelle who abandoned her guardian's house and went straight to that of her sweetheart, whom she only knew by sight, to throw herself into his arms that he might do with her what he would. Nor does Moratín accept the incredible turn of events that leads to the denouement. In the French, the gallant at his window, and the brothers, the commissioner and the scrivener in the street, arrange the marriage by the light of a lantern without finding out who it is that is getting married. Moratín changed all that so that the marriage arrangements take place off stage and are properly announced to the astonishment of the duped Don Gregorio.

Moratín had chosen the foreign dramatist who was most popular on the Madrid stage in the ten years that followed the French invasion, a period in which fifteen of Molière's plays had 228 performances. Peak years were 1811, 1812, and 1815—the latter two being the seasons in which Moratín's translations were performed.[9]

Moratín had had *La escuela de los maridos* ready since 1808, but it was not performed until March 17, 1812. It was put on to honor the saint's day, March 19, of King Joseph Bonaparte. The time could hardly have been less propitious. It was the end of the terrible winter famine of 1811-1812. Furthermore, it was during Lent, and although the French were not strict about theatrical performances, there had not been a show at the Cruz since March 2, and both companies were about to be reformed for the next season. Yet the light-hearted piece, with its tone between comedy and farce and its note of edification, was what the public needed to take its mind off the high price and poor quality of bread. Besides, the part of the young gallant was taken by the greatest actor of his day, Isidoro Máiquez, whom Moratín had got to know and like during the French occupation; and Doña Rosa was played by Pepita Virg, who had created the role of Doña Paquita in *El sí de las niñas*.

Higher admission prices were charged on the 17th and 18th, but regular prices prevailed on the 19th itself. Then the theaters had to close. However, *La escuela de los maridos* came out in an edition of two thousand copies, and in succeeding years it formed a regular part of the repertoire at the Cruz.

III   *A Farce from Molière*

Molière considered *Le Médecin malgré lui* (*The Doctor in Spite of Himself*) a trifling play, but audiences have loved it ever since its première at the Palais Royal in 1666. In the literature of farce it is a masterpiece. The theme went back to a thirteenth-century metrical tale and was a polished version of one of Molière's earlier farces with reminiscences of several sources, including Lope de Vega's *comedia El acero de Madrid* (*Madrid Steel*). The title has been a problem. In French it is a good one, but the usual English translation is awkward. A Spanish version bears the title *El médico por fuerza,* but Moratín, with a stroke of genius, called it *El médico a palos,* which in English becomes ungainly: *A Doctor by Dint of Beating.*

That Moratín should be attracted to Molière's play is understandable, for in his own comedies there is always an element of farce. Spanish dramatists of his day had to create roles for the graciosos in the theatrical companies, and Moratín had the pleasure of years of association with one of the greatest of them, Mariano Querol.

The subject is not far removed from Moratín's concern with a young woman's right to choose her husband. Martina wants to get even with her woodsman husband for a beating he gave her.

It occurs to her to tell some strangers who are looking for a physician that Bartolo is a great doctor, but they can make him practice only by giving him a good drubbing. Thanks to a beating Bartolo is obliged to treat Don Gerónimo's daughter, Paula, whose malady is lovesickness. Bartolo effects the cure by bringing her and Leandro together.

Moratín was as free with Molière's text in his version of *El médico a palos* as he had been with *La escuela de los maridos*. He omitted scenes which were extraneous to the main action so that three characters disappeared: Sganarelle's neighbor M.

El médico a palos
Barcelona, December 5, 1814

Bartolo, a woodsman	Felipe Blanco
Martina, his wife	Barbara Fort
Don Gerónimo, a rich	
property-owner	Vicente Alfonso
Doña Paula, his daughter	
Leandro, Paula's sweetheart	
Juliana, Don Gerónimo's maid and	
wife of Lucas	
Lucas	
Ginés	

Robert, and the peasant Thibaut and his son Perrin. He set the play near Miraflores in the province of Madrid, and changed the characters into Spaniards:

Le Médecin malgré lui	*El médico a palos*
Sganarelle	Bartolo
Martine	Martina
Géronte	Don Gerónimo
Lucinde	Doña Paula
Léandre	Leandro
Jacqueline	Juliana
Lucas	Lucas
Valère	Ginés

He reduced Bartolo's drubbings to three instead of five, and he omitted references that were unseemly for a theater audience of his day. He concluded the play by making more plausible Don Gerónimo's acceptance of Leandro as his son-in-law.

Moratín readied the work for a benefit performance by the gracioso Felipe Blanco. It took place on December 5, 1814, in Barcelona, where Moratín was living after the end of the French occupation. The play was approved by the censor for perform- ance in Madrid in January.[10] It was passed with the suppression of a couple of "damns" and the word "pimp," but the première in Madrid did not occur until November 12. It was part of a program at the Príncipe which celebrated the birthday of the abdicated king Carlos IV, who was living in exile. It played three days, and then before Fernando VII himself had the opportunity to see it the Inquisition obliged the actors to withdraw the play while the censors examined it. One of the examiners was Father José García y Carrillo, who that very week had sent his report on *El sí de las niñas* to the Madrid tribunal. He found nothing to object to in *El médico a palos*, which he described as "a purely amusing piece of no particular consequence."[11] The actors resumed playing it on November 20, and on the 26th His Majesty Fernando VII attended the theater. It remained in the repertoire for many years and was especially popular as part of an evening program of mixed entertainment.

IV   *Voltaire's* Candide

The Age of Enlightenment in Europe was known in Spain as the *siglo de las luces,* and the men of Moratín's generation who grew up in the reign of Carlos III were proud to possess *las luces.* Like many bright young men of the day, Moratín owned sets of Voltaire and Rousseau, although these writers were for- bidden by the Inquisition even to those who had permission to read books that were on the Index. Moratín's travels while he was in his twenties brought him in contact with France, Eng- land, and Italy, and in his letters and travel books he shows his painful sensitiveness to the backwardness of Spain. He was eager to participate in the reforms initiated by Carlos III, and his early life and writings are infused with exuberance and optimism.

In 1800 he was forty years old. The preceding year the gov- ernment instituted the Commission for Theatrical Reform for which he had long struggled, and he was appointed chairman, a post he promptly resigned for reasons that are obscure. He remained as a member with the title of Corrector of Comedies;

this meant that he was a literary censor and editor of the plays that were to be staged. But he did not get on with the chairman of the Commission, who at one meeting very nearly threw a bottle of ink at him. Disillusionment set in, and the Commission itself was abolished. While his great stage successes—*El barón, La mojigata, El sí de las niñas*—followed, each was attended by the hostility and bitterness of the criticasters; and after *El sí* he determined not to write again for the stage.

When the French came to Spain in 1808, Moratín, like many another liberal Spaniard, was torn between patriotism and his admiration for the bearers of light and reform. His timidity, too, influenced his decision to stay on at his post in Madrid as Secretary of the Interpretation of Languages. Then, in 1811, when he was fifty-one, the man who in his twenties had dreamed of a job in a library, was named Royal Librarian, the post that today would correspond to Director of the National Library. But this achievement turned to ashes, for the government of Joseph Bonaparte was already tottering.

It must have been sometime in these years that Moratín turned again to Voltaire's tale *Candide*, for he had completed it when he was obliged, in August of 1813, to flee with the French from Madrid; and he had his manuscript in Valencia in 1814 where a copy was made of it.[12] He had known the work for many years, for there are references in his letters that show that he had read it. In 1787 he admonished the excitable Juan Pablo Forner not to tilt at windmills "on this wretched little globe which the philosophers assure us is the best of all possible worlds." From Italy in 1796 he wrote to Melón asking him to plan to come to his country house in Pastrana and to help him "cultivate his garden."[13]

Whatever optimism he retained after 1808 seeped away in disillusionment. The world of 1810, with Europe under the boot of the Emperor Napoleon, was a denial of Leibnitz' view that all is for the best in this best of possible worlds; and the ridicule that Voltaire heaped upon Dr. Pangloss seemed ironically appropriate. While Moratín was no Candide and had not yet been ousted from his comfortable life in Madrid, ironically he was later to suffer buffetings not unlike those of Voltaire's naive protagonist.

The translation *Cándido, o El optimismo* was probably intended for publication in Madrid during the French occupation. It did not come out then, and it was many years before it appeared in print. In 1838 it was published with a Cadiz imprint, although the critic Menéndez y Pelayo suspects that it was really published in Valencia.[14]

The work is done in Moratín's excellent style. Unlike his work with the plays of Molière, he is not making a stage adaptation, so that he stays near the original. However, the language is Castilian, not French translated into Spanish. Even so, neither the work nor Moratín's translation has been popular in Spain, probably because Spaniards are convinced pessimists who already know that this is not the best of possible worlds.

V Auto de fe

In the sixth chapter of *Candide*, the youthful innocent and Dr. Pangloss ran afoul of the Portuguese Inquisition; they were imprisoned and were obliged to take part in an *auto de fe*. They wore the sanbenito—the yellow robe in which condemned heretics were obliged to parade—and Candide was flogged and Dr. Pangloss was hanged. This adventure of his creatures gave Voltaire yet another opportunity to attack the intolerance, the injustice and the cruelty of the Church.

Moratín read Voltaire over a period of many years. Often he did not agree, as we find in the notes in which he took the Frenchman to task for errors he made about Spain in the *Essai sur les moeurs*.[15] But the spirit of Voltaire entered into his own, and this is nowhere more evident than in the edition which he made of an account that was published originally in 1611 under the title *Relación de las personas que salieron al auto de la fee que . . . celebraron en la ciudad de Logroño en siete y ocho días de noviembre de 1610* (*Account of the Persons who Took Part in the Auto de Fe Held in the City of Logroño on November 7 and 8, 1610*).[16]

The pamphlet reported the culmination of a situation against which the Inquisition had struggled diligently. In the sixteenth century the Suprema had repressed the zealous witch hunting that had swept Europe and had succeeded in moderating to a degree the ardor of persecution. However, the mountainous province of Navarre particularly produced reports of the work of witches and demons. Hair-raising tales of the orgies of witches' sabbaths obliged local authorities to investigate and they concluded that rigorous repression was required. The caution of the previous century was forgotten, and an impressive *auto de fe* was planned. A thousand officials and familiars took part, and two days were required to read the particulars which left the enormous public agape at the monstrous crimes: sickness brought on by a feigned caress, a harvest destroyed by powders, the sucking of infants' blood, feasting on decaying corpses.

The era of the French occupation was propitious for pamphleteering. Napoleon Bonaparte himself from his imperial camp at Madrid abolished the Inquisition in a decree dated December 4, 1808. While the Cadiz government did not abolish the Holy Office outright, it did decree freedom of the press in 1810. A flood of pent-up resentments burst forth on Spain in the form of pamphlets, and the Inquisition was the butt of many of them.

Moratín's pamphlet, which he published under the pseudonym of Bachiller Ginés de Posadilla, appeared both in Madrid in 1811 and in Cadiz in 1812, a fact that shows how close in ideology were those who accepted the French invaders and the liberal wing of the Cadiz government. His printing consists of a prologue which differs slightly in his two editions, the text of the 1611 edition, and his footnotes. In the introduction he suggests the tone that the notes will take: "Now that it is permissible to speak the language of reason and abominate the errors of our ancestors, the *Auto de fe celebrated in Logroño in the year 1610* is again offered to the public, embellished with a few notes in which the editor has purposely not emphasized what is repugnant and horrible in the account but has rather taken the opportunity it offers his pen to ridicule the extravagant absurdities which abound in it."[17]

For example, the report states: "The religious from all the monasteries in the region had hastened in such great numbers to witness the said *auto* that the procession was the largest and most devout that had ever been seen." To this Moratín commented: "Vacation time, fun time, and three weeks of merriment! Stuffing their bellies with food and addling their pates with drink. And in Logroño!" In another part of the report it is related how a certain María de Yurreteguia tried to fend off the Devil and the witches who wanted her to join their sabbath. She invited friends to her house to protect her, but her pursuers entered anyhow. "The Devil and Miguel de Goyburu, king of the sabbath, and other witches hid behind a bench and they stuck their heads over the back to see where María de Yurreteguia was and what she was doing. . . ." Moratín wrote in his note: "So the poor Devil, if he didn't stick his head over the back of the bench, couldn't see a thing!"

It seems likely that Moratín's interest in the Logroño *auto* antedated by many years the publication of his edition. Edith Helman has pointed out the correspondence between several of Goya's *Caprichos* that deal with witches and similar situations which are described in the account of the *auto*.[18] Furthermore, she observes in the manuscript explanations a similarity to the mockingly serious style of Moratín. An example is *Capricho* No. 60, which shows an apprentice witch learning to fly. The comment is: "Gradually she is making progress. She can jump a little now and in time she will know as much as her teacher." The enduring value of Moratín's interest in this subject thus lies in the inspiration which it gave to Goya, for the institution against which the pamphlet was directed did at last pass from the Spanish scene.

VI   *Historian of the Spanish Theater*

After Moratín fled Madrid in 1813 never to return, he lived for a while in Valencia and then in Barcelona, where *El médico a palos* was first produced. Circumstances made life abroad more attractive, however, and he spent most of the rest of his days in Bordeaux and Paris. He turned his attention to writing the history of the Spanish theater which he had begun long before. He inherited the task from his father Don Nicolás, who left the beginning of such a history among his literary papers. Off and on Leandro worked at it all his life. At his death he left in manuscript form the *Orígenes del teatro español* (*Origins of the Spanish Theater*), which was published by the Academy of History.[19] The first substantial study of the Spanish drama before Lope de Vega, it consists of an excellent essay, a catalogue of plays and an anthology.

Moratín compiled another catalogue which covered the period from Lope de Vega to the year 1700, for which he wrote a brief essay not at all comparable to that of the *Orígenes*. For the 1825 Paris edition of his own works, he prepared a history of theater from about 1750 to his own day, and he later revised it to begin with the year 1700; to this he also appended a catalogue. Thus Moratín encompassed, although in an uneven way, the history of the Spanish theater from the beginning to his own day.

In the context of his life, after the buffetings of fortune, his history represents his response to Voltaire's counsel that he should cultivate his own garden.

VII *Summation*

Spaniards laughingly say of themselves that every young man carries an unproduced play in his pocket. The country has a great theatrical tradition which began with the Renaissance and flowered into the outburst of the Golden Age. But its dramatic tradition has not burned with so steady a flame as that of France or England, nor have critics done their task so well in Spain as in other countries. As a result, the Spanish theater since Calderón has not received, either in Spain or abroad, the attention it merits, and no one rightly knows the worth of it. Yet one fact stands out clearly. After the death of Calderón in 1681, Leandro Fernández de Moratín towers above all other dramatists until the twentieth century. The Romantic theater produced great dramas, which entered European culture through the operatic stage. Later, there were important plays such as Tamayo y Baus's *Un drama nuevo* (*A New Drama*), and Nuñez de Arce's *El haz de leña* (*The Faggot*); and José Echegaray and the actors and actresses for whom he wrote thrilled audiences with emotional situations and sonorous language that Spanish audiences adore. Not until Jacinto Benavente began writing at the end of the century, however, does Spain have another dramatist of the stature of Moratín.

Yet it is curious that a man of such scant production in a country that is notable for the fecundity of its writers should loom so large. Lope de Vega is great because embedded in the mass of his work there are plays and parts of plays of the sheerest beauty, and situations and characters of the purest genius. By contrast, Moratín is great for the quality and the polish of his work. He became a model for generations of dramatists, and in a nation where literature has been effusive and even slovenly, a model that combined genius and polish was sorely needed.

Moratín belonged to the first of the new generations of Europeanized Spaniards. His urbanity gave him stature among the sophisticated at the same time that his supposed French sympathies made him suspect to the patriotic. Yet friend and foe were bound to recognize that his own theater was clothed, as he said, in the mantilla and the Spanish skirt; and when he translated Molière he transformed him, without deforming him, into a Spanish mode. As a scholar of the Spanish theater, he summed up the past. As an artist, he created a new future for it.

In the middle of the nineteenth century, the dramatist Ventura de la Vega summarized Moratín's position in the Spanish theater: "Moratín is a model for the artist. Anyone who would write successfully can do no better than to study him. . . .Moratín's reputation will decline in periods of literary decadence, but whenever good taste prevails he will move to the first rank."

Notes and References

Abbreviations and Terms

A. H.	Academia de la Historia, Madrid
A. H. N.	Archivo Histórico Nacional, Madrid
A. V. M.	Archivo de la Villa, Madrid
B. A. E.	Biblioteca de Autores Españoles (I use Arabic numerals for the volume in the total series and Roman numerals if the individual title is published in more than one volume.)
B. M. M.	Biblioteca Municipal, Madrid
B. N.	Biblioteca Nacional, Madrid
B. N. P.	Bibliothèque Nationale, Paris
Expediente	Dossier
f.	Folio
Impreso	Printed (If a MS is marked Impreso, this means that the text is printed but that it has MS notes.)
Legajo	A bundle, box or dossier of documents
MS.	Manuscript
n. d.	No date of impression
n. p.	No place of impression
P. A.	Poeta Arcade, "Arcadian Poet." Moratín was a member of the Arcadian Academy of Rome with the pseudonym of Inarco Celenio. He liked to use the name and the initials P. A. on the title pages of his books.

Preface

1. Federico Ruiz Morcuende, *Vocabulario de D. Leandro Fernández de Moratín* (Madrid: Real Academia Española, 1945), I, vi.

2. For the translation of the title of *El sí de las niñas* I have used the one given it by William M. Davis whose version appears in Angel Flores, ed., *Spanish Drama* (New York: Bantam, 1962).

3. The Latin phrase *Castigat ridendo mores* which I use opposite the Preface, was the motto which the French poet Jean de Santeuil (1630-1697) devised for the portrait of the great seventeenth-century Harlequin Dominique (Giovan Domenico Biancolelli), who put it on the curtain of his theater in Paris.

Chapter One

1. Leandro Fernández de Moratín, *Orígenes del teatro español,* in *Obras de D. Leandro Fernández de Moratín dadas a luz por la Real Academia de la Historia* (Madrid: Aguado, 1830-1831), I, Parte Primera, 53-54.

2. Ludwig Pfandl, *Historia de la literatura nacional española en la edad de oro,* trans. Jorge Rubió Balaguer, 2nd. ed. (Barcelona: Gustavo Gili, 1952), p. 444.

3. Leandro Fernández de Moratín, *Comedias originales,* in *Obras . . . dadas a luz por la Real Academia de la Historia* (Madrid: Aguado), II, Parte Primera, xv-xvi.

4. Santos Diez González, *Instituciones poéticas, con un discurso preliminar en defensa de la poesía y un compendio de la historia poética o mitología para inteligencia de los poetas* (Madrid: Benito Cano, 1793).

5. Ramón de Mesonero Romanos, *Manual histórico topográfico, administrativo y artístico de Madrid,* nueva [3rd.] ed. (Madrid: Antonio Yenes, 1844), p. 63.

6. A. H., MS. 9-29-5/5962, "Varios de historia: [Noticias biográficas de Juan Bautista Conti]," f. 37.

7. "Vida del autor," in Nicolás Fernández de Moratín, *Obras póstumas* [ed. Leandro Fernández de Moratín], (Barcelona: Viuda de Roca, 1821), pp. xxix-xlii.

8. *Ibid.,* pp. xxxvii-xxxviii

9. Juan Antonio Melón, "Desordenadas y mal digeridas apuntaciones," B. N., MS. 18666, No. 24. This MS is printed, with omissions, in Leandro Fernández de Moratín, *Obras póstumas* (Madrid: M. Rivadeneyra, 1867-1868), III, 376-86.

10. *Ibid.,* but only in the MS.

11. B. N., MS. 18666, No. 28. Published by René Andioc, "Broutilles Moratiniennes," *Les Langues Néo-Latines,* No. 172 (mars-avril, 1965), 26-29.

12. Manuel Silvela, "Vida de Don Leandro Fernández de Moratín," in *Obras póstumas de D. Leandro Fernández de Moratín, I,* 24.

13. *Obras póstumas,* I, 64, 98; II, 95. I use this title for the posthumous works of Leandro. In referring to those of his father, I use his name Nicolás in each case.

14. Leandro Fernández de Moratín, "Prólogo" to *Obras dramáticas y líricas* (Paris: Augusto Bobée, 1825), I, xxi. In the following pages Moratín analyzes his definition and in doing so expresses his dramatic theory.

15. The *quintilla* is a strophe consisting of five octosyllabic verses rhyming *ababa, abbab,* etc. The *décima* has ten octosyllabic verses rhyming *abbaaccddc,* etc. The *lira* is a strophe of five verses (the first, third and fourth being heptasyllables and the other two hendeca-

syllables) rhyming *ababb*. The *redondilla* has four octosyllabic verses that rhyme *abba*.

Chapter Two

The title of the chapter is a phrase from Sir Walter Raleigh's poem "A Description of Love."

1. Melón, "Desordenadas y mal digeridas apuntaciones," in *Obras póstumas*, III, 386.

2. Casimiro Gómez Ortega gives an account of the life of Giambattista Conti in A. H., MS. 9-29-5/5962, ff. 36-41, dated August 30, 1782. Gómez Ortega also composed an epigram in honor of his friend which he published years later in *Carminum libri quatuor cum nonnullorum interpretatione hispanica* (Madrid: José Collado, 1817), p. 52. Other details concerning Conti may be found in Vittorio Cian, *Italia e Spagna nel secolo XVIII: Giovambattista Conti e alcune relazioni letterarie fra l'Italia e la Spagna nella seconda metà del settecento* (Torino: S. Lattes, 1896), pp. 8-73; and in Carmine Giustino Mininni, *Pietro Napoli Signorelli: Vita, opere, tempi, amici, con lettere, documenti ed altri scritti inediti, tre illustrazioni ed un autografo* (Città de Castello: S. Lopi, 1914), p. 347. Juan de Dios Mendoza discusses the relationship of Sabina, Moratín, and Conti in "Una leyenda en torno a Moratín," *Razón y Fe*, CLXII (1960), 186, note 14; as does Joaquín de Entrambasaguas, *El Madrid de Moratín* (Madrid: Instituto de Estudios Madrileños, 1960), pp. 20-22.

3. Leandro Fernàndez de Moratín, *Obras*, B. A. E., 2 (Madrid: Real Academia Española, 1944), 589-90.

4. *Obras póstumas*, I, 59-62.

5. Emilio Cotarelo y Mori, *María del Rosario Fernández, la Tirana, primera dama de los teatros de la corte* (Madrid: Sucesores de Rivadeneyra, 1897), p. 244; *Don Ramón de la Cruz y sus obras: ensayo biografico* (Madrid: José Perales y Martínez, 1899), pp. 518-19, 573-75, 602. I have been unable to find the complete cast of the play for its first performance.

6. B. M. M., MS. 1-91-5, *El viejo y la niña*. Autograph revisions by Moratín; censorship by Santos Díez Gonzaléz.

7. *Obras póstumas*, I, 62.

8. B. N., MS. 12963, No. 35, "Letrilla satírica escrita con ocasión de lo que se decía al representarse *El viejo y la niña*."

9. *Obras póstumas*, I, 66.

10. *Ibid.*, 81.

11. Russell P. Sebold, *Tomás de Iriarte: poeta de "rapto racional,"* (Oviedo: Universidad de Oviedo, 1961), pp. 19-38, discusses th subject of the naturalness of poetic style in the eighteenth century.

12. *Diario de Madrid*, 5 de julio, 1790, pp. 836-37.

13. Emilio Cotarelo y Mori, *Iriarte y su época* (Madrid: Sucesores de Rivadeneyra, 1897), pp. 392-93.

14. *Correo de Madrid*, 30 de junio, 7 de julio, 1790.

15. Forner signed himself Lorenzo Garrote [cudgel] in *Correo de Madrid*, 10 de junio, 1790; but in B. N., MS. 9587, "Manuscritos de D. Juan Pablo Forner y Segarra," VI, 252-74, he claims as his the "Papel en defensa de la comedia del *Viejo y la niña.*"

16. B. N., MS. 12963, No. 14, letter from Florian dated Paris, September 11, 1790.

17. Antonio Cánovas del Castillo, *Artes y letras* (Madrid: A. Pérez Dubrull, 1887), pp. 274-75.

18. "Advertencia" to *El viejo y la niña* in *Obras dramáticas y líricas*, I, 5.

19. Gaspar Melchor Jovellanos, *Obras*, ed. Miguel Artola, B. A. E., 85 (Madrid: Real Academia Española, 1955-1956), IV, 163.

20. Emilio Cotarelo y Mori, *Isidoro Máiquez y el teatro de su tiempo* (Madrid: José Perales y Martínez, 1902), p. 333.

Chapter Three

1. Marcelino Menéndez y Pelayo, *Historia de las ideas estéticas en España*, Edición Nacional de las *Obras Completas* (Santander: Aldus, S. A. de Artes Gráficas, 1947), III, 421.

2. C. E. Kany, "Theatrical Jurisdiction of the *Juez protector* in XVIIIth-Century Madrid," *Revue Hispanique*, LXXXI, 2nd part (1933), 382-84.

3. *Obras póstumas*, I, 95-96.

4. *Ibid.*, I, 125-30. Ricardo Sepúlveda, *El Corral de la Pacheca* (Madrid: Fernando Fe, 1888), pp. 267-68.

5. George Ticknor wrote on the back of the title page of his copy of the first edition of *La comedia nueva* (Public Library of the City of Boston: D.170a.16, vol. 1): "The Poet satirized in this piece was Zavala." He is referring to Gaspar Zabala y Zamora. Since Ticknor knew Moratín's friend José Antonio Conde in Madrid and Moratín himself in Paris in 1818, he may possibly have heard some reference to Zabala. Another dramatist of similar vein was Antonio Valladares. Ticknor's note lends credence to Moratín's own affirmation, but the fact remains that Comella saw himself alluded to in the play.

6. Ramón de Mesonero Romanos, *Memorias de un Setentón* (Madrid: La Ilustración Española y Americana, 1880), p. 10, Note 1.

7. José Subirá Puig, *Un vate filarmónico: Don Luciano Comella* (Madrid: Real Academia de Bellas Artes de San Fernando, 1935), 62 pp. Carlos Cambronero, "Comella," *Revista Contemporánea*, CII (1896), 567-82; CIII (1896), 41-58, 187-99, 308-19, 380-90, 479-91, 637-44; CIV (1896), 49-60, 206-11, 288-96, 398-405, 497-509.

8. "Modern Spanish Theatre," *The New Monthly Magazine*, XI (1824), 88-89. The article is signed "G." It has been attributed to both José María Blanco White and Eduardo Gorostiza.

9. B. M. M., MS. 1-152-10, Luciano Francisco Comella, "Fin de fiesta nuevo: El violeto universal o café," four copies without pagination. Censorship dated 1793 and 1817.

10. "Carta de Moratín a Forner," in *Epistolario español*, B. A. E., 62 (Madrid: Sucesores de Rivadeneyra, 1870), 216-17. Francisco Mariano Nifo (1719-1803), a prolific journalist and partisan of the national theater, was also the author of several plays. José Concha was both an actor and a dramatist. Gaspar Zabala y Zamora wrote plays similar to those of Comella and Valladares, who were his contemporaries. Miguel de Higuera was a friend of the actress María del Rosario Fernández, *la Tirana*.

11. Ramón de la Cruz, *El muñuelo: tragedia por mal nombre*, in *Collección de sainetes tanto impresos como inéditos*, ed. Agustín Durán (Madrid: Gabinete Literario and Librería Europea de Hidalgo, 1843), II, 514-26. Cruz uses the dialectal *muñuelo* rather than the normal *buñuelo*.

12. *Diario de Madrid*, No. 52, Feb. 21, 1792, p. 210.

13. Quoted by Ada M. Coe, *Catálogo bibliográfico y crítico de las comedias anunciadas en los periódicos de Madrid desde 1661 hasta 1819*, The Johns Hopkins Studies in Romance Literatures and Languages, 9 (Baltimore: The Johns Hopkins Press, 1935), pp. 47-48.

14. *La comedia nueva, o El café*. Comedia en dos actos por Don Leandro Fernández de Moratín, traducida al alemán por Manuel Ojamar (Dresde: Henríquez Gerlach, 1800.) *Das neue Lustspiel, oder Das Kafeehaus*. Ein Schauspiel in zwei Aufzügen. Aus dem Spanischen des Leandro Fernández von Moratín, übersetzt von Manuel Ojamar (Dresden: Heinrich Gerlach, 1800), 151 pp.

15. *Les Éléments de la conversation espagnole et française, ou dialogues espagnols et français, à l'usage des deux nations*. Ouvrage auquel on a joint la *Nouvelle Comédie, ou le Café*, comédie en deux actes et en prose, en espagnol et en français (Paris: Théophile Barrois Fils, 1803), 191 pp.

16. *Obras póstumas*, II, 169-70.

17. Gérard de Nerval, *Le Nouveau genre, ou le Café d'un théâtre*. Comédie . . . imitée de Leandro Moratín, commencée par Gérard de Nerval et terminée par Arthus Fleury (Paris: J. Barbée, 1860), 79 pp.

18. "Modern Spanish Theatre," *The New Monthly Magazine*, XI (1824), 187. cf. note 8, above.

19. A. V. M., Corregimiento, MS. 1-40-64, "Órdenes a la Compañía de Navarro para que se sugeten a las disposiciones del Sr. D. Leandro Fernández de Moratín, Madrid, 14 de junio de 1799." René Andioc,

"A propos d'une reprise de *La comedia nueva* de Leandro Fernández de Moratín," *Bulletin Hispanique*, LXIII (1961), 54-61.
20. "Modern Spanish Theatre," *ibid.*, Note.
21. *Obras póstumas*, I, 94.
22. B. M. M., MS. 1-95-3 (Impreso), *La comedia nueva, o El café* (n. p., n. d.)

Chapter Four

1. F. Vézinet, "Moratín et Molière," in *Molière, Florian et la littérature espagnole* (Paris: Librairie Hachette et Cie., 1909), pp. 44-45.
2. Phaedrus, *Fabulae Aesopiae*, Book III, Fable 18.
3. N. D. Shergold, *A History of the Spanish Stage from Medieval Times until the End of the Seventeenth Century* (Oxford: The Clarendon Press, 1967), pp. 316-17.
4. Until recently the text of the zarzuela was not known to scholars. René Andioc, by clever deduction and detective work, uncovered a manuscript in the Jesuit Residence in Seville (Fondo Saavedra, Legajo 39). He has published a study and large portions of the text in "Une 'Zarzuela' retrouvée: El barón, de Moratín," *Mélanges de la Casa de Velázquez*, I (1965), 289-321. Basing his conclusions on the differences between the two versions, M. Andioc points out significant features of the theme of the play.
5. Andrés González-Blanco, "Cartas de Moratín a Jovellanos," *La Lectura*, X, No. 3 (1910), 124-25.
6. *Obras póstumas*, II, 112.
7. "Advertencia" to *El barón*, in *Obras dramáticas y líricas*, I, 251.
8. Andrés de Mendoza, *La lugareña orgullosa: Comedia original en tres actos, representada por primera vez en el Coliseo de los Caños del Peral el día 8 de enero de 1803* (Madrid: Imprenta de Sancha, [1803]), pp. [v-vi].
9. A seguidilla is a stanza composed of either four or seven verses. The quatrain consists of alternating seven- and five-syllable verses, with the second and fourth verses in assonance. If the final three verses are added to the quatrain, the first and third are five-syllable in assonance and the second is seven-syllable.
10. B. N., MS. 12963, No. 53, "[Carta de Andrés de Mendoza a Leandro Fernández de Moratín]."
11. Emilio Cotarelo y Mori, *Isidoro Máiquez y el teatro de su tiempo*, p. 157.
12. A. V. M., MS. 2-360-18, "[Resumen de los productos del teatro de los Caños del Peral y su inversión desde 10 de abril de 1803 hasta 10 de enero de 1804]."
13. A. V. M., MS. 2-476-9, "[Cuentas relativas a las comedias del teatro de la Cruz del año de 1803]."

14. *Obras dramáticas y líricas,* I, 252-53.

15. B. N., MS. 12963, No. 7, "[Crítica de *El barón* de D. Leandro Fernández de Moratín]."

16. José Mor de Fuentes, *Bosquejillo de la vida y escritos de Don José Mor de Fuentes, delineado por él mismo* (Barcelona: Antonio Bergnes, 1836), pp. 51-52.

17. Quoted by Ada M. Coe, *Catálogo bibliográfico y crítico de las comedias anunciadas en los periódicos de Madrid desde 1661 hasta 1819,* pp. 25-26.

18. *Obras póstumas,* II, 185.

19. *El Censor,* XVI (1822), 418. Also in *Comedias de Moratín* (Paris: Baudry, 1866), p. xxiii.

Chapter Five

1. Sebastián de Covarrubias, *Tesoro de la lengua castellana o española,* ed. Martín de Riquer (Barcelona: S. A. Horta, 1943), p. 633. The older spelling, still used in Moratín's time, was *mogigata;* modern usage prefers *mojigata.* The masculine form is, of course, *mojigato.* Joan Corominas, *Breve diccionario etimológico de la lengua castellana* (Madrid: Editorial Gredos, 1961), p. 391, considers the word a compound of two words, *mojo* and *gato,* both meaning cat; however, *mojo* is not attested in this sense. He goes on to derive its meaning by the same reasoning as Covarrubias. It would seem that the Arabic source is the logical one.

2. *Obras póstumas,* II, 122.

3. Gaspar Melchor de Jovellanos, *Obras,* Biblioteca de Autores Españoles, 86 (Madrid: Real Academia Española, 1955-1956), IV, 257.

4. *Obras dramáticas y líricas,* II, 4.

5. *Obras póstumas,* I, 157.

6. *Ibid.,* 158.

7. *Ibid.,* 158-59.

8. The entire polemic is to be found in *Variedades de Ciencias, Literatura y Artes,* II (1804), 355-72; III (1805), 228-47, 295-307.

9. *Variedades,* II (1804), 366-67.

10. *Variedades,* III (1805), 245-46.

11. Dartmouth College Library, Ticknor Papers, Case 7. John C. Dowling, "Leandro de Moratín's Answers to Ticknor's Questionnaire on *La mojigata,"* in *Homage to Charles Blaise Qualia* (Lubbock, Tex.: The Texas Tech Press, 1962), pp. 113-19.

12. *El Procurador General del Rey y de la Nación,* VI (1814), 1540-41.

13. Mariano José de Larra, "Representación de *La mojigata," Obras,* B. A. E., 127 (Madrid: Real Academia Española, 1960), I, 341-42.

Chapter Six

1. Pedro Estala, "Discurso preliminar" to Aristophanes, *El Pluto* (Madrid: Imprenta de Sancha, 1794), first pagination, p. 43.

2. Very helpful for the analysis of *El sí de las niñas* is the introduction of Alfredo Lefebvre (ed.), *El teatro de Moratín* (Santiago de Chile: Editorial Universitaria, 1958), pp. 58-71. Also: Charles V. Aubrun, "*El sí de las niñas*, o más allá de la mecánica de una comedia," *Homenaje a Angel del Río*, pp. 29-35 in *Revista Hispánica Moderna*, XXXI (1965).

3. Guillermo Díaz-Plaja, "Perfil del teatro romántico español," *Estudios Escénicos*, No. 8 (1963), 31-34.

4. B. M. M., MS. 71-22, "El sueño." This copy has the censorship date of 1818, but Cotarelo y Mori, *Máiquez*, pp. 109-10, thinks it is the same play in which Máiquez played in 1802.

5. José Francisco Gatti, "Moratín y Marivaux," *Revista de Filología Hispánica*, III (1941), 140-49.

6. Benoît-Joseph Marsollier des Vivetières, *Le Traité nul, comédie en un acte et en prose, mêlée d'ariettes, représentée le 5 Messidor, an 5, sur le théâtre Feydeau* (Paris: Huet, Libraire et Editeur, 1797), 64 pp.

7. Vézinet, "Moratín et Molière," pp. 45-47.

8. Joaquín Casalduero, "Forma y sentido de *El sí de las niñas*," *Nueva Revista de Filología Hispánica*, XI (1957), 38.

9. Juan de Dios Mendoza, S. I., "Una leyenda en torno a Moratín," *Razón y Fe*, CLXII (1960), 183-92, 447-56. Joaquín de Entrambasaguas, with whom Mendoza was studying, had already questioned the legend in *El Madrid de Moratín*, pp. 24-25.

10. Melón's "Desordenadas y mal digeridas apuntaciones," are in B. N., MS. 18666, No. 24, and were published in part in the *Obras póstumas*, III, 376-88. Manuel Silvela's "Vida de Don Leandro Fernández de Moratín" appeared in his own *Obras póstumas* (Madrid: Francisco de Paula Mellado, 1845), II, and was reprinted in Moratín's *Obras póstumas*, I, 1-58. Aribau's "Vida de Don Leandro Fernández de Moratín" is in *Obras de Don Nicolás y de Don Leandro Fernández de Moratín*, B. A. E., 2, xxi-xxxviii.

11. "Prólogo," *Obras dramáticas y líricas*, I, xxi-xxii.

12. The tapestry cartoon is No. 799 in the Museo del Prado collection. The tapestry itself is at the Royal Seat of El Pardo.

13. *The Complete Etchings of Goya*, foreword by Aldous Huxley (New York: Crown Publishers, 1943). Edith Helman, "Moratín y Goya," *Insula*, No. 161 (abril, 1960), 10.

14. Melón, "Desordenadas y mal digeridas apuntaciones," in *Obras póstumas*, III, 380.

15. *Diario de Madrid*, 1806, Part I, January and February.

16. B. N., MS. 12963, No. 48, "Carta de Antonio Nicolás de

Solavide: una invectiva escrita con ocasión de haber visto una representación de *El sí de las niñas.* 25 enero, 1806."

17. B. N., MS. 18666, No. 2, "Crítica de *El sí de las niñas* [seguida del] Juicio imparcial del juicio antecedente."

18. B. N., MS. 12963, No. 3, "Censura crítica de *El sí de las niñas* en forma de crítica."

19. "Carta de un amigo residente en Madrid a otro residente en las montañas de León. Firmado E. P." *Minerva, o El Revisor General,* No. XXII (March 18, 1806), 81-94. "Carta segunda de Don E. P. a su amigo . . ." No. XXXIX (May 16, 1806), 153-61.

20. "Carta de D. J. M. de V. dirigida a los editores desde Cádiz acerca de la comedia *El sí de las niñas,*" *Memorial Literario,* VI (May 16, 1806), 253-62, 289-99.

21. *Obras póstumas,* II, 195-99.

22. Albert S. Cook, *The Art of Poetry: The Poetical Treatises of Horace, Vida, and Boileau* (New York: G. E. Stechert & Co., 1926), p. 10. Cook reproduces the Howes translation of Horace.

23. B. N. P., MS. Fonds Espagnols 442, "Carta crítica de un vecino de Guadalajara sobre la comedia *El sí de las niñas* por Ynarco Celenio (Moratín) y las dos odas de Quintana y Arriaza sobre el combate nabal de Cabo Trafalgar, en 21 de octubre de 1805, con la censura del Juzgado de Imprentas y la repuesta a ella. Año de 1807." A. H. N., Estado, Legajo 3242[1], Expediente 2: Moratín, Leandro Fernández de, Documents 30-40.

24. This section is adapted from my article "The Inquisition Appraises *El sí de las niñas,* 1815-1819," *Hispania,* XLIV (1961), 237-44.

25. Henry Charles Lea, *A History of the Inquisition of Spain* (New York: The Macmillan Co., 1922), IV, 424.

26. A. H. N., Inquisición, Legajo 4484, No. 23. The dossier on *El sí* consists of a title page and 41 numbered folios. It is preceded by the Barcelona dossier containing a title page and four unnumbered folios. Also included is a copy of the play, published without date by Agustín Roca in Barcelona. The edition on which the Madrid censorship was based (Madrid: Villalpando, 1805) is not in the dossier. The other two plays were not on the July 22, 1815 list. One was *La mojigata.* The other was *El no de las niñas,* an adaptation of Goldoni's *Sior Todero Brontolon o sia il vecchio fastidioso* (1761), which had been on the Spanish stage under other titles (*Mal genio y buen corazón, El regañón*) for nearly thirty years. See Coe, *Catálogo bibliográfico y crítico de las comedias anunciadas en los periódicos de Madrid, 1661-1819,* p. 140; Paul P. Rogers, *Goldoni in Spain* (Oberlin, Ohio: The Academy Press, 1941), pp. 92-93.

27. Leopoldo de Cueto, *Autores dramáticos contemporáneos* (Madrid: Fortanet, 1881), II, 221-23.

154 MORATÍN

28. Silvela, "Vida de Moratín," *Obras póstumas,* I, 36-37.
29. *Obras póstumas,* II, 326. Andrés Prieto had played Don Diego in the 1806 première.
30. *Ibid.,* III, 6. The work was published in French: *Le Oui des jeunes filles, comédie-vaudeville en un acte, imitée de l'espagnol,* par MM. Dupeuty, de Villeneuve et Jouslin de la Salle, représentée pour la première fois à Paris, sur le théâtre du Gymnase Dramatique, le 3 mars 1823 (Paris: Pollet, 1824), 32 pp.
31. A. H. N., Consejos: Diversiones Públicas, Legajo 11409, No. 6, "Expediente promovido a instancia de Josefa Virg . . ."
32. A. H. N., Consejos: Diversiones Públicas, Legajo 11386, No. 31, "Licencia para representar en el teatro de Granada la comedia de don Leandro Moratín *El sí de las niñas,* recogida por la Inquisición. 7 de diciembre de 1832."
33. A. H. N., Consejos: Diversiones Públicas, Legajo 11387, No. 22, "Permiso concedido a la Junta de la Capilla de la Congregación de Nuestra Señora de la Almudena de Madrid, propia de los actores españoles, para representar *El sí de las niñas* y *La mojigata,* de Moratín. 10 de diciembre de 1833."
34. Larra, "Representación de *El sí de las niñas,*" *Obras,* B. A. E., 127, I, 345-46.
35. Ventura de la Vega, *Obras escogidas* (Barcelona: Montaner y Simón, 1894), I, 207-34.

Chapter Seven

1. Fernando Lázaro Carreter, "La transmisión textual del poema de Moratín 'Fiesta de toros en Madrid,'" *Clavileño,* IV, Núm. 21 (mayo-junio, 1953), 33-38, shows that Leandro polished and pruned his father's poem before publishing it in the *Obras póstumas,* pp. 78-93. It is this version that appeared in B. A. E., 2, pp. 12-14, and that is consequently generally known.
2. Federico Ruiz Morcuende, "Moratín, Secretario de la Interpretación de Lenguas," *Revista de la Biblioteca, Archivo y Museo del Ayuntamiento de Madrid,* X (1933), 273-90. John C. Dowling, "La noticia de Leandro de Moratín sobre la Interpretación de Lenguas, 1809," *Hispanófila,* Núm. 20 (1964), 49-54.
3. *Epigrams,* Book I, No. xxi. "Si non errasset, fecerat illa minus." *Illa* referred to a hand; Moratín changed the world to *ille.*
4. *Hamlet, tragedia de Guillermo Shakespeare, traducida e ilustrada con la vida del autor y notas críticas por Inarco Celenio, P. A.* (Madrid: Villalpando, 1798), p. 2. Subsequent references: pp. 54, 86, 329, 69.
5. *Obras póstumas,* II, 147.
6. *Examen de la tragedia intitulada Hamlet, escrita en inglés por Guillermo Shakespeare y traducida al castellano por Inarco Celenio, Poeta Arcade.* Escribíalo D. C. C., T. D. D. U. D. F. D. B. (Madrid:

Viuda de Ibarra, 1800), 75 pp. The initials are identified in B. N. MS. 3710, f. 22r, as Don Cristóbal Cladera, Traductor Del Diccionario Universal De Física De Brison.

7. Alfonso Par, *Shakespeare en la literatura española* (Barcelona: Biblioteca Balmes, 1935), I, 105-22. Rudolph Morgan, *Moratín's Hamlet*, Ph. D. dissertation, Stanford University (Ann Arbor: University Microfilms, 1965), 268 pp.

8. This and other quotations are from the prologue to the first edition of Moratín's translation: *La escuela de los maridos, comedia escrita en francés por Juan Bautista Molière y traducida a nuestra lengua por Inarco Celenio, P. A.* (Madrid: Villalpando, 1812), pp. 3-21.

9. Charlotte M. Lorenz, "Translated Plays in Madrid Theatres, 1808-1818," *Hispanic Review*, IX (1941), 376-82.

10. B. M. M., MS. 1-50-13, *El médico a palos*, printed without author, place, publisher, or date. The MS. approval, dated January 19, 1815, begins on p. 60.

11. A. H. N., Inquisición, Legajo 4469, No. 38, "Expediente de calificación de las dos comedias tituladas *Nada con exceso, o Los dos biombos* y *El médico a palos.*"

12. B. N., MS. 6982, Leandro Fernández de Moratín, "Cándido, o El optimismo, traducido de Voltaire."

13. *Obras póstumas*, II, 96, 168.

14. *Cándido, o El optimismo, traducido por Moratín* (Cádiz: Imprenta de Santiponce, 1838), 358 pp.

15. Pablo Cabañas, "Moratín, anotador de Voltaire," *Revista de Filología Española*, XXVIII (1944), 73-83.

16. *Relación de las personas que salieron al auto de la fee que los señores Doctor Alonso Bezerra Holguín, del ábito de Alcántara, Licenciado Iuan de Valle Alvarado, Licenciado Alonso de Salazar Frías, Inquisidores Apostólicos del Reyno de Navarra y su distrito, celebraron en la ciudad de Logroño en siete y en ocho días del mes de noviembre de 1610 años y de las cosas y delitos por que fueron castigados* (Logroño: Juan de Mongastón, 1611), 14 ff. unnumbered.

17. *Auto de fe celebrado en la ciudad de Logroño en los días 7 y 8 de noviembre del año de 1610, siendo inquisidor general el cardenal arzobispo de Toledo Don Bernardo de Sandobal.* Ilustrada con notas por el Bachiller Ginés de Posadilla, natural de Yébenes. (Cádiz: Imprenta Tormentaria, 1812), p. 8. Other quotations are on pp. 13, 45.

18. Edith F. Helman, "The Younger Moratín and Goya: On *Duendes* and *Brujas*," *Hispanic Review*, XXVII (1959), 116-18.

19. The censoring of the Academy edition has been studied by Robert K. Spaulding, "The Text of Moratín's *Orígenes del Teatro Español*," *PMLA*, XLVII (1932), 981-91.

Selected Bibliography

The present study of Moratín is based substantially on documents, manuscripts and contemporary periodicals. I have given the bibliographical references to these materials in the notes rather than in this bibliography.

PRIMARY SOURCES

I give the first edition and significant subsequent editions, plus important collected works. However, I have not seen the first editions of *El viejo y la niña* or the *Auto de fe*.

Besides the pen name Inarco Celenio, Moratín used the following pseudonyms for the particular works listed in this bibliography: Efrén de Lardnaz y Morante, an anagram; Melitón Fernández (Melitón was one of his four baptismal names; this was also the name he used in Barcelona in 1814-1817 to disguise himself); Ginés de Posadilla (a name with a picaresque ring that was in consonance with the mischievous tone of the *Auto de fe*).

1. Individual Works

La toma de Granada por los Reyes Católicos D. Fernando y Dª Isabel. Romance endecasílabo impreso por la Real Academia Española por ser entre todos los presentados el que más se acerca al que ganó el premio. Su autor, D. Efrén de Lardnaz y Morante (Madrid: Joachín Ibarra, 1779), 22 pp.

Lección poética. Sátira contra los vicios introducidos en lo poesía castellana impresa por la Real Academia Española por ser entre las presentadas la que más se acerca a la que ganó el premio. Su autor Don Melitón Fernández (Madrid: Joachín Ibarra, 1782), 32 pp.

La derrota de los pedantes (Madrid: Benito Cano, 1789), 108 pp.

El viejo y la niña. Comedia en tres actos corregida en esta impresión por su autor Inarco Celenio, P. A. (Madrid: Imprenta Real, 1795) [4] + 159 pp.

La comedia nueva. Comedia en dos actos, en prosa, representada en el Coliseo del Príncipe en 7 de febrero de 1792 (Madrid: Benito Cano, 1792), 72 pp.

La comedia nueva. Comedia en dos actos en prosa. Su autor Inarco Celenio, Poeta Arcade (Parma: Juan Bautista Bodoni, 1796), [12] + 128 pp.

La comedia nueva. Edición con introducción, notas y documentos de John Dowling (Madrid: Editorial Castalia, 1970), 346 pp. The critical text is accompanied by a collection of documents which illuminate the play and the theatrical history of the period.

Hamlet. Tragedia de Guillermo Shakespeare traducida e ilustrada con la vida del autor y notas críticas por Inarco Celenio, P. A. (Madrid: Villalpando, 1798), [26] + 379 pp.

El barón. Comedia en dos actos en verso. Su autor Inarco Celenio, P. A. (Madrid: Villalpando, 1803), [10] + 134 pp.

La mogigata. Comedia en tres actos, en verso. Su autor Inarco Celenio, P. A. (Madrid: Villalpando, 1804), [8] + 180 pp.

El sí de las niñas. Comedia en tres actos en prosa. Su autor Inarco Celenio, P. A. (Madrid: Villalpando, 1805), [6] + 146 pp.

Auto de fe celebrado en la ciudad de Logroño en los días 7 y 8 de noviembre del año de 1610 siendo Inquisidor General el Cardenal Arzobispo de Toledo Don Bernardo de Sandobal y Rojas. Ilustrada con notas por el Bachiller Ginés de Posadilla, natural de Yébenes (Cádiz: Imprenta Tormentaria, 1812), 143 pp.

La escuela de los maridos. Comedia escrita en francés por Juan Bautista Molière y traducida a nuestra lengua por Inarco Celenio, P. A. (Madrid: Villalpando, 1812), 128 pp.

El médico a palos. Comedia en tres actos en prosa imitada por Inarco Celenio, P. A., de la que escribió en francés J. B. Molière con el título El médico por fuerza (Madrid: Collado, 1814), 75 pp.

Cándido, o El optimismo [de Voltaire], *traducido por Moratín* (Cádiz: Santiponce, 1838), 358 pp.

Diario (Mayo 1780-Marzo 1808). Edición anotada por René y Mireille Andioc (Madrid: Editorial Castalia, 1967), 387 pp. The abbreviated diaries, expanded and deciphered by the editors, are useful for the life of Moratín, including his theatrical activities.

2. Collected Works

Obras dramáticas y líricas de D. Leandro Fernández de Moratín, entre los Arcades de Roma, Inarco Celenio. Unica edición reconocida por el autor (Paris: Augusto Bobée, 1825), 3 vols. This edition may be regarded as the author's definitive text. Moratín used a copy of it, which lacked title pages and illustrations, to polish his plays once again. The copy, with inked corrections in his handwriting, is in B. N., call number R/2571-3.

Obras de D. Leandro Fernández de Moratín, dadas a luz por la Real Academia de la Historia (Madrid: Aguado, 1830-1831), 4 vols. in 6. This collection contains the first edition of the *Orígenes del teatro español.* However, all the texts must be used with caution because the editors censored certain parts.

Obras de Don Nicolás y Don Leandro Fernández de Moratín, B. A. E., 2 (Madrid: Rivadeneyra, 1846), xxxviii + 656 pp. This is the standard and most accessible collection, and it has been reprinted. However, the relatively deficient scholarly criteria of a hundred years ago require one to use it with caution.

Obras póstumas de D. Leandro Fernández de Moratín publicadas de orden y a expensas del gobierno de S. M. (Madrid: Rivadeneyra, 1867-1868), 3 vols. Containing the travel books, the correspondence and other literary papers from the Biblioteca Nacional, this collection is fundamental for the study of Moratín.

Teatro, ed. F. Ruiz Morcuende. Clásicos Castellanos, 58 (Madrid: Ediciones de "La Lectura," 1924), lvii + 303 pp. Morcuende publishes *La comedia nueva* and *El sí de las niñas* in Moratín's final revision as contained in the B. N. copy of *Obras dramáticas y líricas*, call number R/2571-3.

La comedia nueva. El sí de las niñas. Ediciones, introducciones y notas de John Dowling y René Andioc (Madrid: Clásicos Castalia, 1968), 285 pp. A book that provides sound texts and introductory material based on recent research.

La derrota de los pedantes. Lección poética. Edición con introducción, notas y glosario de John Dowling (Barcelona: Editorial Labor, 1971). Two early works of lively literary criticism appear in modern annotated texts.

SECONDARY SOURCES

1. Books and Monographs

ANDIOC, RENÉ. *Sur la querelle du théâtre au temps de Leandro Fernández de Moratín* (Tarbes: Imprimerie Saint-Joseph, 1970), 721 pp. A ponderous scholarly study of the theatrical disputes of the late eighteenth and early nineteenth centuries.

CAMPOS, JORGE. *Teatro y sociedad en España, 1780-1820* (Madrid: Editorial Moneda y Crédito, 1969), 215 pp. A study of the eighteenth- and early nineteenth-century theater as a channel of the Enlightenment.

CASO GONZÁLEZ, JOSÉ. *Rococó, prerromanticismo y neoclasicismo en el teatro español del siglo XVIII*, Cuadernos de la Cátedra Feijoo, 22 (Oviedo: Universidad de Oviedo, 1970), 29 pp. A tentative effort to classify the eighteenth-century theater.

[CLADERA, CRISTÓBAL]. *Examen de la tragedia intitulada Hamlet, escrita en inglés por Guillermo Shakespeare y traducida al castellano por Inarco Celenio, Poeta Arcade*. Escribíalo D. C. C., T. D. D. U. D. F. D. B. (Madrid: Viuda de Ibarra, 1800). An impassioned but important criticism of Moratín's translation of *Hamlet*. See Chapter 7, Note 6.

Coe, Ada M. *Catálogo bibliográfico y crítico de las comedias anunciadas en los periódicos de Madrid desde 1661 hasta 1819*, The Johns Hopkins Studies in Romance Literatures and Languages, 9 (Baltimore: The Johns Hopkins Press, 1935). This valuable index to the plays performed in Madrid also provides excerpts of contemporary drama criticism.

Cook, John A. *Neo-Classic Drama in Spain: Theory and Practice* (Dallas: Southern Methodist University Press, 1959). Traces the development of neoclassic drama from the time of Luzán through the followers of Moratín.

Cotarelo y Mori, Emilio. *Don Ramón de la Cruz y sus obras: ensayo biográfico* (Madrid: José Perales y Martínez, 1899). The appendixes on actors, actresses and the dramatic companies are very useful for the study of Moratín's theater.

————. *Iriarte y su época* (Madrid: Sucesores de Rivadeneyra, 1897). A fundamental source of background information on the early period of Moratín's literary activities.

————. *Isidoro Máiquez y el teatro de su tiempo* (Madrid: José Perales y Martínez, 1902). The appendixes on the theater companies and on the performances of plays are very helpful.

————. *María del Rosario Fernández, la Tirana, primera dama de los teatros de la corte* (Madrid: Sucesores de Rivadeneyra, 1897). The story of a great actress provides information on the theater in the period when Moratín began to write.

Desdevises du Dézert, George. *L'Espagne de l'ancien régime*, 3 vols. in *Revue Hispanique*, LXIV (1925), LXX (1927), LXXIII (1928). A comprehensive study of Spain in the eighteenth century.

Fernández Guerra, Aureliano. *Lección poética sobre las celebérrimas quintillas de D. Nicolás Fernández de Moratín* (Madrid: Manuel G. Hernández, 1883). Prints in parallel columns the original text of the poem "Fiesta de toros en Madrid" by Moratín senior and the revised version by his son Leandro.

Ferreres, Rafael. *Moratín en Valencia (1812-1814)* (Valencia: Centro de Cultura Valenciana, 1962). Studies an obscure period in Moratín's life and publishes newspaper articles which may be attributed to Moratín.

Herr, Richard. *The Eighteenth Century Revolution in Spain* (Princeton, N. J.: Princeton University Press, 1958). A history of the Enlightenment in Spain.

Lázaro Carreter, Fernando. *Moratín en su teatro*, Cuadernos de la Cátedra Feijóo, No. 9 (Oviedo: Universidad de Oviedo, 1961). Evaluates Moratín's theater within the neoclassic movement.

McClelland, I. L. *Spanish Drama of Pathos, 1750-1808* (Toronto:

University of Toronto Press, 1970), 2 vols. An extensive study of one type of eighteenth-century drama.

MARTÍNEZ RUIZ, JOSÉ. *Moratín: Esbozo por Cándido* (Madrid: Fernando Fe, 1893). An appreciation of Moratín published by Azorín at the age of twenty as one of his first works.

MELÓN R. DE GORDEJUELA, SANTIAGO. *Moratín por dentro*, Cuadernos de la Cátedra Feijóo, No. 16 (Oviedo: Universidad de Oviedo, 1964). Studies the personality and psychology of Moratín.

RUIZ MORCUENDE, FEDERICO. *Vocabulario de D. Leandro Fernández de Moratín* (Madrid: Real Academia Española, 1945). Defines and illustrates every word that Moratín used in his writings.

SARRAILH, JEAN. *L'Espagne éclairée de la seconde moitié du XVIIIe siècle*, 2nd ed. (Paris: Librairie C. Klincksieck, 1964). Provides extensive background on the intellectual climate of Spain during Moratín's formative years.

SHERGOLD, N. D. *A History of the Spanish Stage from Medieval Times until the End of the Seventeenth Century* (Oxford: The Clarendon Press, 1967). This fundamental work presents a thoroughly scholarly treatment of the Spanish theater preceding the neoclassic period.

SUBIRÁ PUIG, JOSÉ. *Un vate filarmónico: Don Luciano Comella* (Madrid: Real Academia de Bellas Artes de San Fernando, 1935). A serious study of a neglected contemporary and rival of Moratín.

VEGA, VENTURA DE LA. *La crítica de El sí de las niñas*, in *Obras escogidas* (Barcelona: Montaner y Simón, 1894), I, 207-34. Like Molière's *Critique de L'Ecole des femmes*, excellent dramatic criticism in dramatic form.

2. Periodical Articles and Essays in Books

ANDIOC, RENÉ. "A propos d'une reprise de *La comedia. nueva* de Leandro Fernández de Moratín," *Bulletin Hispanique*, LXIII (1961), 54-61. Provides documentary evidence of Moratín's insistence on careful production of his plays.

————. "Broutilles Moratiniennes," *Les Langues Néo-Latines*, No. 172 (mars-avril, 1965), 26-33. Gives evidence of a rich creative vein in Moratín.

————. "Une 'Zarzuela' retrouvée: *El barón*, de Moratín," *Mélanges de la Casa de Velázquez*, I (1965), 289-321. A study of the hitherto unknown zarzuela version of *El barón* which provides important insights into Moratín's creative talent.

AUBRUN, CHARLES V. "*El sí de las niñas*, o más allá de la mecánica de una comedia," *Homenaje a Angel del Río*, in *Revista Hispánica Moderna*, XXXI (1965), 29-35. Studying *El sí* as a document of the age, M. Aubrun contrasts characters and situations with Lope's *El acero de Madrid* and Calderón's *La vida es sueño*.

162

MORATÍN

CABAÑAS, PABLO. "Moratín, anotador de Voltaire," *Revista de Filología Española*, XXVIII (1944), 73-83. Analyzes B. N. MS. 18668, No. 1, in which Moratín noted the mistakes that Voltaire makes about Spain in his *Essai sur les moeurs et l'esprit des nations*.

————. "Moratín y la reforma del teatro de su tiempo," *Revista de Bibliografía Nacional*, V (1944), 63-102. Reproduces important documents concerning theatrical reform.

CAMBRONERO, CARLOS. "Comella," *Revista Contemporánea*, CII (1896), 567-82; CIII (1896), 41-58, 187-99, 308-19, 380-90, 479-91, 637-44; CIV (1896), 49-60, 206-11, 288-96, 398-405, 497-509. The first extensive study of the works of an author whose melodramas dominated the theater in the time of Moratín.

CASALDUERO, JOAQUÍN. "Forma y sentido de *El sí de las niñas*," *Nueva Revista de Filología Hispánica*, XI (1957), 36-56. The author applies his well-known critical method to Moratín's masterpiece and produces an outstanding analysis.

COTARELO Y MORI, EMILIO. "Traductores castellanos de Molière," in *Homenaje a Menéndez y Pelayo* (Madrid: Victoriano Suárez, 1899), I, 69-141. Includes an evaluation of Moratín's contribution as a translator of Molière.

DÍAZ-PLAJA, GUILLERMO. "Perfil del teatro romántico español," *Estudios Escénicos*, No. 8 (1963), 29-56. In the tenderness of *El sí* the author discovers the first step toward the Romantic theater.

ENTRAMBASAGUAS, JOAQUÍN DE. "El lopismo de Moratín," *Revista de Filología Española*, XXV (1941), 1-45. Studies Moratín as an admirer of Lope de Vega but who at the same time distrusted his fecundity.

GONZÁLEZ-BLANCO, ANDRÉS. "Cartas de Moratín a Jovellanos," *La Lectura*, X, No. 3 (1910), 53-66, 121-35. The letters themselves are useful, but most are not properly dated and the commentary is inadequate.

GONZÁLEZ PALENCIA, ANGEL. "Una ofuscación de Moratín," *Revista de la Biblioteca, Archivo y Museo del Ayuntamiento de Madrid*, X (1933), 75-82. Recounts Moratín's reluctance to swear formal allegiance to the régime of Joseph Bonaparte.

HELMAN, EDITH F. "The Younger Moratín and Goya: On *Duendes* and *Brujas*," *Hispanic Review*, XXVII (1959), 103-22. Documents the relation between Moratín's notes to the *Auto de fe* and the subject matter of Goya's *Caprichos*.

HUARTE, JOSÉ MARÍA DE. "Más sobre el epistolario de Moratín," *Revista de Archivos, Bibliotecas y Museos*, LXVIII (1960), 505-52. Publishes and comments on 35 autograph letters of Moratín from the private archives of the Marquesses of Valdeterrazo.

Insula, XV, No. 161 (abril, 1960). Articles by Azorín, José Luis Cano, John Dowling, Nigel Glendinning, Edith Helman, Fernando

Lázaro Carreter, Vicente Llorens, Julián Marías, Antonio Odriozola.

KANY, C. E. "Theatrical Jurisdiction of the *Juez protector* in XVIIIth-Century Madrid," *Revue Hispanique*, LXXXI, 2nd part (1933), 382-93. Deals with regulations affecting the theater.

LARRA, MARIANO JOSÉ DE. *Obras*, B. A. E., 127-30 (Madrid: Real Academia Española, 1960). Vol. I has drama reviews of performances of Moratín's plays in the 1830's.

LÁZARO CARRETER, FERNANDO. "La transmisión textual de 'Fiesta de toros en Madrid,'" *Clavileño*, No. 21 (mayo-junio, 1953), 33-38. Demonstrates how the younger Moratín pruned and polished his father's famous poem into the version that we know today.

LEFEBVRE, ALFREDO. "[Introducción y análisis dramático]," in *El teatro de Moratín* (Santiago de Chile: Editorial Universitaria, 1958), pp. 9-74. The analysis of the action of *El sí de las niñas* is especially good.

MARÍAS, JULIÁN. "España y Europa en Moratín," in *Los españoles*, 2nd ed. (Madrid: Revista de Occidente, 1963), pp. 79-119. An excellent assessment of Moratín as an enlightened intellectual of his time.

MENDOZA, JUAN DE DIOS. "Una leyenda en torno a Moratín," *Razón y Fe*, CLXII (1960), 183-92, 447-56. Refutes the latter-day legend that made Moratín's friend Francisca Muñoz the real-life model of Doña Francisca in *El sí de las niñas*.

Moratín y la sociedad española de su tiempo, Revista de la Universidad de Madrid, IX (1960). Number 35, pp. 567-808, was devoted to articles on Moratín by Antonio Domínguez Ortiz, Juan Antonio Gaya Nuño, Luis S. Granjel, Edith F. Helman, Angela Mariutti de Sánchez Rivero, Paul Merimée, Antonio Oliver, and Luis Sánchez Agesta, collected under a general title.

NÚÑEZ DE ARENAS, MANUEL. "Moratín y Cabarrús," in *L'Espagne des Lumières au Romantisme* (Paris: Institut d'Etudes Hispaniques, 1963), pp. 347-51. Studies Moratín's relationship with the famous banker.

PÉREZ DE GUZMAN, JUAN. "La primera representación de *El sí de las niñas*," *La España Moderna*, XIV, No. 168 (diciembre, 1902), 103-37. Describes the première of *El sí* but does not cite sources.

————. "Los émulos de Moratín," *La España Moderna*, XVII, No. 195 (marzo, 1905), 41-57. Describes the rivalries and enmities which surrounded Moratín.

RUIZ MORCUENDE, FEDERICO. "Moratín, Secretario de la Interpretación de Lenguas," *Revista de la Biblioteca, Archivo y Museo del Ayuntamiento de Madrid*, X (1933), 273-90. Describes and documents the work of Moratín as an official in the governments of Carlos IV and Joseph Bonaparte.

SPAULDING, ROBERT K. "The Text of Moratín's *Orígenes del Teatro Español,*" *PMLA,* XLVII (1932), 981-91. Studies the effects of censorship on the first edition of Moratín's history of the Spanish theater.

VÉZINET, F. "Moratín et Molière," in *Molière, Florian et la littérature espagnole* (Paris: Librairie Hachette et Cie., 1909), pp. 11-178. For long the only extensive study of Moratín's theater, it propagated the view of Moratín as a pallid imitation of the French master.

VILLEGAS MORALES, JUAN. "*El sí de las niñas* de Leandro Fernández de Moratín," in *Ensayos de interpretación de textos españoles* (Santiago de Chile: Editorial Universitaria, 1963), pp. 99-142. An analysis of the action of the play.

3. Doctoral Dissertations

KERSON, PILAR REGALADO DE. "Don Leandro Fernández de Moratín y la polémica del teatro de su tiempo" (diss. Yale, 1966). An extensive study of Moratín's role in the disputes about traditional and neoclassic drama.

MORGAN, RUDOLPH, "Moratín's *Hamlet*" (diss. Stanford, 1965). A thorough investigation into all aspects of Moratín's introduction, translation and notes as well as Cristóbal Cladera's criticism.

ROONEY, SISTER ST. DOMINIC. "Realism in the Original Comedies of Leandro Fernández de Moratín" (diss. Minnesota, 1963). Places Moratín as a link between the tradition of Ruiz de Alarcón and the nineteenth-century problem play.

Index

The asterisk indicates a character in a particular literary work; the author and title of the work are given in parentheses. Roles (e.g., Clytemnestra) which do not refer to a specific play are not so marked.

Titles are indexed in the language, usually the original, in which I most frequently use them. A translation of the title may normally be found in the text at the first citation. The author's surname follows titles except for works by Moratín himself, anonymous works, and the names of periodicals.

*Abbé (in *El Abuelo y la nieta* by Comella), 51

Abuelo y la nieta (El) (Comella), 51

Academy, French, 133

Academy, Royal Spanish, 13, 16, 25, 76

Academy of History, 14, 124, 125, 142, 145

Academy of San Fernando, Royal, 107

Academy of Sciences, Naples, 56

Acero de Madrid (El) (Lope de Vega), 136

Acknowledgments, 9, 10

Actors in premières, 8, 9, 30, 31, 43, 53, 54, 61, 69, 72, 73, 78, 82, 83-84, 93, 109-10, 133, 137, 138

Adelphi (Menander, Terence), 80, 89, 132

Aduladores (Los), 111

Afrancesados, 7, 90, 91

*Agnès (in *L'Ecole des femmes* by Molière), 105

Aguilar, Marquess of, 113

*Agustina, Doña (in *La comedia nueva*), 40, 42, 43, 44, 45, 53, 54, 58

Alcalá de Henares, 92, 93, 94, 95, 98

Alegret, Antonio, 120

Alfonso, Vicente, 137

Álvarez Acero, Bernardo, 48

*Alvaro, Don (in *Don Alvaro* by Duke of Rivas), 91, 96

Amateur productions, 37, 46, 64, 67, 76, 82, 112, 113, 124

America, 28, 34, 43, 51

Ancien régime in Spain, 8

Andioc, René, 146, 149, 150

*Angélique (in *L'Ecole des mères* by Marivaux), 104, 105

Angoulême, Duke of, 91

*Antón (in *El barón*, zarzuela), 66, 67

*Antonio, Don (in *La comedia nueva*), 43, 45, 54, 126

*Antonio, Don (in *La crítica de "El sí de las niñas"* by Ventura de la Vega), 126, 128

Apuntaciones sueltas de Inglaterra, 60

Aranda, Count of, 26, 39, 40, 109

Aranjuez, 72, 124

Arapiles, Battle of, 53

Arce y Reynoso, Ramón José de, 116

Archivo de la Villa, Madrid, 145

Archivo Histórico Nacional, Madrid, 145

°Areusa (in *La Celestina* by Fernando de Rojas), 24
°Argante, Madame (in *L'Ecole des mères* by Marivaux), 104
Aribau, Buenaventura Carlos, 107, 152
°Ariste (in *L'Ecole des maris* by Molière), 134, 135
Aristophanes, 92, 152
Aristotle, 24, 33
°Aristotle (in *El maestro de Alejandro* by Fernando de Zárate), 57
Armona, José Antonio, 50
°Arnolphe (in *L'Ecole des femmes* by Molière), 105
Arriaza, Juan Bautista, 113, 114, 153
Art of Poetry (Horace), 114, 115
Artasona, Marquess of, 113
Arte de escribir en prosa y verso (Gómez Hermosilla), 20
Arte nuevo de hacer comedias en este tiempo (Lope de Vega), 16
Arteaga, Esteban de, 36, 92
Arteaga, Joaquina, 84
Artola, Miguel, 148
Asdrúbal (Comella), 49
Asombro de Salerno (El), 55
Ataulfo (Montiano), 19
Athaliah, 30
Athalie (Racine), 18
Aubignac, Abbé d', 86
Aubrun, Charles V., 152
Auto de fe celebrado en la ciudad de Logroño en los días 7 y 8 de noviembre del año de 1610, 14, 129, 139-42, 155
Autobiographical themes in plays, 106, 107, 108
Autos de fe, 9, 14, 90, 140-42
Autos sacramentales, 49
Avare (L') (Molière), 60, 105, 125
Avecilla, Bernardo, 133
Aventuras del galanteo (Las), 55
°Azucena (in *El Trovador* by García Gutiérrez), 91

Baisers (Dorat), 86

Barbas, 16, 31, 53, 71, 83
Barbieri, José, 53
Barcelona, 14, 52, 120, 123, 137, 138, 142
Baron, Michel, 80
Barón (El), 13, 14, 52, 53, 60-75, 76, 82, 83, 84, 85, 102, 109, 125, 139
Barón (El), zarzuela, 63-68, 72, 82, 103
°Bartolo (in *El médico a palos*), 137
°Basilio (in *La lugareña orgullosa* by Mendoza), 69
Bayle, Pierre, 85
°Beatriz, Doña (in *El viejo y la niña*), 28, 29, 31
Beaumarchais, Pierre-Augustin Caron de, 24, 33, 40, 56
Beaumont, Francis, 80
Becerra Holguín, Alonso, 155
Benavente, Faustina, Dowager Countess of, 64
Benavente, Jacinto, 28, 143
Bench of Burgesses, 39
°Benigno, Don (in *La crítica de "El sí de las niñas"* by Ventura de la Vega), 126
Bermejo, María, 29, 30
Bernabeu, Francisco, 30
Bernascone, Ignacio, 27
Bernascone, Isabel, 27
Beyermón, María Teresa, 46, 50
Biancolelli, Giovan Domenico, 145
Biblioteca de Autores Españoles, 145
Biblioteca Municipal, Madrid, 145
Biblioteca Nacional, Madrid, 145
Bibliothèque Nationale, Paris, 145
Blair, Hugo, 112
Blanco, Felipe, 137, 138
Blanco White, José María, 149
°Blasa (in *El viejo y la niña*), 31
Boda (La) (tapestry cartoon by Goya), 108
Boileau, Nicolas, 133, 153
Bonaparte, Joseph, 7, 14, 90, 129, 135, 139

Bonaparte, Napoleon, 7, 113, 139, 141

Bourgeois gentilhomme (Le) (Molière), 56, 60

Bouzas, Father Francisco Xavier, 120, 121, 122, 123

Box office receipts, 32, 33, 55, 58, 72, 74, 84, 85, 110, 111, 136

Bretón de los Herreros, Manuel, 117

Briones, Joaquina, 69, 71

British in Spain, 7, 84, 113

Buen Retiro Park, Madrid, 21, 22

Buena esposa (La) (Comella), 49

Caballero, Marquess of, 114, 115

Cabañas, Pablo, 155

Cabarrús, Francisco, Count of, 13, 63, 64

Cabo Conde, Isidora, 13

Cadalso, José, 52

Cadiz, 28, 33, 64, 90, 112, 123, 140, 141

Cadiz, Constitution of, 7, 116, 123

Cádiz, Fray Diego de, 38

Caesar, Julius, 33, 36, 77

*Calamocha (in *El sí de las niñas*), 93, 95, 96, 98, 99, 103, 113, 119, 121, 127

Calderón de la Barca, Pedro, 16, 17, 23, 63, 80, 81, 82, 123, 143

Calle, Teodoro de la, 71

Calle de la Puebla (now Fomento), Madrid, 27

Calle del Fomento (formerly Calle de la Puebla), Madrid, 27

Cambronero, Carlos, 148

Camões, Luis de, 122

Campo de Alange, Count of, 114

Candide (Voltaire), 138-140, 141

*Candide (in *Candide* by Voltaire), 139, 140

Cándido, o El optimismo (trans. by Moratín), 139, 155

Cañizares, José, 74

Caños del Peral Theater, Madrid, 17, 38, 39, 55, 69, 70, 71, 72, 83, 110, 111, 150

Cánovas del Castillo, Antonio, 148

Caprara, Joaquín, 69, 133

Caprichos (etching series by Goya), 108, 142

*Carlos, Don (in *La crítica de "El sí de las niñas"* by Ventura de la Vega), 126, 127

*Carlos, Don (in *El sí de las niñas*), 93, 94, 95, 96, 97, 98, 99, 100, 101, 102, 103, 105, 113, 119, 120, 121

Carlos III, 21, 26, 138

Carlos IV, 7, 30, 110, 116, 138

"Carta crítica de un vecino de Guadalajara" (Bernardo García), 113, 114

Casa de Bernarda Alba (La) (García Lorca), 28

Casalduero, Joaquín, 105, 152

Casamiento desigual (El). See: *Viejo y la niña (El)*

*Casilda (in *La crítica de "El sí de las niñas"* by Ventura de la Vega), 126, 127

Castellanos, Francisco (El Tirano), 29

Castle Spectre (The) (Lewis), 87

Cecchi, Giovanni, 80

Cecilia (Comella), 46, 47

Cecilia viuda (Comella), 47

Censor (El), 124

Censorship, 29, 30, 39, 50, 51, 59, 89, 90, 91, 114, 115, 116-23, 124, 125, 138, 139

Centeno, Fray Pedro de, 51

Cervantes, Miguel de, 15, 24, 62, 74

*Champagne (in *L'Ecole des mères* by Marivaux), 104

Choleric Man (The) (Cumberland), 80

Chorizos, 39, 54

Chronology, 13, 14

Cian, Vittorio, 147

Cid (Le) (Corneille), 133

Cid (El) (trans. by Tomás García Suelto), 72

Cifra (La), 55

Cifuentes, Count of, 50
Cladera, Cristóbal, 35, 46, 131, 155
Claques, 39, 40, 73
°Clara (in *Gúardate del agua mansa* by Calderón), 81, 82
°Clara, Doña (in *La mojigata*), 76, 77, 78, 79, 83, 84, 87, 88, 89, 93, 109, 126
Clásicos Castellanos, 108
°Claudio, Don (in *La mojigata*), 77, 78, 79, 81, 83, 88, 91
Clavigo (Goethe), 40
Clavijo y Fajardo, José, 40
°Cléante (in *L'Avare* by Molière), 105
"Clori" (María García), 84
Clytemnestra, 30
Coe, Ada M., 149, 151, 153
Colman, George, 80
Comedia (Golden Age), 8, 15, 16, 21, 25, 33, 34, 62, 72, 81, 92, 103
Comedia de figurón, 81
Comedia de magia, 17, 49
Comedia de teatro, de ruido, or *de cuerpo,* 16, 17
Comedia nueva (*La*), 16, 23, 35, 38-59, 63, 72, 82, 108, 125, 126, 131
Comedies by Moratín, 8, 23, 25
Comella, Luciano Francisco, 46, 47, 48, 49, 50, 51, 52, 54, 123, 148, 149
Comella y Beyermón, Joaquina, 46, 50
Commedia dell'arte, 62
Commission for Theatrical Reform, 138
°Commissioner (in *La escuela de los maridos*), 133
Committee of the Chapel of the Congregation of our Lady of Almudena, 124
Concha, José, 54, 149
Conde, José Antonio, 92, 106, 114, 115, 116, 148
Contador, Tomás, 133
Conti, Antonio, 27

Conti, Giambattista, 20, 28, 146, 147
Conti y Bernascone, Sabina, 27, 147
Contrato anulado (*El*). See: *Traité nul* (*Le*) by Marsollier
Convento de la Victoria, 117
Cook, Albert S., 153
Corneille, Pierre, 60, 72, 133
Corominas, Joan, 151
Corrales, 17
Correo (*El*), 35, 36, 49
Correspondence of Moratín, 9, 23, 60, 64, 92, 107, 123, 124, 131, 138, 139
Corresponsal del Censor (*El*), 104
°Cosme (in *La escuela de los maridos*), 133, 135
Cotarelo y Mori, Emilio, 147, 148, 150, 152
Covarrubias, Sebastián de, 76, 151
Cristiani, Eugenio, 69, 71, 133
Cristóbal Colón (Comella), 49
Crítica de "El sí de las niñas" (*La*) (Ventura de la Vega), 125
Criticism and critics, 85, 86, 87-89, 90, 91, 111-23, 125, 139
Critique de "L'Ecole des femmes" (*La*) (Molière), 125
Cross of the Royal Order of Spain, 7
Cruz, Ramón de la, 32, 55, 64, 130, 149
Cruz Theater, Madrid, 14, 17, 23, 38, 39, 53, 55, 61, 70, 72, 74, 78, 83, 84, 93, 109, 110, 111, 124, 125, 127, 136, 150
Cubas, Félix de, 43, 54
Cueto, Leopoldo de, 153
Cumberland, Richard, 80

°Damis (in *L'Ecole des mères* by Marivaux), 104, 105
Davis, William M., 145
Décima, 146
Defensa de Melilla (*La*) (Nicolás Fernández de Moratín), 21
Derrota de los pedantes (*La*), 13

Diario de los Literatos de España, 20

Diario de Madrid, 19, 32, 35, 46, 50, 55

Diary of Moratín, 60, 107, 129

Díaz-Plaja, Guillermo, 152

Dictionary (Bayle), 85

Diderot, Denis, 24, 33, 80

°Diego, Don (in *La crítica de "El sí de las niñas"* by Ventura de la Vega), 126

°Diego, Don (in *El sí de las niñas*), 93, 94, 95, 96, 97, 99, 100, 101, 102, 103, 105, 109, 113, 115, 119, 121, 122, 124, 154

Díez, Matilde, 59

Díez González, Santos, 19, 31, 32, 50, 51, 52, 53, 146, 147

Discreta enamorada (*La*) (Lope de Vega), 103, 132

Discursos sobre las tragedias españolas (Montiano), 18, 19

Dissimili (*I*) (Cecchi), 80

Dominique, 145

Don Alvaro (Duke of Rivas), 28, 96

Don Quijote (Cervantes), 24, 62

Don Roque. See: *Viejo y la niña* (*El*)

Doña Perfecta (Pérez Galdós), 28

°Dorante (in *Le Bourgeois gentilhomme* by Molière), 60

Dorat, Claude-Joseph, 86

Dorimond, Louis, 132

Drama nuevo (*Un*) (Tamayo y Baus), 37, 143

Ducis, Jean-François, 71, 130

Duque de Viseo (*El*) (Quintana), 87

Durán, Agustin, 149

Echegaray, José, 143

Ecole des femmes (*L'*) (Molière), 105

Ecole des maris (*L'*) (Molière), 14, 80, 132-36

Ecole des mères (*L'*) (Marivaux), 104, 105

Ecole des pères (*L'*) (Baron), 80

Edward III, 48

Élémens de la conversation espagnole et française (*Les*), 56

°Eleuterio, Don (in *La comedia nueva*), 40, 41, 42, 43, 44, 45, 53, 58, 91, 126

°Eleuterio. Don (in *La crítica de "El sí de las niñas"* by Ventura de la Vega), 126, 127

°Elvira, Doña (in *Macías* by Larra), 27, 28

Enciso Castrillón, Félix, 104

England, 13, 60, 130, 138

English theater, 80, 130, 131, 143

Enlightenment in Spain, 7, 138

°Enrique de Cárdenas, Don (in *La escuela de los maridos*), 133, 135, 136

Entrambasaguas, Joaquín de, 147, 152

Entre bobos anda el juego (Rojas Zorrilla), 104

°Eraste (in *L'Ecole des mères* by Marivaux), 104

°Ergaste (in *L'Ecole des maris* by Molière), 135

Eruditos a la violeta (*Los*) (Cadalso), 51, 52

Esclava del Negro Ponto (*La*) (Comella), 49, 50

Escosura, Patricio de la, 107

Escriche, Baroness of, 113

Escuela de los maridos (*La*) (trans. by Moratín from Molière), 14, 80, 132-36, 137

Espíritu de los mejores diarios literarios que se publican en Europa (Cladera), 46

Essai sur les moeurs (Voltaire), 140

Essay on Criticism (Home), 131

Essay on Criticism (Pope), 112

Estala, Pedro, 22, 26, 92, 152

Esteve, Pablo, 48

°Eugenia (in *Gúardate del agua mansa* by Calderón), 81

Eugénie (Beaumarchais), 40

Examen de la tragedia intitulada "Hamlet" (Cladera), 131

Famine of 1811-12, 135
Fandango, 110
Farce, 136, 137
Fathers (The) (Fielding), 80
°Faustina (in *La lugareña orgullosa* by Mendoza), 69
Federico II en el campo de Torgau (Comella), 47
Federico II en Glatz (Comella), 47
Federico II, Rey de Prusia (Comella), 47
Fedra, (La) (Paisiello), 55
°Felix, Don. See: °Carlos, Don (in *El sí de las niñas*)
Femme industrieuse (La) (Dorimond), 132
°Fermina (in *El barón*), 60, 61, 62, 66, 72
°Fermina (in *El barón*, zarzuela), 64, 65, 66
Fernández, María del Rosario (La Tirana), 29, 149
Fernández, Melitón (*pseud.*), 157
Fernández de Moratín, Leandro: life, 13-14; afrancesado, reputation as, 7, 138, 139, 143, 144; dramatist, 8, 23-25, 32, 33-34, 35-36, 55, 57, 58, 63, 74, 75, 93, 101, 103, 105, 106, 108, 125, 128, 134, 143; master of language, 8, 25, 56, 75, 76, 82, 103, 122, 124, 125, 143; literary reputation, 7, 8, 144; fecundity, 22, 23, 123, 143; improvisations, 21-23
Fernández de Moratín, Miguel, 21, 109
Fernández de Moratín, Nicolás, 13, 19, 20, 21, 23, 27, 129, 142
Fernando VII, 7, 91, 117, 123, 124, 125, 138
Fielding, Henry, 80
Fiesta de toros de Juan Tuerto (La), 111

Fiesta de toros en Madrid (Nicolás & Leandro Fernández de Moratín), 129
Figurón, 62, 81
Fin de fiesta, 32, 47, 51, 52
Flanders, 13
Fletcher, John, 80
Fleury, Arthus, 56, 149
Flores, Angel, 145
Florian, Claris de, 36, 148, 150
Fomento, calle del, Madrid, 27
Fonda de San Sebastián, 20, 42
Forner, Juan Pablo, 30, 36, 54, 139, 148, 149
Fort, Barbara, 137
France, 13, 14, 22, 23, 29, 60, 63, 122, 138, 142
°Francisca, Doña (in *El sí de las niñas*), 93, 94, 95, 96, 97, 98, 99, 100, 101, 102, 105, 106, 109, 113, 115, 118, 119, 121, 122, 124, 136
°Francisco (in *Hamlet*), 130, 131
°Frederick, Seneschal (in *El gran cerco de Viena*), 40, 41
French in Spain, 7, 14, 53, 70, 83, 90, 91, 113, 116, 135, 136, 138, 140, 141
French theater, 56, 60, 79, 80, 124, 132, 133, 134, 143
°Frosine (in *L'Avare* by Molière), 105

Gaceta, 90
Gallegas celosas (Las) (Ramón de la Cruz), 32
García, Bernardo, 113, 114, 115, 116, 123
García María, 78, 83, 84, 133
García Vicente, 69, 71
García Asensio, Miguel, 26
García de la Huerta, Vicente, 21
García de la Prada, Manuel, 83, 84
García Hugalde, José, 43, 54, 58
García Lorca, Federico, 28
García Parra, Manuel, 43, 53, 58, 61, 72
García Porrero, Fray Agustín, 120

García Ugalde, Juana, 31, 32, 43, 53, 54
García y Carrillo, Fray José, 117-21, 122, 138
Garrick, David, 80
Garrote, Lorenzo (*pseud.*), 148
Gatti, José Francisco, 152
Germany, 13
°Gerónimo, Don (in *El médico a palos*), 137
°Géronte (in *Le Médecin malgré lui* by Molière), 137
Gertrude, St., 118
Gijón, 37
Gil y Zárate, Antonio, 117
°Ginés (in *El médico a palos*), 137
°Ginés (in *El viejo y la niña*), 31
Godoy, Diego, Duke of Almodóvar, 68, 110
Godoy, Luis, 30
Godoy, Manuel, 13, 30, 68, 72, 85, 87, 90, 92, 110, 113, 114, 115, 116
Goethe, Johann Wolfgang von, 40
Golden Age, 8, 15, 16, 21, 25, 33, 43, 143
Goldoni, Carlo, 23, 62, 153
Gómez Hermosilla, José, 20
Gómez Ortega, Casimiro, 20, 147
González-Blanco, Andrés, 150
Gorostiza, Eduardo, 47, 149
Goya, Francisco de, 107, 108, 109, 142, 152, 155
Goyburu, Miguel de (in *Auto de fe ...*), 142
Graciosos, 16, 31, 39, 53, 54, 83, 84, 95, 96, 136, 138
Gran cerco de Viena (*El*), 17, 40, 41, 42, 45, 48, 52
Granada, 124, 154
°Gregorio de Velasco, Don (in *La escuela de los maridos*), 133, 135
Guadalajara, 93, 95, 114, 115
Guárdate del agua mansa (Calderón), 80, 81
Guardian (*The*) (Garrick), 80
Guerrero, Alvaro, 35
Gutiérrez de la Torre, Dámaso, 70

Guzmán, Antonio, 59
°Guzmán de Alfarache (in novel by Mateo Alemán), 24

°Hamlet (in *Hamlet*), 131
Hamlet (trans. by Ramón de la Cruz), 130
Hamlet (trans. by Moratín), 14, 46, 130-32, 134, 154
°Harpagon (in *L'Avare* by Molière), 60, 105, 106
Hartzenbusch, Juan Eugenio, 107
Haz de leña (*El*) (Núñez de Arce), 143
Hechos heroicos y nobles del valor godo español (Moncín), 55
Hecuba, 30
Helman, Edith, 142, 152, 155
°Hermógenes, Don (in *La comedia nueva*), 35, 40, 42, ` 44, 45, 46, 50, 53, 58, 72, 86, 1, 102, 126, 131
°Hermógenes, Don (in *La crítica de "El sí de las niñas"* by Ventura de la Vega), 126, 127
Hermosa, Vicente, 59
Higuera, Miguel de la, 54, 149
Hijos de Nadasti (*Los*) (Comella), 52
Home, Henry, 131
Homer, 122
Horace, 18, 24, 114, 153
°Horace (in *L'Ecole des femmes* by Molière), 105
Hurtado de Mendoza, Antonio, 132
Huxley, Aldous, 152

Illescas, 61, 66, 75, 104
Inarco Celenio (*pseud.*), 145, 153, 155, 157
Inca Yupanqui, Manuel de, 113
Index, the, 138
Indolente (*El*) (Comella), 51
°Inés, Doña (in *Don Juan Tenorio* by Zorrilla), 28, 91
°Inés, Doña (in *La mojigata*), 77, 78, 79, 83, 84
Infantes, José, 69
Inquisition, Portuguese, 140

Inquisition, Spanish, 89, 90, 91,
    116-23, 124, 138, 140, 141, 153,
    154, 155
Instituciones poéticas (Santos Díez
    González), 19
Instituto Theater, Madrid, 125, 127
Intereses creados (Los) (Bena-
    vente), 28
Interpretation of Languages, Secre-
    tary, 14, 129, 139, 154
Iphigénie (Racine), 131
°Irene, Doña (in El sí de las niñas),
    93, 94, 95, 96, 97, 98, 100, 101,
    102, 104, 105, 109, 113, 115,
    119, 121, 122, 124, 127, 128
Iriarte, Tomás de, 30
°Isabel (in El barón), 61, 62, 67,
    68, 72
°Isabel (in La lugareña orgullosa
    by Mendoza), 69, 70, 71
°Isabel, Doña (in El viejo y la
    niña), 28, 31, 32, 34, 53
°Isabelle (in L'Ecole des maris by
    Moliére), 135
Italian theater, 36, 37, 56, 80
Italy, 13, 14, 27, 36, 56, 60, 82,
    106, 129, 138, 139

Jacoba (La) (Comella), 47
°Jacqueline (in Le Médecin malgré
    lui by Molière), 137
°Jacques, Maître (in L'Avare by
    Molière), 60
Jealous Wife (The) (Colman), 80
°Jourdain, Monsieur (in Le Bour-
    geois gentilhomme by Molière),
    56, 60
Jovellanos, Gaspar Melchor de, 21,
    30, 37, 64, 82, 88, 148, 150, 151
°Juan, Don (in El viejo y la niña),
    27, 28, 31, 34
°Juan, Uncle (in La mojigata), 77,
    78, 79, 83, 87
°Juan Tenorio, Don (in Don Juan
    Tenorio by Zorrilla), 91
Judge Protector of Theaters, 38,
    39, 50, 57, 58
°Juliana (in El médico a palos),
    137

°Juliana (in La escuela de los mari-
    dos), 133, 135
Juno (in Phaedrus' fable), 63

Kany, C. E., 148
°King of Poland (in El gran cerco
    de Viena), 41

Lardnaz y Morante, Efrén (pseud.),
    157
Larra, Mariano José de, 28, 91,
    125, 151, 154
Laserna, Blas, 48
Latorre, Carlos, 59
Lázaro Carreter, Fernando, 154
Lea, Henry Charles, 153
°Léandre (in Le Médecin malgré
    lui by Molière), 137
°Leandro (in El barón, zarzuela),
    64, 65
°Leandro (in El médico a palos),
    137
°Leandro (in La lugareña orgullosa
    by Mendoza), 69
Lección poética, 13
Lecciones sobre la retórica (trans.
    by Munárriz), 112
Lefebre, Alfredo, 152
°Leonardo (in El barón), 61, 62,
    63, 66, 67, 68, 72
°Léonor (in L'Ecole des maris by
    Molière), 134, 135
°Leonor, Doña (in Don Alvaro by
    Duke of Rivas), 28, 96
°Leonor, Doña (in La escuela de
    los maridos), 133, 135
°Leopold, Emperor (in El gran
    cerco de Viena), 40, 41, 42
Lewis, Matthew "Monk," 87
Liberals, 7, 116
"Licoris" (Sabina Conti y Bern-
    ascone), 26, 27
Lidón, José, 64
Lira, 146
°Lisette (in L'Ecole des maris by
    Molière), 135
°Lisette (in L'Ecole des mères by
    Marivaux), 104
Lista, Alberto, 75

Llaguno y Amírola, Eugenio, 18
Loa, 47
Logroño, 140-42, 155
London theater, 13
López, Francisco, 43, 54, 58
López, Tomás, 83
López de Ayala, Ignacio, 19
Lorenz, Charlotte M., 155
Louis XIV, 132
Louis XVI, 26
*Lucas (in *El médico a palos*), 137
*Lucas (in *Le Médecin malgré lui*
by Molière), 137
*Lucía (in *La mojigata*), 78, 84
*Lucinde (in *Le Médecin malgré
lui* by Molière), 137
Lucrecia (Nicolás Fernández de
Moratín), 19, 38
Lugareña orgullosa (La) (Men-
doza), 68, 69, 70, 71, 72, 74
*Luis, Don (in *La mojigata*), 77,
78, 79, 83
Luna, Rita, 50, 61, 72
Luzán, Ignacio de, 18, 20, 23

Macías (Larra), 28, 91
Madrid, 13, 14, 26, 27, 29, 32,
36, 38, 53, 63, 70, 82, 106, 124,
125, 134
Maestro de Alejandro (El) (Zá-
rate), 57
Magdalena cautiva (Valladares de
Sotomayor), 55
*Mágico de Salerno Pedro Vayalarde
(El)* (Salvó y Vela), 17
Mágico prodigioso (El) (Calde-
rón), 17
Máiquez, Isidoro, 69, 71, 104, 133,
136
*Manolo: tragedia para reír, o
sainete para llorar* (Ramón de
la Cruz), 54
*Manuel, Don (in *La escuela de
los maridos*), 133, 135
Manuel, Miguel de, 50, 51
Manuel de los Dolores, Fray, 120
Manuscripts extant, 83
Manzanares River, 26, 53
*Marchioness (in *La crítica de "El

sí de las niñas" by Ventura de
la Vega), 126, 127
*Margarita (in *El gran cerco de
Viena*), 41
María Cristina, Queen, 124
Mariage forcé (Le) (Molière),
60
*Mariane (in *L'Avare* by Molière),
105
*Marido hace mujer y el trato muda
costumbre (El)* (Hurtado de
Mendoza), 132
*Mariquita, Doña (in *La comedia
nueva*), 43, 44, 45, 53, 58
Marivaux, Pierre Carlet de Cham-
blain de, 104, 105, 152
*Marquess (in *La lugareña orgull-
osa* by Mendoza), 69, 70, 71
Marsollier, Benoît-Joseph, 104, 105,
112, 152
Marston, John, 80
*Marta (in *Marta la piadosa* by
Tirso de Molina), 80, 81
Marta la piadosa (Tirso de Molina),
80, 81
Martial, 130
*Martín, Don (in *La mojigata*), 77,
78, 79, 83, 126
*Martina (in *El médico a palos*),
136, 137
*Martine (in *Le Médecin malgré lui*
by Molière), 137
Martínez, Francisca, 29
Martínez, Manuel, theatrical com-
pany of, 13, 29
Más ilustre fregona (La) (Cañi-
zares), 74
Médecin malgré lui (Le) (Mo-
lière,), 14, 136-38
Médico a palos (El), 14, 136-38,
142
Médico por fuerza (El). See:
Médecin malgré lui (Le)
Medina-Sidonia, Duke of, 20, 21
*Melibea (in *La Celestina* by Fer-
nando de Rojas), 24
Melilla (Africa), 21
Melón, Juan Antonio, 21, 22, 26,

27, 46, 70, 82, 92, 107, 109, 114, 116, 131, 139, 146, 147, 152
Memorial Literario, 26, 35, 55, 74, 75, 112
Menander, 36, 60, 80
Mendoza, Andrés de, 68, 69, 70, 71, 72, 150
Mendoza, Juan de Dios, 106, 108, 147, 152
Menéndez y Pelayo, Marcelino, 38, 140, 148
Menestral sofocado (El) (Comella), 49
Mesonero Romanos, Ramón de, 19, 146, 148
°Michoacán, Bishop-elect of (in El sí de las niñas), 119, 121, 127
Milton, John, 122
Minerva, 112
Minims, Order of, 120
Mininni, Carmine Giustino, 147
Miraflores, 137
Mojigata (La), 14, 76-91, 109, 126, 127, 132, 139, 151
Mojigato, 151
Molière, 9, 14, 56, 60, 62, 74, 79, 89, 105, 125, 132-38, 140, 144, 150, 155
Molina, Tirso de, 16
°Mónica, Aunt (in El Barón), 60, 61, 62, 67, 68, 70, 72, 75, 91, 102, 109
°Mónica, Aunt (in El barón, zarzuela), 66, 67, 68
°Mónica, Doña (in La lugareña orgullosa by Mendoza), 69, 70, 71
°Montepino, Baron (in El barón), 60, 61, 62, 66, 67, 70, 72, 83, 91
°Montepino, Baron (in El barón, zarzuela), 65, 66
Montiano y Luyando, Agustín de, 18, 19
Mor de Fuentes, José, 74, 151
Moral, Pablo del, 48
Morales Guzmán y Tovar, Juan, 57, 58

Moreto, Agustín, 60, 62
Morgan, Rudolph, 155
Mort de César (La) (Voltaire), 30
Mortara, Marquess and Marchioness of, 46
°Mudo (in El muñuelo by Ramón de la Cruz), 54, 55
Munárriz, José Luis, 112
°Muñoz (in El viejo y la niña), 28, 31, 32, 34, 53, 72, 91
Muñoz (El). See: Viejo y la niña (El)
Muñoz, Father Rafael, 122
Muñoz, Francisca Gertrudis, 106, 107
Muñoz, Santiago, 106, 107
Muñuelo, 149
Muñuelo (El): tragedia por mal nombre (Ramón de la Cruz), 54
Music in drama, 48, 49, 51, 54, 63, 64, 65, 66, 69, 103, 124

Napoli Signorelli, Pietro, 23, 36, 37, 56, 75, 82, 147
Navarre, 140, 155
Navarrete, Father, 22
Navarro, Luis, theatrical company of, 57, 149
Naves de Cortés destruidas (Las) (Nicolás Fernández de Moratín), 13, 19
Negrete y Adorno, Agustín María, 114
Negrete y Adorno, Manuel María, 114
Nelson, Lord, 113
Neoclassic movement, 18, 19, 20, 21, 23, 24, 30, 33, 51, 55, 82, 112, 130
Nerval, Gérard de, 56, 149
Neue Lustspiel (Das), oder Das Kaffeehaus (trans. by Manuel Ramajo), 56
Nifo, Franciso Mariano, 54, 149
Night Thoughts (Young), 86
Nouveau genre (Le), ou le Café d'un théâtre (trans. by Fleury), 56

Nouvelle comédie (La), ou Le Café (trans. anon.), 56
Núñez de Arce, Gaspar, 143

Obras póstumas, 107
Ojamar, Manuel (*pseud.*), 56, 149
°Ophelia (in *Hamlet*), 131
Orígenes del teatro español, 14, 23, 129, 142, 155
Ortiz de Muñoz, María, 106, 107
Ossorio y Bernard, M., 107
Otelo (trans. by Teodoro de la Calle), 71
Othello (Shakespeare), 71
Oui des couvents (Le), 112

Palais Royal Theater, Paris, 136
Palma, Josefa, 59
Panduros, 39
°Pangloss, Dr. (in *Candide* by Voltaire), 139, 140
°Panza, Sancho (in *Don Quijote* by Cervantes), 24, 62
°Panza, Teresa (in *Don Quijote* by Cervantes), 24, 62
°Paquita (in *La crítica de "El sí de las niñas"* by Ventura de la Vega), 126, 127, 128
Par, Alfonso, 155
Pardo, Royal Seat of El, 63, 152
Parisitaster, or The Fawn (Marston), 80
°Pascual (in *El barón*), 61, 62, 72
Pastrana, 38, 92, 139
°Paula, Doña (in *El médico a palos*), 137
Paz, Coleta, 58, 61, 72
Peace, Prince of the. *See:* Godoy, Manuel
°Pedro, Don (in *El barón*), 61, 62, 66, 67, 72, 75, 83
°Pedro, Don (in *El barón,* zarzuela), 66, 67, 68
°Pedro, Don (in *La comedia nueva*), 43, 44, 45, 53, 126
°Pedro, Don (in *La crítica de "El sí de las niñas"* by Ventura de la Vega), 126, 127, 128

°Pedro, Don (in *La lugareña orgullosa* by Mendoza), 69, 70, 71
Pelayo (Quintana), 87
Peñíscola, 14
°Pepe (in *La escuela de los maridos*), 133
Pepita Jiménez (Valera), 28
°Pepito (in *La lugareña orgullosa* by Mendoza), 69
Père de famille (Le) (Diderot), 80
Pérez de Castro, 82
Pérez Galdós, Benito, 28
°Perico (in *La lugareña orgullosa* by Mendoza), 69
°Perico (in *La mojigata*), 77, 78, 79, 83, 87, 88
°Perrin (in *Le Médecin malgré lui* by Molière), 137
Petimetra (La) (Nicolás Fernández de Moratín), 19, 23, 38
Pfandl, Ludwig, 146
Phaedrus, 63, 150
Philip IV, 15
Pinto, Antonio, 61, 72, 73, 83, 92
°Pipí (in *La comedia nueva*), 43, 44, 54, 58
Pla, José, 59
Plautus, 75
Plutus (Aristophanes), 92, 152
Poeta Arcade, 145
Poética (Luzán), 18, 20
Poetry by Moratín, 9, 20, 23, 24, 29, 129
Polaco, Father, 39
Polacos, 39
Ponce, Antonio, 61, 72, 83
Pope, Alexander, 112
Posadilla, Ginés de (*pseud.*), 14, 141, 155, 157
Prado, Madrid, 126, 152
Prado, Antonia, 69, 71
Pratique du théâtre (Abbé d'Aubignac), 86
Première performances, casts of. *See:* Actors in premières
Premio de la constancia (El), 54
Prieto, Andrés, 93, 109, 124, 154

Príncipe Theater, Madrid, 13, 14, 17, 31, 32, 38, 39, 42, 43, 53, 55, 70, 87, 125, 127, 133, 138
Procurador General del Rey y de la Nación (El), 90
Prose dramas, 34, 35, 56, 63, 82, 103, 134
Puebla, calle de la, Madrid, 27

Qualia, Charles Blaise, 151
Querol, Mariano, 31, 32, 43, 53, 58, 61, 72, 83, 87, 136
°Quijote, Don (in *Don Quijote* by Cervantes), 62
Quintana, Manuel José, 74, 87-89, 113, 114, 116, 153
Quintillas, 127, 146

Racine, Jean, 18, 21, 131
Raleigh, Sir Walter, 147
Ramajo, Manuel, 56, 149
Reales Estudios de San Isidro, 19, 51
Redondilla, 147
Reform, theatrical, 8, 17, 18-25, 29, 32, 33, 35, 36, 40, 50-51, 52, 54, 55, 56, 57, 58, 59, 70, 138
Refundiciones, 16
Regañón General (El), 71
Reglas del drama (Las) (Quintana), 87
Relación de las personas que salieron al auto de la fee que . . . See: *Auto de fe celebrado en la ciudad de Logroño . . .*
Renaissance, 143
Revista Española (La), 91, 125
Ribera, Eusebio, theatrical company of, 29, 30, 32, 53, 72
Ribera, María, 58, 61, 72, 93, 109
Riego, Rafael de, 123
Riquer, Martín de, 151
°Rita (in *El sí de las niñas*), 93, 94, 95, 96, 97, 98, 99, 103, 113, 119, 121
Rivas, Duke of, 28, 96
°Robert, M. (in *Le Médecin malgré lui* by Molière), 137

Robles, Antonio, 57
Rochel, Polonia, 43, 53
Rogers, Paul P., 153
Rojas Zorrilla, Francisco de, 62, 104
Romantic period, 23, 28, 34, 56, 59, 91, 92, 96, 125, 143
Romea, Francisco, 59
Romea, Julián, 59
Ronda, Francisco, 69
°Roque, Don (in *El viejo y la niña*), 27, 28, 29, 31, 32, 34, 53, 91, 101
°Rosa, Doña (in *La escuela de los maridos*), 133, 135, 136
Roscius, 57
Rousseau, Jean Jacques, 138
Royal Conservatory, Madrid, 124
Royal Librarian, 7, 139
Rubert, Francisco, 39
Rubín, Santos Manuel, 104
Rubió Balaguer, Jorge, 146
°Rufino, Don (in *El violeto universal* by Comella), 52
Ruiz de Alarcón, Juan, 16, 60
Ruiz Morcuende, Federico, 8, 108, 145, 154

Sainetes, 19, 22, 32, 47, 49, 54, 111
Salazar Frías, Alonso, 155
Salvó y Vela, Juan, 17
San Antonio, Fray Magín de, 120
San Sebastián, Fonda de, 20, 42
Sandoval, Bernardo de, 155
Santa Coloma, Marchioness of, 113
Santevil, Jean de, 145
Santiago, Marchioness of, 82
Scornful Lady (The) (Beaumont and Fletcher), 80
Sebold, Russell P., 147
Segovia, 21, 109
Seguidilla, 150
Semiramis, 30
Señorito mimado (El) (Iriarte), 30
Sententiae (Publilius Syrus), 77
Sepúlveda, Ricardo, 148
°Serafín (in *La crítica de "El sí de las niñas"* by Ventura de la Vega), 126, 127

°Serapio, Don (in *La comedia nueva*), 43, 44, 54, 58, 126

°Serapio, Don (in *La crítica de "El sí de las niñas"* by Ventura de la Vega), 126, 127

°Servant (in *La escuela de los maridos*), 133

°Sganarelle (in *L'Ecole des maris* by Molière), 134, 135

°Sganarelle (in *Le Médecin malgré lui* by Molière), 137

Shadwell, Thomas, 80

Shakespeare, 9, 14, 71, 130-32, 154, 155

Shergold, N. D., 150

Sí de las niñas (*El*), 8, 9, 14, 23, 37, 56, 63, 82, 92-128, 132, 136, 138, 139

Siglo de las luces. *See*: Enlightenment in Spain

Silva y Palafox, María del Pilar, 26

Silvela, Francisco Agustín, 22

Silvela, Manuel, 14, 22, 23, 56, 106, 111, 123, 146, 152, 153

Silvela de Figuera, Victoria, 57

°Simón (in *El sí de las niñas*), 93, 94, 98, 99, 100, 103, 105, 113, 120

°Simplicio, Don (in *La escuela de los maridos*), 133

Sitio de Calés (*El*) (Comella), 48, 52

Sitios Reales Theater, 40

Sofonisba (Comella), 48

Solavide, Antonio Nicolás de, 111, 123, 152, 153

°Solimán (in *La esclava del Negro Ponto* by Comella), 50

Solís, Dionisio, 72, 109

Soto, Fulgencio de (Cristóbal Cladera?), 35, 46, 131

Spanish College, Bologna, 82

Spaulding, Robert K., 155

Squire of Alsatia (*The*) (Shadwell), 80

Steele, Sir Richard, 80

Suárez, Joaquín, 69, 133

Subirá Puig, José, 148

Sueño (*El*) (adapt. from French by Enciso Castrillón), 104

Switzerland, 13

Syrus, Publilius, 77, 87, 89

Talassi, Angelo, 20

Talma, François-Joseph, 71

Tamayo y Baus, Manuel, 37, 143

°Tartuffe (in *Le Tartuffe* by Molière), 79, 80, 88, 106

Tartuffe (*Le*), *ou L'Imposteur* (Molière), 79, 89, 125

Tasso, 122

Tender Husband (*The*) (Sir Richard Steele), 80

Terence, 33, 36, 60, 75, 80, 81, 82, 89, 132

Terror (Paris), 13, 130

°Teruel, Lovers of (in *Los amantes de Teruel* by Hartzenbusch), 91

Theatrical season, 38, 44, 58, 110, 136

Thebaid, 133

°Thibaut (in *Le Médecin malgré lui* by Molière), 137

Ticknor, George, 89, 90, 91, 148, 151

Tineo, Juan, 88, 89, 91

Tirana (La) (María del Rosario Fernández), 29, 149

Tirano (El) (Francisco Castellanos), 29

Tirso de Molina, 80, 81, 82

Titles of respect, 61

Toledano, José, 113

Tolrá, Father José, 120, 121, 122

Toma de Granada (*La*), 13

Tonadilla, 42, 48, 54, 84, 110, 111

°Toribio Cuadrilleros, Don (in *Gúardate del agua mansa* by Calderón), 81

Torre, Gertrudis, 69, 133

Torre, Manuel de la, 31, 32, 43, 53

Traditionalists, 7

Trafalgar, Battle of, 113, 114, 153

Traité nul (*Le*) (Marsollier), 104, 105, 112

Translations, 14, 129

Translations by Moratín, 9, 80, 129, 130-40
Travel books by Moratín, 9, 23, 60, 138
*Trovador (in El Trovador by García Gutiérrez), 91
Tudó, Pepita, 110
Tutor (El), 92

Unities, 18, 24, 34, 55, 112
Urquijo, Mariano Luis de, 30

Vaca, Francisco, 83
Valencia, 14, 84, 139, 140, 142
Valencia, Archbishop of, 59, 91
Valera, Juan, 28
*Valère (in L'Ecole des maris by Molière), 135
*Valère (in Le Médecin malgré lui by Molière), 137
Valladares de Sotomayor, Antonio, 127, 148, 149
Valle Alvarado, Juan de, 155
Valverde, Francisco, 106
Variedades de Ciencias, Literatura y Artes, 87, 88
Vega, Lope de, 8, 15, 16, 21, 23, 74, 103, 123, 131, 132, 136, 142, 143
Vega, Ventura de la, 125, 144, 154
Venus, 84
Vergil, 122
Verse dramas, 34, 35, 56, 63, 82, 134
Vézinet, F., 60, 105, 150
Viaje de Italia, 60
Victoria, Convento de la, 117
Vida, Marco Girolamo, 153
Vieja y el niño (La), 37
Viejo y la niña (El), 8, 13, 26-37, 38, 46, 47, 53, 54, 57, 62, 63,

68, 72, 75, 82, 83, 85, 92, 101, 107, 108, 109
Villafranca, Marchioness of, 92
Violeto universal o El café (El) (Comella), 51, 52
Virg, Josefa, 83, 84, 93, 109, 124, 133, 136, 154
Virginia (Montiano), 19
*Vizier (in El gran cerco de Viena), 41, 42
Voltaire, 9, 14, 30, 130, 138-40, 143, 155

War of Independence, 23, 116
Wellington, Duke of, 84
Women, position of, 27, 28, 62, 63, 77, 78, 79, 80, 81, 82, 93, 100, 103, 115, 118, 121, 122, 128, 132, 136

Young, Edward, 86
Yurreteguia, María de (in Auto de fee...), 141

Zabala y Zamora, Gaspar, 54, 148, 149
*Zafir of Alexandria (in La buena esposa by Comella), 49
*Zaque (in El muñuelo by Ramón de la Cruz), 55
*Zara (in La buena esposa by Comella), 49
Zaragoza, 93, 94, 95, 98, 112, 113
Zárate, Fernando de, 57
Zarzuela, Palace of La, 63
Zarzuelas, 48, 63, 64, 65, 66, 67, 68, 82, 150
Zorrilla, José, 28
Zorrilla de Velasco, Dr., 120, 122